Bed, Breakfast & Bike
Pacific Northwest

A Cycling Guide
To Country Inns

by Carrie and Jon Muellner

White Meadow Press
P.O. Box 56
Boonton, NJ 07005

Cover art by Karen Strattner. Cover design by Debbie Jorgensen. Illustrations in the book courtesy of the innkeepers.

Maps created in Freehand 5.0 on a Macintosh IIvx and Performa 6115 by Jon Muellner.

Also Available From White Meadow Press:
Bed, Breakfast & Bike/Mid-Atlantic
Bed, Breakfast & Bike/New England
Bed, Breakfast & Bike/Northern California
RIDE GUIDE/Hudson Valley and Sound Shore
RIDE GUIDE/North Jersey, 2nd Edition
RIDE GUIDE/Central Jersey
RIDE GUIDE/South Jersey
Please use the order form on Page 278.

Library of Congress Catalog Card Number: 95-60718
ISBN 0-933855-09-5

CONTENTS

PREFACE

This book is not just for "cyclists". If you own a bicycle and haven't been on it for awhile, but keep meaning to take it for a spin, there are plenty of rides here for you. If you're in training for a long ride and want to get away for the weekend, this book is for you, too. Most of the ride routes in the book are between 15-40 miles long, but we have often given suggestions for making the rides longer or shorter so that you can adapt the routes to your needs. We've listed at least one additional attraction along each of the routes, be it a walk on the beach or a tour of a winery, a kayak trip or a Shakespeare play, so it's certainly possible to turn a 15-mile ride into an all-day event and include non-cycling members of the family, too.

Bicycling is an excellent way to get to know a new area. After a fabulous breakfast and a stimulating conversation with fellow guests, there's nothing like heading off into a bright sunny morning for a day of adventure and exercise. Bicycling allows you to see and hear and smell the finer details of a place: Orcas playfully breaching offshore, bear cubs hiding in an apple tree, the crispness of a fall day or the smell of coffee beans roasting. On a bicycle, whole worlds open up.

However, we think of riding as a way to explore, not an all-consuming activity. Each B&B we visited has created a unique, comfortable atmosphere, and we want to be sure you have some time to enjoy the inn itself. Soak in the hot tub, curl up with a good book by the fire or put your feet up on the porch rail and talk to the other guests. You'll meet fascinating people from all over the world and come away feeling pampered and refreshed.

This the fourth Bed, Breakfast and Bicycling book in the series from White Meadow Press. In keeping with the intent of the series, we selected B&Bs or inns in the Northwest that would make good "base camps" for a cycling vacation, and then consulted guide books, local bike shops, innkeepers and bicycling clubs to select appropriate routes from each inn. We personally visited each inn in the book, and rode each route we've suggested. We've provided descriptions of the inns we selected and a detailed map and cue sheet for each ride. The rest is up to you: whether your bike is buried in a dusty corner of the garage or is a finely-tuned racing machine, we hope you'll use this book to put together your own memorable cycling vacation.

ACKNOWLEDGMENTS

For some reason, people are fascinated with bike tourists. They want to know where you're from, where you've been, where you're going, and most importantly, if you need anything. And wonderful things happen at B&Bs; people talk for hours at breakfast, chat in the evening by the fire, and find things in common with guests from across the globe. The combination of traveling by bicycle and staying in B&Bs is magical.

Many times during the course of our research we were amazed at the generosity extended to us by total strangers, like the gentleman on a twenty-minute ferry ride who offered to let us stay at his house, or the two mountain bicyclists we met in the woods who beat us back to our cars and had cold beers in frosted mugs waiting for us when we emerged from the trail. We had many memorable conversations over breakfast with fellow guests, and were constantly impressed with the rich variety of people who visit B&Bs.

Again and again we met friendly and compassionate folks. If we ever doubted the inherent goodness in fellow human beings, the process of traveling and writing this book has taught us otherwise.

All of the innkeepers we met were exceptionally warm and welcoming; their hospitality and eagerness to help made our job especially rewarding.

We'd like to especially thank the following people for going out of their way to make us feel welcome, help us out in some way, or provide the support we needed to complete this project:

Brad & Melissa Williams
Mac & Amy Lee
Monte & Donna McAllister
Mike and Mo Shipton
Loragene Gaulin
Jason Davis
Matt Johnson
Robin Stephani

Tom & Ann Hennessy
Ursula Bates
Lou & Rikki Meyers
Monty & Karen Turner
Ned & Kate Schumann
Jim & Marilyn Muellner
Tom Andrews
Matthew Schoenfeld

And a final note of thanks to our editor and publisher, Dan Goldfischer, whose patience and hard work made this book possible.

HOW TO USE THIS BOOK

Bed, Breakfast and Bike/Pacific Northwest is divided into seven sections, with an additional chapter including recipes from each inn at the end. The sections are divided either by geographical location ("Western Washington") or terrain ("San Juan and Puget Sound Islands"). The brief introduction at the start of each section will describe the general characteristics of the area covered. The sections are presented alphabetically.

Information about the B&B

The inns in each area are listed alphabetically. Each chapter contains specific information about the inn or B&B we visited and a description of the ambiance, decor, food and overall experience. Where it was applicable, we have also included information about interesting sites in the area, particularly good restaurants in the neighborhood and unique historical features of the B&B or its locale.

The heading for each chapter looks like this:

> B&B Name
> Owner's Name
> Address of Inn
> Phone Number
> Rates

Each description begins with some general information: the owners' names, the address and phone number of the inn, and the room rates. The rates listed range from the least expensive room available to the most expensive, and were correct as of December 1994. We did not specify whether or not smoking is allowed at each individual inn: it isn't. Most of the inns allowed smoking outdoors, although a few did not want smoking anywhere on the property, so if you smoke, ask about the smoking policy when you make reservations.

All the B&Bs we visited include a full breakfast in the room rates; a few of the inns also offer dinner for an additional fee. Several inns offer complimentary tea in the afternoons, complete with freshly baked cookies or scones. In any event, you won't go hungry!

The number of rooms in each establishment is listed in the description; the majority of the inns we visited had 4-6 rooms.

Cycling

In each chapter we have provided information on terrain, road conditions, traffic and the nearest bike shop. The terrain of each route is described briefly before each cue sheet; additional commentary is found in the cue sheet itself. Many areas we rode were undergoing varying degrees of construction, so what we described as a gravel road may well be a paved one now. Also, we rode primarily during the week, so our opinion of traffic flow may be different from yours if you visit on a weekend! Whenever possible, we called upon the bike shops listed in each chapter, and can heartily recommend the majority we visited. If you plan to be in an area for more than a couple of days, do stop in and see if the local shop has a group ride planned—you'll no doubt be invited along.

We rode mountain bikes with road tires on all the routes listed, in order to cover the most territory with the fewest number of flats. The vast majority of roads in rural areas do not tend to favor skinny tires! While we have designated mountain bike rides as such, a mountain bike, "city bike", or cross-bike will be most appropriate for most of the rides listed here; being drawn to the dirt, we've often included small off-road detours.

Bring a patch kit, pump and tire levers and know how to use them (make sure the glue in the patch kit has not dried out). A little simple bike knowledge can make a flat tire just another part of a great ride, instead of the end of one.

Ride descriptions contain information on **Terrain**, what the general area is like for riding; **Road Conditions** tells which roads to look out for and overall surface condition. **Traffic** will point out the busiest spots; **Nearest Bike Shop** shows where to go to get the best information or repairs in the area. **Best Time to Ride** points out the best seasons for riding; **Mountain Biking Opportunities** gives the location of the closest off-road riding.

Cue Sheets

Cue sheets are done in clear, point-to-point fashion. The headings listed from left to right are as follows:

Pt.-Pt. is for mileage between highlights, turns, stop signs or points of interest. None are marked below 0.1 and some less than this figure are listed as 0.0 (such as a quick right, and then left turn). Off-road distances are approximate.

Cum. is overall cumulative distance to that point.

Dir. signifies which direction to go at that point.

Abbreviations in the Dir. column represent:
L Left
R Right
CL Curve left
CR Curve right
S Straight
– Point of interest/highlight
TA Turnaround (used for out and back routes)
X Cross

Streets at which you need to turn, stop and continue or points of interest are signified by **bold type**. All other streets and landmarks are in plain type.

Maps
The maps included in each chapter are intended to give you a sense of the route, not to be your only guide to the area. As mentioned earlier, the Visitor's Center in almost any town is a helpful source for good maps; some areas even have maps especially designed for cyclists, detailing the best routes in the area. The local bike shop and the innkeepers at your B&B are also good sources for regional maps. We highly recommend you pick up a good map of the area you'll be riding in before heading out—if nothing else you'll feel more confident when you take that interesting detour! For off-road riding it is imperative that you take a map (and compass) and know how to use it.

BEFORE YOU GO

The thought of spending a weekend based at a luxurious B&B and leisurely touring the countryside by bicycle sounds pretty ideal. There are a few details to attend to before you throw your bike on top of the car and head out, however. We mention the following things not to spoil your fun, but to ensure you enjoy the Bed, Breakfast and Bicycling experience to its utmost!

Be Prepared

While we made every attempt to provide accurate maps and cue sheets for each chapter, we do not recommend relying solely on the maps included here. Most Visitors Centers or Chambers of Commerce can provide excellent local maps for free; if you will be riding off-road it would be worth paying a few dollars for a local trail map. The bike shops in most towns have good maps and are happy to help you with additional route planning as well.

Regardless of the length of your ride, always bring water and a light snack. There's nothing worse than fixing a flat in the blazing sun and being out of food and water. Despite the huge breakfast you may have consumed, you'll be ready for a snack after a few hours of riding, and those corner stores aren't always right on your route! Off-road it can be downright dangerous to run out of food and water.

Before leaving on your trip, take a jaunt over to the local bike shop for a tune-up. Have the cables tightened, tires inflated, the chain lubricated and derailleurs adjusted. Once you're underway, make sure at least one person on your ride has basic bike repair tools (and knows how to use them)! At the very least, carry a spare tube, tire patch kit and a pump. Thirty miles may not be a long ride, but it's a heck of a long walk. . .

Training

The routes in this book were chosen for recreational cyclists; that is, riders who enjoy getting out and seeing an area by bicycle, but who are not necessarily training for the Tour de France. However, you will enjoy your cycling vacation much more if you have been riding regularly. Getting out on your bicycle just two to three times a week will make a difference in your overall conditioning. Read the ride descriptions before heading out on your trip; some routes are more suited to less-energetic cyclists than others. The off-road rides included in this book are generally more strenuous and more technically challenging than the road rides; you should be comfortable riding on singletrack before attempting to do these rides.

What to Wear

We have a saying here in the Northwest: "If you don't like the weather, just wait a minute." More than once we headed out in cycling shorts and t-shirts and found we had to stop and put on all our rain gear at some point in the ride. Thankfully, the reverse is often true, but the point is: no matter how nice (or awful) the day is, be ready for a change. Particularly in the mountains or along the coast, storm fronts can move in quickly, and temperatures can change 20° in as many minutes. Always have a warm pullover and a waterproof jacket with you. If you're riding in the fall, rain pants can make the difference between a great ride and a miserable one. Conversely, it doesn't hurt to have shorts on under your bike tights when you set out on a chilly morning; you could be overheating by noon! You don't need to tow your entire wardrobe behind you, but a few extra layers will allow you to adapt to a variety of weather conditions.

And one more thing: don't leave home without an ANSI- or SNELL-approved helmet. Regardless of how competent you are on a bike, how remote your route is or how slowly you might be riding—wear one. Accidents can—and do—happen in every imaginable situation, and the risk simply isn't worth it.

Riding in Traffic or On the Trail

While we tried to select routes with the least amount of traffic, it was often necessary to ride through a busy area to get to the open roads. Routes with especially heavy traffic areas are marked in each cue sheet. Some routes are more appropriate for experienced riders, although the majority of routes are suitable for riders of any ability. After all, even experienced cyclists prefer a quiet ride!

If you've chosen to try some of the off-road rides, be courteous to other trail users such as hikers and horseback riders. If you encounter horses, dismount and stand beside your bike while speaking calmly to the horse and rider. Keep your bike under control at all times, and stay on the trail. Do not ride in any areas posted off-limits to bicyclists!

When to Go

The Northwest is at its finest in July, August and September. June can be rainy and October is unpredictable, but for three months one is almost guaranteed glorious weather: 75° sunny days, no humidity and clear blue skies. Unfortunately, most tourists are also aware of this window of opportunity, and flock to the Northwest en masse during this time. If you can schedule your riding after Labor Day, you'll be glad you did. If you must vacation during the peak summer months, make every attempt to go midweek. Traffic on the roads will be reduced, ferry lines will be shorter and you'll have a much easier time getting reservations at inns. Also, plan to stay at least two days; by the time you get to your destination and unpack, meet the innkeepers and stroll the grounds, get your riding gear on and head out the door, it'll be time to go again already if you aren't staying a second night. We planned a short and a longer route from each inn, allowing you to take a ride your first day, and then go for a longer tour the second.

BICYCLING IN THE PACIFIC NORTHWEST

The Pacific Northwest has rapidly achieved a reputation as a bicyclist's mecca, offering some of the most varied terrain in the world. Ranging from rugged coastline to dense rain forests, rolling plains to sweet-smelling fruit orchards, and jagged mountain peaks to green valleys dotted by farms, there is truly something here for everyone. A madrona-lined road suddenly opens up to reveal islands emerging from sparkling water. An arduous mountain climb offers breathtaking vistas with every pedal-stroke. A rapid descent is suddenly halted by the sight of Orcas breaching off shore.

There are delights to be found year-round here. Pedal through acres of blooming tulip fields in La Conner in the spring, or pause on a country road to watch the peaches being harvested near Leavenworth. Enjoy the dry sunny days of summer, and stop for a quick swim in one of hundreds of lakes, rivers and bays. In autumn plan a wine-tasting tour in Walla Walla, or ride up to Goat Wall in Mazama for a 360° view of fall color in the mountains. Even in the winter, a wet ride may be rewarded by a spectacular sun break and a rainbow over the Columbia River.

The physical beauty of our region is complemented by an ample variety of cultural, historical and educational attractions, many of which we've tried to incorporate on the rides chosen for this guide. The inns themselves often have a rich history, and the innkeepers generally have a wealth of information about the area; on innkeepers' advice, we discovered wineries, museums, historical sites, festivals and unique attractions.

The rain in the Northwest is legendary, and frankly somewhat exaggerated. While the average rainfall ranges from 19" on the northern Olympic Peninsula to 150" in the rain forest, it rarely rains from July to September. Eastern Washington and Oregon have hot, dry summers, while the Western half of the region has average daytime temperatures around 75-80°. With no humidity and very few insects, summers here are just about perfect!

Despite rapid growth in the Northwest during the past few years, one is never more than a fifteen minute pedal away from quiet open roads. In addition to the breadth of unspoiled landscape, many cities are courting bicyclists with excellent urban cycling facilities as well. The city of Eugene, Oregon, has changed two-way roads into one-way car lanes with wide bike lanes going in either direction throughout its core. At each intersection there are signs posted specifically for bicycle traffic in addition to the car traffic signage. Buttons to push for the "Walk" sign are placed on the curb at bicycle height. As a result of these bicycle-friendly improvements, it seems almost everyone in Eugene commutes by bicycle!

The Oregon Department of Transportation has dedicated 1% of its total annual revenue to maintaining and improving bicycle facilities in the state, and as a result, riding Highway 101 south down the coast has become a popular bicycling vacation in the Northwest. With smooth, wide shoulders, special lights through tunnels to alert cars to cyclists' presence and special bicycle-only rest stops along the way, riding on the highway is as enjoyable as on many backroads. Stores along the highway offer special deals to bicyclists, taking advantage of the ever-growing number of tourists choosing to see the beautiful Oregon Coast by bike.

Whether you choose to stick to peaceful backroads or experience the thrill of a city by bike, the territory covered in this book—over 70 rides from 32 different inns— should keep you busy for quite awhile. Whatever your cycling ability or your taste in accommodations, we hope you'll use this book to discover the splendor of the Pacific Northwest and the joys of exploring by bicycle.

INN LOCATOR

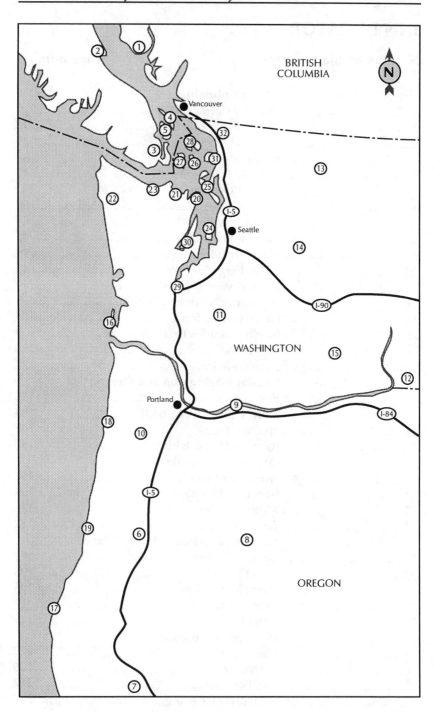

BRITISH COLUMBIA INNS AND RIDES

W e loved this little corner of Canada. The people we met were enthusiastic, helpful and unbelievably generous; at the same time, the lush green landscapes and picturesque islands were among the prettiest we've seen. The inns and rides we covered encompass the southwest portion of the mainland, the lower half of Vancouver Island and two of the Gulf Islands. While the culturally diverse city of Vancouver and the very British city of Victoria are enticing urban oases, we couldn't justify going anywhere near them by bicycle. Feel free to incorporate these exciting metropolises in your itinerary, but plan on leaving your bike on the roof rack.

You're never far from the water in British Columbia; spectacular fjords divide the southern mainland dramatically, while Vancouver Island and the smaller Gulf Islands are surrounded by the Straight of Georgia to the east and the vast Pacific to the west. As such, ferry trips are a part of travelling in this area. In the peak summer months ferry travel is a chore, but by early September the traffic has subsided and the wait is substantially reduced. In any case, when you plan to take a ferry, bring a book!

Drivers in British Columbia are less accustomed to bicyclists than their neighbors to the south, which makes for some hairy riding in places. Highway 101 along the Sunshine Coast (Roberts Creek) should be avoided as much as possible, although we did use a portion of it to link an otherwise splendid ride back to the **Country Cottage B&B.**

On Vancouver Island the traffic is only heavy on Highway 19, the major north-south thoroughfare. Riding from **Greystone Manor** in Courtenay we were able to avoid all but a mile or two of nasty traffic, and other than crossing the highway, riding from the **Pine Lodge Farm B&B** in Mill Bay was equally pleasant.

The Gulf Islands are a more pristine version of Washington's San Juan Islands: smaller in size, much less traffic, and far fewer inhabitants. Consequently, there are fewer services available and the roads have not received the same repair attention, so be sure to bring extra food and water. Pay particular attention to narrow shoulders!

Sutil Lodge on Galliano Island rents kayaks from the inn, and a twilight trip out on the bay is not to be missed—it'll give you an opportunity to work your upper body after a long day of pedaling, too!

Saltspring Island is the largest of the Gulf Islands, and has the most comprehensive services in the chain of islands. **The Old Farmhouse** is well located on the north side. Nearby Ganges is a fun little town to pedal around, and offers a surprisingly diverse assortment of bakeries, cafes and restaurants.

We mentioned Denman and Hornby Islands in the Greystone Manor chapter, and want to urge again that you visit these little gems. It is possible to ride both islands entirely in one day, though you may want to drive to the ferry landing and spare yourself the 20-mile round trip to and from the inn. Park at the ferry dock and wheel your bike onto the ferry—one ticket will allow you to see both islands. We didn't leave ourselves enough time to explore the myriad parks and beaches, but thoroughly enjoyed the quiet roads and spectacular scenery.

One last note on the following chapter: the rates listed are in U.S. dollars unless otherwise noted. U.S. travellers have been enjoying a tremendously favorable exchange rate in Canada for the past year, making an otherwise pricey trip a real bargain, but rates change rapidly. Inquire about current exchange rates when you call for reservations.

COUNTRY COTTAGE BED & BREAKFAST
Philip and Loragene Gaulin
1183 Roberts Creek Road
General Delivery
Roberts Creek, B.C. Canada V0N 2W0
(604) 885-7448
Rates: $65-115 (Canadian)

Roberts Creek is nestled into steep woods which slope down to the water along the Sunshine Coast. Although just a ferry trip and a short drive from Vancouver, this tiny town (one grocery store, a restaurant and a post office) has all the charm of a remote retreat. For perspective, take a short coast down the hill from the Country Cottage at twilight. You'll wind up at a small waterside municipal park, dazzled by a stunning view of the sun setting over Texada Island in Georgia Strait, with views of mountainous Vancouver Island off in the distance.

The Country Cottage is a lovingly restored home tucked behind tall green hedges, surrounded by tended rose gardens and natural landscaping. Loragene will enthusiastically greet you with tea or lemonade and a plate of cookies hot from the oven. The main house opens into the front parlor, with a delightfully cluttered array of old toy trucks, books and magazines, an antique postcard collection and a dollhouse arranged around the doily-covered armchairs, coffee tables, weaving loom and player piano. Admire the wood inlay in the hardwood floor, which Philip painstakingly created during the initial remodelling of the house.

Around the corner is the sunny kitchen where breakfast is served. Above the table sun pours through a bank of windows, where an antique bottle collection lines the sill and twigs artfully weave above each window. Red and blue walls with dark wood wainscotting and oil lamps on the table and hutch lend a cozily rustic feel to the room, where Loragene does all the cooking over a 1927 wood stove. A screen door leads out to the porch lined with tall rubber work boots, pulled on for trips out to the garden in back or the henhouse just beyond.

Upstairs in the main house is the Rose Room, a bright alcove room with a peaked roof and white wrought iron bed. A "double wedding ring" pattern white quilt nicely complements pale pink and white walls. An unusual half-bath off the bedroom more closely resembles a sitting room than a bathroom, with a glass

ceiling keeping the large room bathed in sun, a white wicker reading chair and warm brick and wood floor. The elegant pedestal sink was recovered from the controversial remodelling of the famous Empress Hotel in Victoria.

The B&B's namesake, the Country Cottage, is a picture-perfect little white cottage across the driveway, surrounded by climbing roses twining about the white picket fence, mature fruit trees and window boxes bursting with geraniums. Two stately green Adirondack chairs beckon from a tidy square of lawn. Through the cheerful red door of the cottage, a small foyer leads to the living room with pine floors, small couch and antique rocker, brick hearth and antique woodstove from Norway. The kitchen, in the far corner, is decorated simply in blue and white, right down to the dishes stored in the antique hutch and the throw rugs on the floor. Stained glass hangs in the four big windows which look out on the garden. A simple log cabin pattern quilt and tasteful flower prints decorate a small bedroom off the living room. The cottage has its own private bath with a tub.

Although all three room choices were special, our accommodations in the Cedar Lodge, which Loragene describes as "a treehouse for active adults," were our favorite. This cozy hideaway, perfect for two or three couples, is found on the back side of the property, nestled among huge cedar and Douglas fir trees and up a flight of stairs. You enter from a deck overlooking the trees and meadow, where the Gaulin's two sheep graze. Coming in through the glass door you are surrounded by warm wood walls and ceiling, with a painted red floor and an inviting river-rock fireplace. Three large skylights and a wall of windows overlooking the deck allow light to stream in through the trees. An overstuffed couch and armchair, Craftsman-era Morris rocker and straight-back chair, all loaded with patterned pillows, form a comfortable grouping near the fire. Large wool rugs in a Native American design, a green and red blanket over the couch, and warm throws over the back of each chair all add to the authentic lodge feeling, but the artwork throughout the lodge is most convincing. Old postcards of hunting and fishing expeditions, light fixtures, cabinet handles and even a cribbage board made of deer antlers, a pair of wood and gut snowshoes, a collection of flyfishing rods and a pair of wooden skis are among the numerous artistic touches the Gaulins have added.

A long counter with a deep sink above and cupboards below separates a fully-equipped spacious kitchen from the living room. In one corner of the main room a few steps rise up to a wide bed enclosed by warm wood walls on three sides and open to the room on the other. The bed is covered with a red wool blanket and lots of stuffed pillows, on which a stuffed bear reclines. The bear will be waving at you when you arrive, and when you come in the evening, he will magically be propped up against the pillows reading a book!

Off the main room and through French doors, a step down takes you to a small foyer which leads up a ladder to another loft bed, or in to the bathroom with clawfoot tub, or out a door onto the deck. From this door you walk down a ramp to the sauna house, which has a private bedroom next door to the sauna room. The ceiling in the bedroom slopes to the window which looks out through the woods; the beige walls, bent willow shelves, green Hudson Bay blanket and red flannel sheets all contribute to the sense of being in a cabin deep in the woods.

We stayed two nights in the Cedar Lodge, and difficult as it was to tear ourselves away in the morning, breakfast made it worth the trek across the lawn each morning! The first morning we began with a fruit plate, coffee and orange juice, before diving into an English muffin topped with salmon, tomato, capers and a poached egg smothered in a delicate cheese sauce. Spicy sausage and a fresh nasturtium blossom shared the plate. As Loragene tries to alternate between savory and sweet entrees, the next morning our main course was a large helping of crusty french bread baked with fruit and melted chocolate inside!

Fortunately, you'll have no trouble working off breakfast on the rides from here, in fact you may want to digest a bit before heading off on the uphill portion of the Roberts Creek Loop!

BIKING FROM COUNTRY COTTAGE B&B

Terrain
Highway 101 is on the flat shore of the Strait of Georgia, but everything else goes up from there. Most loops for mountain biking go up and come down again, so it's an even give and take. The Sechelt-Roberts Creek Loop begins with a substantial climb for about five miles.

Road Conditions
Road surfaces are not overly maintained and have some serious shoulder variation. Logging roads are active haul roads and should be used with caution. Some are restricted (mostly for combustion-engines, not bikes), but check first with the Ministry of Forests office.

Traffic
With Highway 101 being the main thoroughfare to Powell River, it has an exceptional amount of high speed traffic. If there is a ferry going out of Langdale expect people to be going all out to make it. Except for the ride to Gibsons, mountain biking is your safest bet.

Nearest Bike Shop
Trail Bay Sports
5504 Trail Ave.
Sechelt, B.C., Canada V0N 2W0
(604) 885-2512

Or   The Real Bicycle Shop
934 Davis Rd.
Gibsons, B.C., Canada V0N 2W0
(604) 886-7192

Best Time to Ride
Late spring through early fall.

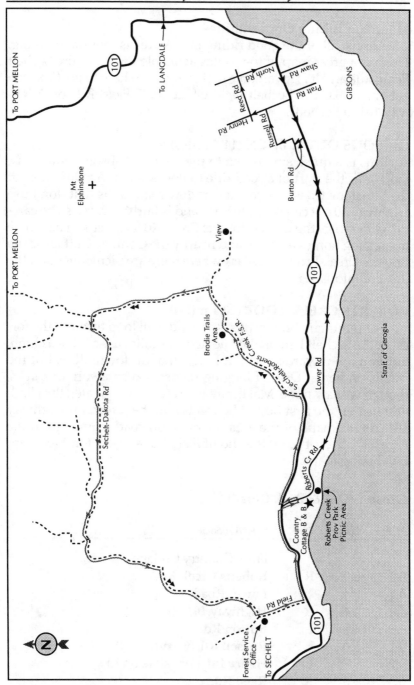

Gibsons Out & Back ——— Roberts Creek Loop ———

Mountain Biking Opportunities

Almost all of the good riding in this area is mountain biking. There is a great map of the routes available for the entire Sechelt Peninsula and it is invaluable in finding out where to go. (You can get one at B.C.F.S. Sechelt Field Office, 1975 Field Rd., off Highway 101 in Sechelt).

GIBSONS OUT & BACK (14.7 miles)

This is a quick spin down to the town of Gibsons, either as a loop or as the start of a road ride to Port Mellon. As with most of the Sunshine Coast, there are very few road loops that don't use Highway 101. It can be quite busy and is fairly narrow, so be careful. Otherwise, the Lower Roberts Creek Rd. is quiet and has some interesting homes along it, and nearby the Country Cottage is the Roberts Creek Provincial Park where there are picnic sites and the most fabulous sunsets.

ROBERTS CREEK LOOP (20.1 miles)

For mountain bikers, this is a wonderful loop through the forest of the Sechelt Peninsula. The first five miles are a bit of a climb, but you are rewarded with a long, smooth downhill. All of the ride is on Forest District logging roads so keep aware of trucks, though we saw none. Make sure to bring enough water, the climb will use up the first bottle! Be careful on the return on Highway 101. As for maps of the area for more off-road riding, go to the Forest District office at the end of Field Rd. and ask for the mountain biking maps.

Gibsons Out & Back (Road)

Pt.-Pt.	Cum.	Dir.	Street/Landmark
			From Country Cottage
0.0	0.0	R	**Roberts Creek Rd.**
0.4	0.4	L	**Lower Road**
4.0	4.4	R	**Highway 101**
0.5	4.9	L	**Burton Rd.**
0.1	5.0	L	**Russell Rd.** (Curves to R)
0.7	5.7	L	**Henry Rd.** (Tire store on L)
0.3	6.0	R	**Reed Rd.**
1.2	7.2	R	**North Rd.** (very busy intersection)

0.5	7.7	R	Highway 101 (R turn lane)
0.3	8.0	X	Shaw
0.5	8.5	X	Pratt Rd.
1.6	10.1	L	**Lower Road**
4.1	14.2	R	**Roberts Creek Rd.**
0.5	14.7	–	Country Cottage on L

Roberts Creek Loop (MTB)

Pt.-Pt.	Cum.	Dir.	Street/Landmark
			From Country Cottage
0.0	0.0	L	**Roberts Creek Rd.**
0.4	0.4	R	**Highway 101**
0.9	1.3	L	**Sechelt-Roberts Creek Forest Service Rd.** (gravel and uphill)
1.3	2.6	S	**Pass Roberts Flume Rd. on L**
1.4	4.0	–	View at end of road to R (unmarked)
1.6	5.6	–	Road levels out
0.4	6.0	S	**Pass spur road on R**
0.6	6.6	–	Steep descent
0.2	6.8	CL	**Sechelt-Dakota Forest Service Rd.** (downhill—you'll love it)
0.2	7.0	S	**Pass spur road on R**
3.3	10.3	S	**Pass spur road on R**
3.0	13.3	–	Awesome views of Strait of Georgia
1.7	15.0	S	**Pass Airport-Sechelt Rd.**
0.5	15.5	L	**Field Rd. (paved)**
1.0	16.5	L	**Highway 101**
3.2	19.7	R	**Roberts Creek Rd.**
0.4	20.1	–	Country Cottage on R

GREYSTONE MANOR
Mike and Mo Shipton
4014 Haus Road
RR6 Site 684-C2
Courtenay, B.C. Canada V9N 8H9
(604) 338-1422
Rates: $45-58

Bicyclists with a passion for gardens will have two treats in store at the Greystone Manor. In addition to its proximity to fabulous rides down forest paths, through rolling countryside and out to delightful little islands, this B&B has the most magnificent garden we saw all summer. When Mike and Mo Shipton moved to British Columbia from their native England in 1990, the inn was surrounded by nothing but a daunting expanse of lawn. Five years later, one and a half acres of former lawn is a medley of flower beds, native plants, vegetable gardens and specimen trees, ablaze in color from early spring well into the fall. Contoured paths weave through the garden, happening upon benches to sit and gaze with admiration at the effect achieved by this ambitious effort. The gardens slope gradually to the banks of Comox Harbor, where an interesting breakwater has been formed by shipwrecks from years ago.

The house itself was built in 1918 by a Scottish lumber baron, back when the booming logging and mining industries filled the Comox Valley with diverse ethnic groups. At one time the largest Chinatown north of San Francisco could be found in nearby Cumberland, although all that remains of that legacy today is a small museum in town and an interpretive sign on the side of the road.

Four guest rooms are available at the Greystone Manor: the Twin, Double, Queen and Maid's Rooms. All these spotlessly clean rooms are located upstairs, and share the two baths in the hall. One of the baths is a modern addition with a shower, while the other features a clawfoot tub and antique combination towel, glass and soap rack. Steam radiators in all the rooms reminded us of our Midwest upbringings with their comforting soft gurgling throughout the night. The bedrooms are all modestly appointed, very quiet and have lovely garden or water views.

The Twin Room is done in soft pinks and purples, with floral print wallpaper and two twin beds. Tall trees and the wooded drive are visible from this alcove room.

The Double Room is light and cheerful, with broad windows revealing views of the gardens below and the harbor beyond. Reading lights above the double bed let you stay up late and plan the next day's ride!

Down a remarkably narrow hallway is the Maid's Room, with a coved ceiling and view out through the trees to a hint of garden below. White walls, a white wicker nightstand and colorful flowered curtains brighten the snug room.

The Queen Room has the best view in the house: sitting up in bed we could see the gardens, the harbor and the Coast Mountains off in the distance. White ruffled curtains accent bold floral print wallpaper in mauve and light pinks.

Downstairs guests are free to enjoy the parlor and dining room. The parlor in the front of house has plush carpet and dark wood panelling, with a large couch and loveseat grouped about a cozy glass-front woodstove. A baby grand piano in the corner invites you to play, or you can browse the scrapbooks filled with before and after pictures of the ambitious landscaping project underway. China plates line the ledge around the room, while potted plants sit in the bay window relishing the sun.

Across the wide foyer, the dining room offers seating for up to eight people at a long table covered with an elegant red cloth. The same dark panelling gives the room an distinguished feel, while the lace curtains in the window brighten it up. More china is displayed on the ledge about the room and in an antique hutch. We helped ourselves to orange and raisin muffins and fresh fruit with our coffee and juice, and then were served some deliciously fluffy apple pancakes with a fresh raspberry sauce. We lingered over breakfast talking to the Meyers from Illinois about what to see and do in the area, and finally headed off to see the nearby town of Cumberland.

On our way back from this pleasant ride we paused in the remains of an old orchard to read a roadside sign detailing the rise and fall of Cumberland's Chinatown. As we read the sign we heard a noise in the apple tree beside us, and glanced up to spot a baby bear high up in the branches. Wandering over for closer examination, we noticed a second baby up in the tree! Amazed at our good fortune in spotting *two* bears in one day, we moved in a little closer to take a picture, and suddenly were looking straight at Mama Bear, who was not high up in the tree, but right at eye level—and less than pleased to see us! Needless to say, we pedaled on. Keep your eyes open while you ride this area; you never know what you might run into!

BIKING FROM THE GREYSTONE MANOR

Terrain

Most of the countryside spills down from the Forbidden Plateau into the Comox Valley, which has the Strait of Georgia as its eastern boundary. The valley is flat, with good views of both Georgia Strait and the Mount Washington area. Denman and Hornby Islands offer rolling hills with some spectacular traffic-less roads traversing the shoreline.

Road Conditions

In the Comox Valley, roads are in fair condition, with some shoulders on the country roads. Denman and Hornby roads have good surfaces. Comox Lake Road becomes increasingly rough as you get near the lake. Fitzgerald Rd. is gravel, but smooth enough for a road bike.

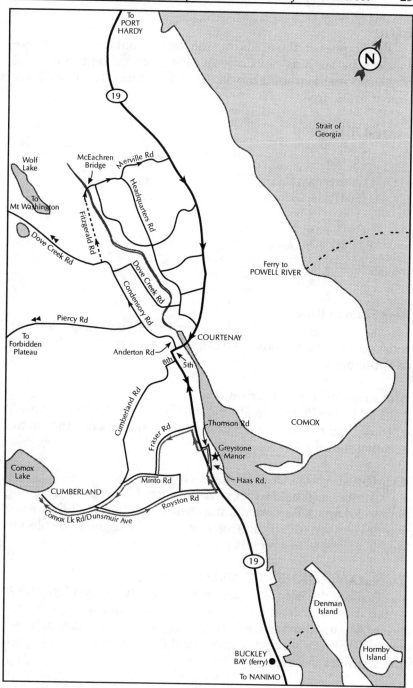

North Farm Loop ——— Cumberland Loop ·········

Traffic

Fairly quiet on the roads outside the city, but the Island Highway can be busy, as can Cliffe Ave. In-town riding can be a bit crazy, especially around the 5th St. intersection. The islands are almost traffic free.

Nearest Bike Shop

Pedal Pushers
137 5th St.
Courtenay, B.C. 8H9
(604) 334-4845

Or   Cyclepath
2130 Cliffe Ave.
Courtenay, B.C. 8H9
(604) 338-0886

Best Time to Ride

May through September for mountain biking, road biking almost year round. Comox Lake Dam area has a mountain bike race in September.

Mountain Biking Opportunities

Forbidden Plateau in Strathcona Provincial Park has a variety of trails, and the Mt. Washington Resort offers its facilities in the summer months.

CUMBERLAND LOOP (16.8 miles)

Cumberland holds a lot of history for this area. Cairns along Sutton Rd. mark the communities here in the 1880s to 1920s. Keep your eyes open for wildlife too—we saw a bear and two cubs sitting in an apple tree on this route!

DENMAN/HORNBY ISLANDS

Explore the islands at your own pace. The second ferry takes you to Hornby Island with its incredible windblown rock formations. All island roads are fairly rolling but mostly quiet between ferries. This is a great day trip—start early so you can ride back the ten miles in daylight.

NORTH FARM LOOP (25.2 miles)

Following the Tsolum River valley, this route meanders through areas northwest of Courtenay and provides some pastoral contrast to the rapidly growing Comox Valley. A possible side trip would be to ride out Piercy Rd. toward the Mt. Washington Ski Area for some better views of the valley below.

Cumberland Loop (Road)

Pt.-Pt.	Cum.	Dir.	Street/Landmark
			From Greystone Manor
0.0	0.0	R	**Haas Rd.**
0.2	0.2	–	Haas changes to **Thomsen Rd.**
0.1	0.3	R	**Island Highway 19**
0.9	1.2	L	**Fraser Rd.**
1.8	3.0	R	**Minto Rd.**
0.8	3.8	L	**Cumberland Rd.**
1.8	5.6	CL	**Cumberland changes into Fourth St.**
0.3	5.9	R	**Dunsmuir Ave.**
0.3	6.2	–	Cumberland Museum on R
0.1	6.3	L	**Sutton Rd.**
2.6	8.9	–	Comox Lake Park (beach)
		TA	
2.6	11.5	R	**Dunsmuir Ave./Royston Rd.**
0.6	12.1	–	Cumberland Miner's Park on R
4.0	16.1	L	**Island Highway 19**
0.6	16.7	R	**Hilton** (CL into **Haas**)
0.1	16.8	–	Greystone Manor on R

Denman/Hornby Islands (Road)

Pt.-Pt.	Cum.	Dir.	Street/Landmark
			From Greystone Manor
0.0	0.0	L	**Haas Rd.** (changes to **Hilton**)
0.1	0.1	L	**Island Highway 19** (good shoulder)
0.5	0.6	X	**Royston Rd.**
7.9	8.5	–	Rest area on R (restrooms)
1.9	10.4	L	**Ferry Dock for Denman Island**
		TA	Reverse route to return

North Farm Loop (Road)

Pt.-Pt.	Cum.	Dir.	Street/Landmark
			From Greystone Manor
0.0	0.0	R	**Haas Rd.**
0.2	0.2	–	Haas changes to **Thomsen Rd.**
0.1	0.3	R	**Island Highway 19**
1.9	2.2	X	26th (Island Hwy changes into **Cliffe Ave.**)
0.6	2.8	X	17th Ave. (go straight to City Centre)
0.5	3.3	X	8th St.
0.1	3.4	R	**5th** (Pedal Pushers on L)
0.1	3.5	L	**Anderton** (immediate L before bridge)
0.4	3.9	X	Putledge River (Anderton changes to **Condensory Rd.**)
1.4	5.3	X	Piercy Rd. (good views, farms, mountains)
3.0	8.3	CL	**Orr Rd.**
1.1	9.4	R	**Fitzgerald Rd.** (unmarked gravel road, goes into a beautiful, quiet grove)
0.9	10.3	–	Fitzgerald changes to pavement
0.7	11.0	R	**McEachren bridge**
0.8	11.8	CR	**Headquarters Rd.**
1.1	12.9	CL	**Headquarters Rd.**
0.2	13.1	X	Headquarters changes to **Merville**
1.2	14.3	R	**Island Highway 19** (good shoulder, views to L, downhill)
6.8	21.1	X	Headquarters Rd.
0.3	21.4	X	Ryan Rd. (at Courtney River bridge, get in L lane with traffic-very busy intersection)
0.4	21.8	L	**Cliffe Ave.**
0.2	22.0	X	8th (heavy traffic next two miles)
0.4	22.4	X	17th
0.7	23.1	X	26th
1.8	24.9	L	**Thomson Rd.**
0.1	25.0	R	**Haas Rd.**
0.2	25.2	–	Greystone Manor on L

PINE LODGE FARM BED & BREAKFAST
Barbara and Cliff Clarke
3191 Mutter Road
Mill Bay, B.C. Canada V0R 2P0
(604) 743-4083
Rates: $75-85

Pine Lodge Farm sits on 28 acres of gently sloping hillside covered in madrona (arbutus this side of the border), with stunning views of sparkling Mill Bay, Saanich Inlet and Satellite Channel. Former owners of a Victoria antique shop, Cliff and Barbara joke that they built the B&B eleven years ago to have a place to house all the antiques they'd collected. And that would have been reason enough, as they've amassed some impressive pieces over the years.

The lodge was built around the most impressive of the collection: the balcony of the old Capitol Theatre in Victoria. When the 1914 structure, built entirely of Canadian fir, was torn down, Cliff saved the balcony and railings, using the pieces to create the second floor passageway which connects the bedrooms and overlooks the grand living room below. Stained glass from the theater was also salvaged and used throughout the living room, as were doors, windows, chandeliers and other furnishings from razed turn-of-the-century buildings around Victoria.

The result is a fitting showcase for the rest of the museum-like antique collection, which includes prints and engravings, an organ, a grandfather clock, red velvet chairs, an enormous china hutch filled with one-of-a-kind place settings, model ships, an old musket, a piano, an inlaid wood rocker, beautiful china lamps and glass-front bookshelves housing first-edition rare books. Perhaps the most unique of the assortment is the collection of Dolton whiskey jugs, dating from the 1870s. (Our favorite of these was the monk-figurine jug!) Wide fir floors polished to a rich shine sparkle beneath deep red oriental rugs. Couches and end tables are grouped beside the massive river rock fireplace which extends the height of the two-story room. Broad windows the length of the room take advantage of the splendid water view.

Upstairs there are seven rooms, each with a private bath. The rooms are similar in size and decor, with antique armoires, dressers and chairs throughout. Thick carpet and pine paneling warms each room, decorated simply with prints and engravings. Most

rooms have queen-sized beds, although Room 5 has two twin beds and Room 2 has a double. Rooms 2 through 6 have woodsy views toward the back of the property, while 1 and 7 face out over the full-length porch to the water. All the guests are welcome to recline on the porch and watch the ferry traversing Satellite Channel.

You'll wake in the morning to the sound of roosters crowing—the Clarkes keep 100 chickens on the farm—and smell your breakfast cooking downstairs. Breakfast is served from 7:30 to 9 a.m. in the dining room, which opens off the living room. A long table with leaves to accommodate a houseful of guests dominates the room, while the shiny broad pine floor and wood cookstove add a cozy touch. A few unique pieces grace the room, such as the spinning wheel in the corner, the antique telephone and the china hutch displaying pewter plates and mugs, but the view of the water will really command your attention.

Breakfast is a hearty farm meal: orange juice and coffee, fresh eggs cooked the way you like them, bacon, toast, an assortment of homemade jams and a helping of crisp hash brown potatoes. Pine Lodge Farm is a stop for the Sea-to-Sky bike tour, so the Clarkes are accustomed to accommodating bicyclists' appetites! As guests arrive at the table, Cliff and Barbara bustle about chatting and fixing breakfast; guests are welcome to loll about the table after eating, but the Clarkes will be off to open their country furniture store in nearby Cowichan Bay after fixing the meal.

One of our favorite rides from Mill Bay was a simple loop out along the water, taking advantage of little traffic and beautiful views through the trees, which ended up at a delightful provincial park—a great spot for a swim or a picnic. The Shawnigan Lake Loop is a tad more demanding, but explores the woods, farms and lake to the west of Mill Bay, offering a different perspective on this tranquil spot.

BIKING FROM PINE LODGE FARM B&B

Terrain

Mill Bay is a quiet little town on the east shore of Saanich Inlet and offers a bit of farmland near the water and hills as you go further to the west. It is the link off Highway 1 to Shawnigan Lake and the Koksilah River Provincial Park directly to the west. Most of the area is popular recreational area and caters to hikers, bikers and water sports.

Road Conditions

Island Highway has a good shoulder, most other roads are narrow. Shawnigan Lake Roads (east and west) are rough in places and are narrow and winding. Mill Bay Rd. has an excellent surface.

Traffic

Because there are few paved roads the traffic can be heavy on the weekends, especially around Shawnigan Lake. Fortunately, most people are not travelling at high speed. Mill Bay Rd. is exceptionally pleasant to ride.

Nearest Bike Shop

Cycle 'n Sports
P.O. Box 208
#9 - 2720 Mill Bay Rd.
Mill Bay, B.C. V0R 2P0
(604) 743-7433

Best Time to Ride

Almost year round riding possible, with the winters being fairly wet and cool. June through early October is best.

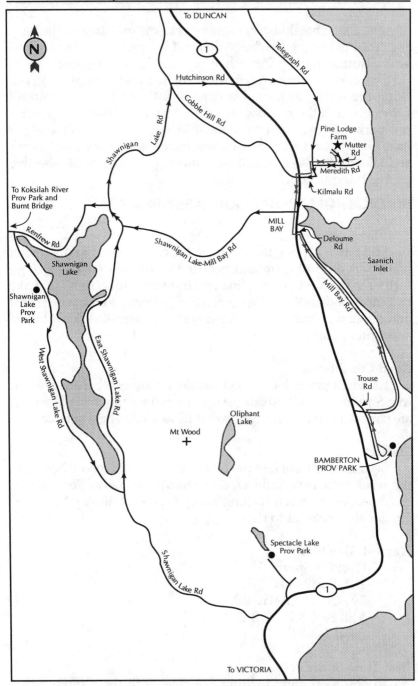

Shawnigan Lake Loop ——— Bamberton Out & Back ———

Mountain Biking Opportunities

Koksilah River Provincial Park at the end of Renfrew Rd. has a large selection of trails from the casual fire road to extremely technical singletrack. Most mountain bikers you meet can tell you which trails are best. Try to get a park map before you go, but remember, trails are not marked.

BAMBERTON OUT & BACK (15.2 miles)

Mill Bay Road is beautiful, leading to the Bamberton Provincial Park where it would be conceivable to sit for a whole day watching the water. A tranquil spot to escape to. A short stretch on Highway #1 is the only difficulty.

SHAWNIGAN LAKE LOOP (26.0 miles)

This loop follows the shore of Shawnigan Lake and provides some lovely views and water access at the park. Shawnigan Lake Road is narrow so stay to the right. Aitken & Fraser is a good place to grab a cool drink on your way by.

Bamberton Out & Back (Road)

Pt.-Pt.	Cum.	Dir.	Street/Landmark
			From Pine Lodge Farm
0.0	0.0	S	**Mutter Rd.**
0.3	0.3	R	**Merideth Rd.**
0.4	0.7	L	**Telegraph Rd.**
0.3	1.0	R	**Kilmalu Rd.**
0.3	1.3	L	**Highway Route #1**
0.5	1.8	X	Shawnigan Lake Rd.
0.4	2.2	L	**Deloume Rd.**
0.1	2.3	R	**Mill Bay Rd.**
4.2	6.5	L	**Trouse Rd.**
0.1	6.6	L	**Bamberton Rd.**
1.0	7.6	–	Bamberton Beach parking area (picnic areas, restrooms, swimming, sunrises)
		TA	
0.0	7.6	S	**Bamberton Rd.**
1.0	8.6	R	**Trouse Rd.**
0.1	8.7	R	**Mill Bay Rd.** (great views)

4.2	12.9	L	**Deloume Rd.**
0.1	13.0	R	**Highway Route #1**
0.4	13.4	X	Shawnigan Lake Rd.
0.5	13.9	R	**Kilmalu Rd.**
0.3	14.2	L	**Telegraph Rd.**
0.3	14.5	R	**Merideth Rd.** (uphill)
0.4	14.9	L	**Mutter Rd.**
0.3	15.2	–	Pine Lodge Farm straight ahead

Shawnigan Lake Loop (Road)

Pt.-Pt.	Cum.	Dir.	Street/Landmark
			From Pine Lodge Farm
0.0	0.0	S	**Mutter Rd.**
0.3	0.3	R	**Merideth Rd.**
0.4	0.7	L	**Telegraph Rd.**
0.3	1.0	R	**Kilmalu Rd.**
0.3	1.3	L	**Highway Route #1** (cross with light)
0.5	1.8	R	**Shawnigan Lake Rd./Mill Bay Rd.** (narrow shoulder; hilly; moderate traffic)
3.3	5.1	R	**Shawnigan Lake Rd.** (Aitken & Fraser General Store on corner)
0.3	5.4	L	**Renfrew Rd.**
2.7	8.1	L	**W. Shawnigan Lake Rd.**
1.5	9.6	–	W. Shawnigan Lake Park (trails, restrooms, swimming)
0.2	9.8	L	**W. Shawnigan Lake Rd.** (beautiful, rolling hills)
4.1	13.9	L	**Shawnigan Lake Rd.** (lake views; narrow shoulder)
4.7	18.6	X	Shawnigan Lake Rd./Mill Bay Rd.
0.3	18.9	R	**Shawnigan Lake Rd.**
2.8	21.7	R	**Hutchinson Rd.**
1.1	22.8	X	Highway Route #1
1.2	24.0	R	**Telegraph Rd.**
1.3	25.3	L	**Merideth Rd.** (uphill)
0.4	25.7	L	**Mutter Rd.**
0.3	26.0	–	Pine Lodge Farm straight ahead

SUTIL LODGE
Tom and Ann Hennessy
637 Southwind Road
Galliano Island, B.C. Canada V0N 1P0
(604) 539-2930
Rates $50-75 (Canadian)

G alliano Island is a heavily wooded, narrow outcropping in the Northern Gulf Islands. Popular among hikers and bicyclists alike, the island attracts those looking to escape the bustle of urban existence. You'll have no trouble doing that in this tranquil paradise; in fact, other than a couple of restaurants and a gas station, you won't be bothered by civilization at all! Make a stop at the cash machine before getting on the ferry, since there are no banks on the island. Dining choices on the island are somewhat limited, but we enjoyed the Hummingbird Pub, a popular local hangout with a remarkably comprehensive menu and a good selection of microbrews.

Ideally located on 20 acres of forest and fields at the base of Montague Harbor, the site now home to Sutil Lodge was a native settlement for 3500 years; artifacts in the harbor dating much later have been found. Towering maples at the water's edge are thought to be "conference trees" for the Coast Salish people who lived on these shores two centuries ago.

The green and white clapboard home has an interesting contemporary history, too. Built in 1928, it was run as a fishing lodge from 1929 to 1948, then used as a private residence until the 1960s, when it was again opened to the public. In the 60s, artists and "free-thinkers" travelling the coast came to rent the little cabins at the edge of the harbor for $20 a month. The 16 little cabins have dwindled to 8, and prices have gone up a bit, but under Tom and Anne Hennessy's care since 1986, Sutil Lodge still evokes memories of the past while providing modern amenities.

The lodge is comfortably furnished with 1930s decor, creating a homey atmosphere that encourages lounging about. The living room has dark wood floors with a worn oriental rug in the center, a low round table in front of the woodstove, several overstuffed armchairs and a burgundy velvet couch. A vase of fresh flowers atop a lace doily sits on a round table beside the multipaned window, through which one views the water lapping at the shore and Mt. Prevost off in the distance. Old photos on the turquoise walls

step back through time to show the lodge looking much as it does today, with visitors from the 30s and 40s reclining in Adirondack chairs on the lawn. Scrapbooks throughout the room are filled with brochures for the lodge from the 40s and 50s, as well as photos of the family that ran the resort for several decades.

All six of the rooms share the two upstairs and one downstairs baths. The smaller single bedroom downstairs, which views the orchard and woods behind the house, was occupied when we visited. The upstairs rooms have low-ceilings and cozy alcoves created by the eaves of the house. We had the cedar-paneled room in the front corner, with hypnotic views of the harbor from the bed on a ledge built under the window. The green and white bedspread complemented cheerful white wicker chairs and dhurrie rugs over dark wood floors. A 1920s dresser with attached round mirror and small desk at the foot of the bed rounded out the furnishings.

Across the hall is a small room with views of apple and cedar trees, perfect for a single traveller. Down the hall in the front of the house are two more rooms facing the water, both with beds under the window and dhurrie rugs on the dark floors. The room closest the stairs has a nautical feel—crisp navy and white curtains match the bedspread and throw pillows. A leather slingback chair and small desk provide places to sit and admire the view, also reflected in the unusual mirror framed by horse tack.

The bright room in the far front corner has unfinished cedar panelling and the same throw rugs and snug alcove bed under the window as the other waterside rooms. A unique loveseat has been fashioned from an antique iron baby's crib.

The last room is in the northeast corner, facing the orchard and cedars. The unfinished cedar walls and light polished floors accent the fun artwork hanging on the walls. A dresser and wicker trunk have been painted blue to match the blue and white curtains hanging in the window. The bed is snugly nestled into the cozy corner alcove.

For several years prior to purchasing Sutil Lodge, the Hennessys had operated a sailboat charter operation on their 1000 square-foot catamaran, the Great White Cloud. Since opening the inn they have continued to offer charter trips on the boat, which are combined with kayaking trips using the boat as a base. While the boat is moored elsewhere on the island, a fleet of kayaks is kept at the Lodge. After a long day riding, consider renting a kayak in the evening and paddling out through the sheltered cove to see the sun set over the islands. Watching the sky turn all shades of pink and orange before slipping behind the horizon was breathtaking. As we slowly paddled home, the stars came out and phosphorescence magically created sparkling swirls in the water with each paddle stroke.

You'll need the extra exercise for the spread that awaits you in the morning. Breakfast is served in the dining hall adjacent to the house. The hall is reminiscent of summer camp, with dark wood floors, a fireplace and low windows looking out at the ancient maples and harbor just beyond. Oars, deer antlers, fishing rods and old photos decorate the walls while the woodstove chases away the morning chill. If you wander in early you can start with the juice, coffee, toast and cereal set out on the sideboard as you read the morning's menu, propped up on a restored freezer chest. Forewarned by the menu, we saved room for the next round of goodies: a baked breakfast casserole of apples and blueberries topped with creme fraiche, served with buttermilk currant scones and toasted veggie herb bread. We completed our feast with a choice between whole-grain pumpkin waffles with cranberry maple sauce and eggs any style served with Canadian bacon or smoked salmon. Ann makes a "picnic breakfast" available for people who have to leave early to catch a ferry, but we couldn't imagine dashing away from here!

When you do pedal off, you'll be in for some great rides. If you want additional routes, stop in and see Matthew at Galliano Bicycle Rental and Repair—he's got a wealth of information about where to ride on the island, and may even be persuaded to join you for a ride.

BIKING FROM SUTIL LODGE

Terrain

Galiano is truly "the jewel of the Gulf Islands". The terrain is comprised of both salt water views and arbutus-covered bluffs. From Dionisio Point the land rises up to the Bluffs above Georgeson Bay, then down again more sharply to the south at Bellhouse Park on Active Pass Inlet. Water is almost always in view. Bodega Ridge has a short trail which leads to a spectacular viewpoint.

Road Conditions

The island is narrow and long, with one main road which is narrow and winding. The road into Dionisio Park is gravel to dirt and very rough. Georgia View Rd. is gravel, but flat, very rideable as of October 1994, but logging and some developments are in progress. Some changes will be occurring with Cook Rd. as well—check with Galiano Bikes on status. Porlier Road is narrow and hilly, has no views and is heavily traveled.

Traffic

There is not much traffic, except when the ferry comes in, but watch out for blind corners. Keep to the right; speed limits are generally around 30 m.p.h. Logging rigs and machinery are operating on Georgia View Rd.

Nearest Bike Shop

Galiano Bicycle
139 S. Warbler Rd.
Galliano Island, B. C. V0N 1P0
(604) 539-2806
(Matthew will deliver rental MTB and does emergency road repair stops!)

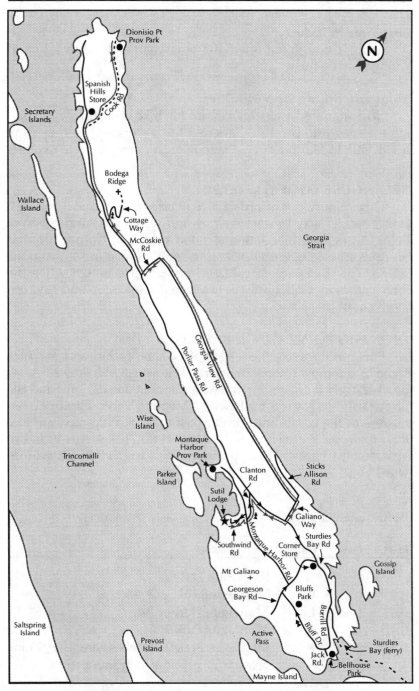

Dionisio Pt Prov Park

Spanish Hills Store

Secretary Islands

Cook Rd

Bodega Ridge

Cottage Way

McCoskie Rd

Georgia Strait

Wallace Island

Porlier Pass Rd

Georgia View Rd

Wise Island

Trincomalli Channel

Montague Harbor Prov Park

Parker Island

Clanton Rd

Sticks Allison Rd

Sutil Lodge

Galiano Way

Montaque Harbor Rd

Southwind Rd

Corner Store

Sturdies Bay Rd

Gossip Island

Mt Galiano

Georgeson Bay Rd

Bluffs Park

Saltspring Island

Prevost Island

Active Pass

Burrill Rd

Bluff Dr.

Sturdies Bay (ferry)

Jack Rd.

Bellhouse Park

Mayne Island

Bellhouse Loop ——— Dionisio Point Out & Back ———

Best Time to Ride

Spring through fall offers the best weather, though July and August can be busy.

Mountain Biking Opportunities

No designated area, but a mountain bike is useful for traversing the road into Dionisio Park and for traversing Georgia View Road. Talk to Matthew at Galiano Bikes for any places to explore.

BELLHOUSE LOOP (14.5 miles)

This is short, but affords a nice overlook of Active Pass Inlet. It is a perfect way to start the day and watch the sunrise before breakfast or as a nice late afternoon ride. The Corner Store at Sturdies and Georgeson Roads is the only year round store on the island. The roads are narrow but are not busy except when the ferry comes in. Galiano Bikes is a nice place to stop and find out more about the island.

DIONISIO POINT OUT & BACK (33.8 miles)

This route travels the length of Galiano Island and explores some of the most interesting parts. It is worth starting this after breakfast so you have the time to explore Dionisio Point and the Bodega Ridge Nature trail (with "Meghan", the self-appointed hostess of the community trail). Best to walk bikes up trail and lock them on the trail, this is a "must do" hike with views of Trincomali Channel. Treat this area with respect and it will reward you.

Bellhouse Loop (Road)

Pt.-Pt.	Cum.	Dir.	Street/Landmark
			From Sutil Lodge
0.0	0.0	R	**Southwind Rd.** (gravel)
0.4	0.4	L	**Montague Harbor Rd.**
0.2	0.6	R	**Montague Park Rd.**
0.9	1.5	–	Montague Park (lock bikes here; Grey Point beach trail; picnic area, restrooms)
		TA	
0.9	2.4	L	**Montague Harbor Rd.**

0.3	2.7	L	**Clanton Rd.** (uphill)
0.7	3.4	R	**Portlier Pass Rd.**
2.4	5.8	L	**Sturdies Bay Rd.** (Hummingbird Tavern on L)
1.4	7.2	R	**Burrill Rd.**
0.4	7.6	L	**To Bellhouse Provincial Park**
0.4	8.0	–	Bellhouse Provincial Park (view of Active Pass inlet; great sunrise; ferries)
		TA	
0.4	8.4	L	**Burrill Rd.**
1.1	9.5	–	Burrill changes to **Bluff Dr.** (uphill past farm to Bluffs Park)
0.8	10.3	–	Galiano Bikes to R on Warbler Rd. S (Bluff Dr. turns to gravel)
0.3	10.6	–	Bluffs Park Trailhead on L (lock up bikes and hike trails)
0.8	11.4	R	**Georgeson Bay Rd.** (paved)
0.7	12.1	L	**Montague Harbor Rd.** (uphill, then fast downhill)
1.9	14.0	L	**Southwind Rd.** (gravel)
0.5	14.5	L	Sutil Lodge driveway

Dionisio Point Out & Back (Road/MTB)

Pt.-Pt.	Cum.	Dir.	Street/Landmark
			From Sutil Lodge
0.0	0.0	R	**Southwind Rd.** (gravel)
0.4	0.4	R	**Montague Harbor Rd.**
0.1	0.5	L	**Clanton Rd.** (uphill)
0.7	1.2	R	**Porlier Pass Rd.**
1.3	2.5	L	**Galiano Way**
0.6	3.1	L	**Georgia View Rd.** (turns to gravel)
6.5	9.6	L	**McCoskie Rd.**
0.3	9.9	R	**Porlier Pass Rd.**
4.0	13.9	R	**Cook Rd.**
0.9	14.8	–	Entrance of Dionisio Point Provincial Park
2.1	16.9	–	Dionisio Point (awesome views of Coon Bay; lock up bikes and hike around)
		TA	
3.0	19.9	L	**Porlier Pass Rd.**

3.0	22.9	–	Cottage Way on L (1.0 mile uphill to the Bodega Ridge Nature Trail)
1.0	23.9	L	**McCoskie Rd.**
0.3	24.2	R	**Gravel road at barrier** (changes to **Georgia View Rd.**, paved)
6.5	30.7	R	**Galiano Way**
0.6	31.3	R	**Porlier Pass Rd.**
1.3	32.6	L	**Clanton Rd.**
0.7	33.3	R	**Montague Harbor Rd.**
0.1	33.4	L	**Southwind Rd.** (gravel)
0.4	33.8	L	Sutil Lodge driveway

THE OLD FARMHOUSE
Karl and Gerti Fuss
1077 North End Road
Salt Spring Island, B.C. Canada V8K 1L9
(604) 537-4113
Rates: $125-150 (Canadian)

Salt Spring is the largest and most populated of the Gulf Islands; as such it offers the most varied riding opportunities among the islands. The little town of Ganges, at the heart of the island, offers a diverse collection of shops and galleries to poke through, and you'll have no trouble finding a bite to eat at one of the many restaurants and cafes. We heartily recommend a meal at the Pomodori, a tremendously innovative establishment featuring deliciously creative dishes in a fun atmosphere.

The Old Farmhouse is just a few miles from either the Crofton ferry or town, set back from the road on a quiet lane lined with fruit trees and sunflowers. The 100-year-old heritage house was entirely renovated to add a new wing when Karl and Gerti bought the place in 1987, but the appeal of this charming farmstead has not diminished. Madrona, wild cherry, plum and pine trees flourish on the property; paths winding through the lot pass an inviting hammock, quiet benches, picnic tables, a croquet field and herb gardens. Morris the cat will be happy to accompany you on a tour. You are welcome to sample the grapes growing on the arbor, and Gerti encourages people to "take as many apples as you can carry."

The house itself is as delightful as the property. The guest parlor is bright and cheerful, with a window seat in the large bay window covered in a sunny floral pattern to match the two comfortable armchairs and chaise lounge nearby. Light pine floors are covered by oriental rugs which surround a cozy woodstove. High ceilings and fresh white wainscoting add to the light feel of the room. Down a few steps one enters the hall to the new addition, which houses four guest rooms, each with a private bath and secluded balcony. Architect Richard Blagborne designed the addition to mesh perfectly with the existing structure and yet add luxurious comfort to the new rooms.

Each of the rooms is spotless and elegant. A sherry decanter and delicate glasses are set out in the rooms, and in the morning, coffee

appears on a tray outside each door. Starched duvets cover the feather beds, while fresh cut flowers and roses from the garden grace each room.

On the first floor one finds the Blue and Peach Rooms. The Blue Room has wide polished pine floors covered with rag rugs, white wainscotting and soothing blue floral wallpaper to match the coverlet on the double bed. Leaded glass French doors lead out to the balcony covered by a grape arbor.

Next door is the Peach Room, furnished much like the Blue Room but with a soft peach wallpaper and pine headboards on the two twin beds. The east-facing balcony is a perfect spot to greet the morning with a cup of coffee.

Upstairs are the Pink and Rose Rooms, each with high ceilings, queen size beds with pine headboards, and lovely views of the gardens and trees below. A tiny pink floral print paper covers the walls in the Pink Room, while sun streams in through a triangular window above the French doors to the geranium-covered balcony. The bathroom has a tub and shower with skylight above.

We stayed in the Rose Room, very similar to the Pink Room except for the deep rose and white accent wallpaper. Like the Peach Room, this east-facing room takes advantage of the morning sun, and we enjoyed the sunrise from the balcony chairs.

Breakfast is served at 9 a.m. in the dining room downstairs. Another bright room with a built-in china hutch at one end and sunny window at the other, skylights in this room make it cheerful on the dreariest of days. The long table is elegantly set with European china and silver, set off by bouquets of fresh flowers in the center. We had an appetizing assortment of poppyseed muffins, croissants and raisin buns—*all* baked fresh that morning—and a bowl of just-picked raspberries in creme fraiche before being served a mouth-watering slice of orange soufflé. Our meal was accompanied by dark coffee and a healthy blend of orange and banana juice. After breakfast Gerti packed up the remaining pastries for us all to enjoy during the day.

In addition to making hospitality an art form, the Fusses are a great source of information about the island, and are happy to help you make dinner reservations, figure out which ferry to take, or plan an additional bike route. You'll have no trouble enjoying your stay at The Old Farmhouse!

BIKING FROM THE OLD FARMHOUSE

Terrain

Saltspring Island has a great variety of hilly, open roads interspersed with trees and farms, all radiating from Ganges, the main town and center of most of the island's facilities. Mount Maxwell overlooks the center of the island, with beautiful Ruckle Park hugging the east side. Beaver Point is ideal for watching ferries, starfish, crabs and birds.

Road Conditions

Roads tend to be narrow, two-lane affairs with narrow to no shoulders. Stewart Rd. through Peter Arnell Park changes to gravel for a short distance, but most other road surfaces are asphalt-paved.

Traffic

The main roads, Fulford-Ganges Rd., Lower Ganges Rd. and Vesuvius Bay Rd., carry the bulk of the traffic through the island and can be busy around ferry time. Ferries come in from three points: Long Harbor on the east shore, Vesuvius Bay on the northwest side and Fulford Harbor in the south. Ganges is a busy place in the summer, so in-town riding requires you to stay aware.

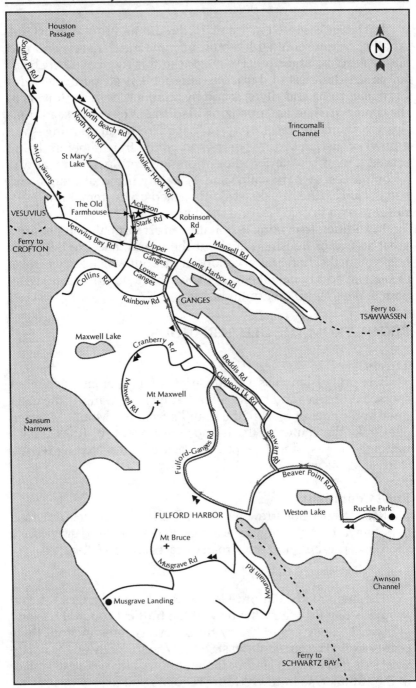

Ruckle Park Loop -----------   Sunset Loop ———

Nearest Bike Shop
   Island Spoke Folk Ltd.
   104 McPhillips
   P. O. Box 494
   Ganges, Salt Spring Island, V8K 2T5
   (604) 537-4664/Fax (604) 537-4664

Best Time to Ride
   May through October has the warmest weather and the most activities going on, but the climate is moderate year 'round and the off-season offers more solitude.

Mountain Biking Opportunities
   Check with the informative Spoke Folk, they can tell you where to go. Smaller gravel roads go out to Musgrave Landing and Mt. Bruce on the island's south end. Check out Mansell Mountain Bike Trails off Mansell Road.

RUCKLE PARK LOOP (32.8 miles)
   You'll get a full taste of Saltspring Island on this route. The picnic area at Beaver Point is one of the most idyllic places imaginable. The terrain is rolling with a few long climbs (namely Lee's Hill). An option may be to stop in Fulford Harbor for lunch at the tavern. Traffic is fairly heavy around Ganges and Fulford Harbor, but the remaining roads have low to moderate traffic.

SUNSET LOOP (14.9 miles)
   Sunset is the perfect time for riding this loop. It makes a great pre-dinner ride, with some steep, short climbs, but mainly it's just a pleasant route through the northwest end of Saltspring. The route can be done in reverse to get the Vesuvius Pub in after the ride, but the climb back up on North Beach Road is steep.

Ruckle Park Loop (Road)

Pt.-Pt.	Cum.	Dir.	Street/Landmark
			From The Old Farmhouse
0.0	0.0	L	**North End Rd.**
0.6	0.6	L	**Upper Ganges Rd.**
1.5	2.1	R	**Upper Ganges Rd.**
0.7	2.8	L	**Fulford Harbor Rd.** (stay on main road through town)
0.3	3.1	–	Island Spokefolk bike shop to R
0.8	3.9	L	**Beddis Rd.**
3.2	7.1	R	**Cusheon Lake Rd.** (Beddis Beach is straight ahead)
0.6	7.7	L	**Stewart Rd.** (steep climb)
0.4	8.1	–	Gravel section
0.5	8.6	–	Peter Arnell Park (views)
0.6	9.2	–	End of gravel
0.7	9.9	L	**Beaver Point Rd.**
3.7	13.6	–	Enter Ruckle Provincial Park (restrooms)
0.9	14.5	– TA	Beaver Point picnic area (perfect lunch spot)
4.6	19.1	L	**Beaver Point Rd.**
1.6	20.7	CR	**Beaver Point Rd.** (Fulford Harbor to L)
0.7	21.4	CR	**Fulford-Ganges Rd.** (Climb up Lee's Hill– long uphill)
7.0	28.4	–	Mt. Maxwell Park to L on Cranberry Rd.
1.1	29.5	CL	**Lower Ganges Rd.** (Watch for traffic)
0.4	29.9	R	**Upper Ganges Rd.**
0.7	30.6	L	**Upper Ganges Rd.**
1.5	32.1	R	**North End Rd.**
0.7	32.8	–	The Old Farmhouse on R

Sunset Loop (Road)

Pt.-Pt.	Cum.	Dir.	Street/Landmark
			From The Old Farmhouse
0.0	0.0	L	**North End Rd.**
0.5	0.5	R	**Vesuvius Bay Rd.** (Vesuvius Pub to L)

2.0	2.5	R	**Sunset Dr.** (a couple steep climbs)
4.2	6.7	**CR**	**North End Rd.**
1.6	8.3	L	**North Beach Rd.** (steep downhill)
1.9	10.2	S	**Walker Hook Rd.** (Fernwood Seaside Market to R; government dock to L)
3.2	13.4	S	**Stark Rd.** (past Robinson Rd. on L)
1.1	14.5	R	**Acheson Rd.**
0.1	14.6	L	**North End Rd.**
0.3	14.9	–	The Old Farmhouse on L

CENTRAL OREGON INNS AND RIDES

There is no way to succinctly sum up the terrain of "Central Oregon." The areas we covered in this section range from rolling open hills to steep valleys formed by the mighty Columbia River to undulating desert plateaus. Oregon is less populated than its northern neighbor, and offers hundreds of miles of empty roads and wide open areas, all with spectacular views. There's not much flat riding in Central Oregon—you have to stick to the coast for that—but the panoramic vistas afforded by even a short climb make the effort pay off.

A couple of the areas we rode are well known for outdoor activities other than bicycling, but the city of Eugene is considered a bicycling mecca. Bicycle clubs throughout the country look to a few cities for guidance on bicycle facility planning, and Eugene happens to be one of them. Several years ago the city rerouted downtown car traffic, creating one-way car streets and two-way bike lanes on most arterial routes. Bicyclists have their own directional signs, and buttons to push to make the light change are mounted curbside at bike height. Businesses are bike-friendly too—there's an abundance of bicycle parking all over the downtown area. As a result of all this good planning, bicyclists are everywhere in Eugene. It's fun to get a glimpse of what it could be like if bicycling were taken seriously as a means of transportation. . .

Despite the fun we had riding around downtown, we did a couple of rides from the **Campus Cottage B&B** that got out in the country for awesome views of the surrounding river valley. There's a nasty section of road getting out of town, but once you get out a bit you have a treat in store. For a casual afternoon ride we recommend pedaling along the river trail on either side—the path continues for several miles beyond the section we included on our loops.

Far south, just a few miles from the California border, the landscape surrounding Ashland changes dramatically to massive rolling dry hills, punctuated by irrigated farmland and ancient oak trees. Ashland is internationally known for having one of the oldest Shakespeare festivals in the country, but also offers great riding opportunities. We stuck to the road on our rides from **Country Willows B&B**, but the folks from the bike shop raved about the local mountain bike trails, so you may want to bring your fat tires, too.

Bend is well known as a ski town; people from all over the Northwest flock there for powder skiing which is virtually non-existent in the rest of this region. The town is encircled by mountains and desert, a combination which allows spectacular views of the surrounding peaks while riding on relatively flat terrain. There are miles of mountain bike trails here, many of which are located in the forest along the Deschutes River. Bring your mountain bike for your trip to the **Lara House B&B**, since the Deschutes Trail Ride is largely off-road and offers unbelievably nice singletrack meandering along the river.

Hood River is another town renowned for something other than bicycling: windsurfers hail Hood River as paradise. The steady wind up the Columbia River gorge creates a consistent blast that allows windsurfers to reach mind-boggling speed on the fast-moving river. If you get the urge to give it a try, there are about five shops in this little town that rent gear and offer lessons. If you decide to stick to your bike you'll still have a great time—the steep climbs out of town from the **State Street Inn** lead to fun winding roads with views of Mount Hood not too far in the distance. The Sam Hill Out & Back ride follows the river on a spectacular road that dips and winds along a fairly steep rock face which drops to the water.

You don't even have to get on your bike to enjoy astounding views from the **Youngberg Hill Farm** in McMinnville—the inn is already located on one of the highest hills in the area! (In fact, the mile-long driveway feels positively vertical after a ride.) Surrounded by its own vineyard, the inn overlooks the acres and acres of farmland encompassing McMinnville. One of the rides we did from here heads down into the flat land and meanders through the farms, while the other heads up into the hills behind the house on a winding steep road. Fortunately, what goes up must come down, and the steep climb is rewarded with a teeth-rattling downhill on a dirt road through the woods.

In addition to some excellent rides, the inns in this section offer countless other activities to enjoy, including windsurfing, a night at the theater and wine tasting tours. You're sure to relish the unspoiled beauty and diverse terrain of Central Oregon.

CAMPUS COTTAGE B&B
Ursula Bates
1136 19th Avenue
Eugene, OR 97403
(503) 342-5346
Rates: $85-120

Eugene has got to be the most bicycle-friendly town in the Northwest, so it's only fitting that Campus Cottage has one of the Northwest's friendliest innkeepers. Unfortunately, after 13 years as an innkeeper (Campus Cottage was the first B&B in Eugene), Ursula Bates spends more and more of her time in California, and would like to find a buyer for the inn, so visit soon! Of course, if the inn doesn't sell she has backup plans to expand and remodel.

As much as we enjoyed Ursula herself, the Campus Cottage will continue to be charming in her absence. Built in 1922, the B&B is a wonderful example of an Arts & Crafts, bungalow-style home. Three of the four rooms open off the living room, the fourth, The Cottage, has separate entrances from outside and through the kitchen. The living room and dining room stretch across the front of the house, with hardwood floors, braided rugs, a big couch in front of the fireplace, a few chairs around a little round table, and a huge pile of magazines to read. Everything is done simply and in keeping with the period of the house, with Ursula's decorating flair evident in the Radio Flyer filled with plants and the old crib with one side removed to create a little couch in the dining area.

We stayed in The Cottage, a newer addition to the room choices at Campus Cottage. Spacious, with a private bath, the room is at once bright and cozy. Cream carpet complements the green, pink and cream plaid spread on the queen-sized oak bed, while in the sitting area a white wrought iron daybed with a green spread serves as a couch in front of a sunny bay window. A ceiling fan hangs from the wide-beam white painted peaked ceiling. Modern extras, which blend in seamlessly, include a small writing desk with a phone, books and a television set stacked in the tall wicker shelf and a small refrigerator. The period decor continues in the private bath, with a clawfoot tub and shower, dried flower arrangements and jelly jar drinking glasses on lace doilies.

A BED & BREAKFAST INN

Back through the house, at the far end of the living room, is the Sun Room, a small charming room with light pine paneled ceiling and walls and deep teal carpet. Light streams in from the many windows (it is, after all, the former sun porch) with old stained glass hanging in them, while ivy winds around the window sills. A built-in bookshelf above the quilt-covered bed and an antique dresser complete the furnishings. Down one step at the end of the room is a small private bath with tub and shower.

The Suite and the Guestroom are both entered through a glass door from the living room. The Suite is the former master bedroom, and is the largest of the available rooms. Hardwood floors throughout the suite are painted a deep rose color; the sitting area is wallpapered to match. A marvelous antique twin sleigh bed acts as a couch in the sitting room, while an antique desk and chair and pillow-laden wicker armchair round out the decor. The sunny bedroom has quiet white walls and a light coverlet on the queen-sized brass bed, further brightened with braided throw rugs on the floor and lots of healthy houseplants throughout the suite. The private bath for the Suite is reached through the small foyer between the Suite and the Guestroom; a refrigerator and coffee maker is available here for guests of either room.

The Guestroom is a cozy blue and white room, with white floors and ceilings, soft blue doors and accents and a pretty floral wallpaper on the walls. An overstuffed blue armchair sits in the south-facing window to take advantage of the sun. A white bedspread covers the queen-sized pine bed. A porcelain sink and mirror are located right in the room, while the private bath has a shower.

Breakfast in the morning is simple but delicious. Good coffee is available early, and breakfast is served around 9 a.m. We had granola topped with blueberries and yogurt accompanied by hot scones to start, then were each served a baked egg in a cup, with chunky homemade salsa on top. Breakfast conversation tends to be lively, since guests are often connected to the nearby University and are frequently return visitors to the inn.

We didn't stay at too many inns this summer where we didn't have to use our car once. Restaurants, a bike shop and miles of good riding are just minutes away by bike, even though the Campus Cottage is in a residential neighborhood, with big trees and many older homes. We rode everywhere in Eugene, taking advantage of the miles of bike lanes and bike-friendly motorists. While Eugene itself is fun to explore, and the bike path along the river is a wonderful ride in itself, don't miss the great roads and remarkable views afforded by getting out of town a few miles.

BIKING FROM THE CAMPUS COTTAGE

Terrain
Much of the area is relatively rolling hills with a few substantial hills thrown in. The routes chosen here are winding and offer wonderful views of the McKensie River Valley and the southern Eugene area from the crest of Dillard Road.

Road Conditions
Generally the roads in and around Eugene are well maintained. The city takes a certain pride in providing good bicycle routes through the city and the bike paths are a great way to separate yourself from the traffic and enjoy the parks in the center of the city.

Traffic
Coburg Road is very busy, but does allow a moderately sized safety zone to ride along with traffic. But try to avoid riding it during rush hour. Once out of the city the roads are quiet and quite pleasant. Watch the crossing from A Street to D Street on Mill. Franklin is busy most of the time.

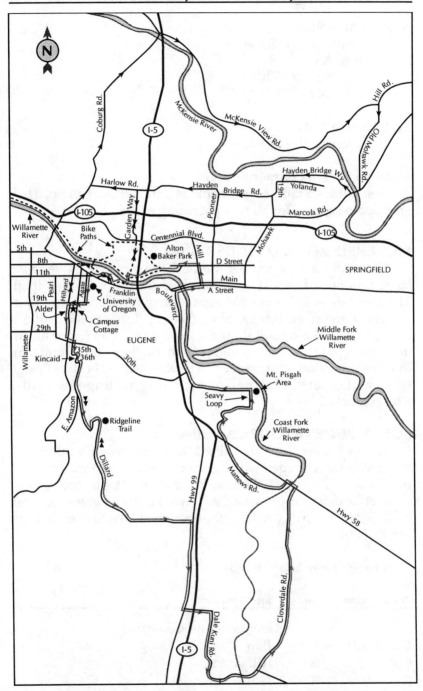

McKensie River Loop ———   South Eugene Loop ----------

Nearest Bike Shop
>   Paul's Bicycle Shop
>   2480 Alder
>   Eugene, OR 97405
>   (503) 342-6155

Best Time to Ride
Early spring through late fall.

Mountain Biking Opportunities
Best bet is to talk to the people at Paul's Bicycle Shop. They are good resources for all types of riding in the area.

MCKENSIE RIVER LOOP (28.0 miles)

This route is very popular for the Eugene crowd, as we saw a large number of cyclists making their way around this loop. McKensie View Drive is a fun road with quite a few turns winding above the river. Be careful on Coburg Road, as the traffic is heavy, but there is a good shoulder to travel on. Feel free to meander along the bike paths on your way back, they are a wonderful in-town excursion in themselves. The Knickerbocker Bike Bridge is named after the father of bicycling in Eugene, Willie Knickerbocker.

SOUTH EUGENE LOOP (30.4 miles)

After the long climb up Dillard Road (the only big hill on the loop), you are rewarded with some fine views of the valley where the Coast Fork of the Willamette River winds its way south. Give yourself enough time to visit the Howard Buford Recreation Area off of Seavy Loop. If you have the energy you could even hike up Mt. Pisgah!

McKensie River Loop (Road)

Pt.-Pt.	Cum.	Dir.	Street/Landmark
			From Campus Cottage
0.0	0.0	L	**19th**
0.3	0.3	R	**Hillyard St.**
0.1	0.4	X	18th
0.4	0.8	X	13th

0.1	0.9	X	12th
0.0	0.9	X	E. 11th
0.2	1.1	X	E. Broadway
0.0	1.1	**CR**	**E. 8th Ave.** (follow sign to South Bank Trail)
0.1	1.2	**R**	**Paved bikepath** (the Riverbank Trail system)
0.6	1.8	**R**	**T intersection** (to R is Autzen bridge, under railroad tracks, straight past the U. of O. annexes)
0.2	2.0	**L**	**Path before Franklin Blvd.**
0.1	2.1	X	Riverfront Pkwy. to Mill Race Path
0.2	2.3	**R**	**Bikepath**
0.1	2.4	**L**	**Bikepath leads onto Garden Ave.** (road CR, changes to Walnut St.)
0.3	2.7	**L**	**Franklin Blvd.** (stay on sidewalk bikepath opposite traffic side)
0.4	3.1	**L**	**Knickerbocker Bike Bridge**
0.2	3.3	X	Paved bikepath and follow dirt/wood chip path straight ahead. I-5 bridge towers above)
0.1	3.4	X	Paved bikepath and go over bridge
0.8	4.2	**R**	**Bikepath parallels S. Garden Way**
1.0	5.2	**L**	**Harlow Rd.**
0.2	5.4	X	light near Sweetgum
0.5	5.9	X	Palamino
0.3	6.2	**R**	**Coburg Rd.**
0.2	6.4	X	Tandy
0.2	6.6	X	Bailey Lane
0.1	6.7	X	Cal Young
0.1	6.8	X	Wilkensie
0.5	7.3	X	Beltline Rd. (south entrance)
0.1	7.4	X	Beltline Rd. (north entrance)
0.1	7.5	X	Chad Dr.
0.3	7.8	X	Crescent Ave.
1.8	9.6	**R**	**McKensie View Rd.** (winding; great views)
5.9	15.5	**R**	**Hill Rd.**
0.4	15.9	**CR**	**Old Mohawk Rd.**
1.4	17.3	**R**	**Marcola Rd.** (market on L)
0.2	17.5	**R**	**Hayden Bridge Rd.** (winding)
1.6	19.1	**L**	**23rd Ave.**
0.2	19.3	**R**	**Yolanda**
0.2	19.5	**L**	**19th**

0.2	19.7	R	**Hayden Bridge Rd.**
1.1	20.8	X	5th (bike lane)
0.8	21.6	X	Pioneer
0.1	21.7	X	Game Farm
0.3	22.0	X	Hartman
0.2	22.2	X	Gateway
0.1	22.3	X	Beverly
0.4	22.7	L	**South Garden Way** (bike path merges to L)
1.0	23.7	L	**Bike path**
0.8	24.5	X	Bike path (follow wood chip path straight)
0.1	24.6	X	Bike path intersection (**cross Bike Bridge**)
0.2	24.8	R	**Bike path** (up to Franklin Blvd.)
0.4	25.2	R	**Bike path along sidewalk of Franklin**
0.3	25.5	R	**Bike path** (on Walnut)
0.1	25.6	L	**Bike path** (on Garden)
0.1	25.7	R	**Bike path**
0.2	25.9	X	Riverfront Parkway
0.1	26.0	R	**Bike path**
0.2	26.2	L	**Bike path "T" intersection**
0.6	26.8	L	**Bike path** (to 8th)
0.1	26.9	CL	**E. 8th** (to Broadway)
0.0	26.9	X	E. Broadway (onto **Hillyard**)
0.2	27.1	X	E. 11th
0.0	27.1	X	E. 12th
0.1	27.2	X	E. 13th
0.4	27.6	X	E. 18th
0.1	27.7	L	**19th**
0.3	28.0	–	Campus Cottage on R

South Eugene Loop (Road)

Pt.-Pt.	Cum.	Dir.	Street/Landmark
			From Campus Cottage
0.0	0.0	L	**19th**
0.2	0.2	L	**Alder St.**
0.4	0.6	X	E. 24th Ave. (Paul's Bike Shop on R)
0.4	1.0	X	E. 28th Ave.
0.2	1.2	X	E. 30th Ave.
0.2	1.4	X	E. 32nd Ave.

0.2	1.6	CL	**E. 35th Ave.**
0.1	1.7	R	**Kincaid St.**
0.0	1.7	CL	**E. 36th Ave.**
0.0	1.7	R	**Kincaid St.**
0.3	2.0	R	**E. 39th Ave.**
0.1	2.1	L	**E. Amazon Dr.**
0.5	2.6	L	**Dillard Rd.** (begin climb—2 miles)
2.0	4.6	–	Ridgeline Trail to R (crest of hill; views)
3.5	8.1	R	**Highway 99** (after RR tracks)
1.9	10.0	L	**Dale Kuni Rd.**
2.2	12.2	L	**Cloverdale Rd.**
5.8	18.0	L	**Highway 58**
0.2	18.2	L	**Matthews Rd.** (immediately after bridge)
2.3	20.5	X	Highway 58 onto Seavy Loop Rd.
2.0	22.5	L	**Seavy Loop Rd.** (Mt. Pisgah area to R)
1.5	24.0	X	Franklin Blvd.
0.3	24.3	R	**Franklin Blvd.** (heavy traffic)
0.5	24.8	S	**Pass freeway entrance**
1.5	26.3	R	**South "A" St.** (over Willamette River)
0.3	26.6	L	**Mill St.**
0.0	26.6	X	Main St.
0.3	26.9	L	**West "D" St.**
0.3	27.2	L	**Bike path**
0.5	27.7	CL	**Bike path** (enter Alton Baker Park)
0.3	28.0	CR	**Bike path under footbridge**
0.2	28.2	L	**Wood chip trail** (after crossing under I-5)
0.1	28.3	S	**Across Knickerbocker Bridge** (bike path then curves up to sidewalk on Franklin Blvd.)
0.7	29.0	R	**Walnut to Garden** (bike path)
0.3	29.3	R	**Bike path**
0.0	29.3	L	**Bike path**
0.2	29.5	L	**Riverfront Pkwy.**
0.1	29.6	X	Franklin (Riverfront changes to Agate)
0.0	29.6	X	E. 13th
0.2	29.8	X	E. 15th
0.3	30.1	R	**E. 19th**
0.2	30.3	X	University
0.1	30.4	–	Campus Cottage on L

COUNTRY WILLOWS B&B INN
Dan Durant and Dave Newton
1313 Clay Street
Ashland, OR 97520
(503) 488-1590
Rates: $90-155

Ashland is one of our favorite towns in the Northwest. We've been drawn there in the past by the annual Shakespeare festival (which runs from February to October but is at its peak in the summer months), but had no idea there was so much wonderful riding nearby! A variety of good restaurants, fun shops and a beautiful green downtown park surround the theater square, while just a few miles out of town the land opens into rolling hills and wide open vistas.

Just a few miles from the downtown core, on a dead-end street heading up into the hills, sits the Country Willows B&B. The old farmhouse, completely restored in 1985, sits on a gently sloping five-acre hill, with spectacular views of the Cascades to the east and the Siskiyous to the west. Adding to the farm feeling are horses in the field behind the house, a gaggle of geese meandering about the property, two Newbian goats (aptly named Porche and Juliet), and a rabbit named Redford in a hutch near the garden. A dog and two cats round out the menagerie, though they are restricted to the innkeepers' quarters and you'll only see them outside.

After a long ride (and the final climb up to the inn), you'll be excited to discover a crystal-clear swimming pool and hot tub behind the house. After a refreshing dip, you're welcome to wander through the new organic garden or the grape arbor and flower garden. Many of the breakfast items come from the garden, and Dan makes jam and jelly from the grapes (for sale in the dining room). A bent willow double swing hanging beneath one of the many willows on the property provides a pleasant spot to get out of the sun.

Inside the inn guests share the sunny living room, where large corner picture windows look out to the Cascades. Two couches and a rocking chair group around a coffee table stacked with information about the area, complete with restaurant guides, theater schedules, play reviews and "things to do" books. White walls and plush blue carpet make this a soothing room, with tasteful artwork and a narrow floral border around the ceiling.

The living room opens to the dining room, where the carpet gives way to polished oak floors covered with oriental rugs, and the walls are covered in a rich floral print paper. Two small tables are set for breakfast in the dining room, while the majority of guests choose to dine on the sun porch. The glassed-in sun porch has several tables for two and a buffet where juice, iced tea, coffee and glasses are set out for guests throughout the day. A small refrigerator is available for guests' use.

Across the entrance foyer from the living room is the den, a dark paneled, cozy winter room, with tons of books, puzzles, games and videos available to while away an evening. Two handsome striped couches are arranged in front of the fireplace.

The four bedrooms in the main house are upstairs. Each room has a large dried flower wreath on the door, glorious goosedown pillows and comforters, fresh flowers, fluffy robes in the closet and a private bath well-stocked with Country Willows soaps, shampoo and lotions. Independent heat and air conditioning controls are found in each room. Guests share the second-floor balcony, a perfect spot to watch the sunrise while curled up with a cup of coffee in a cushioned bent-willow armchair.

The Cedar and Oak Rooms, both front corner rooms, face the porch and get wonderful morning sun streaming in. The Cedar Room, in pale pink, white and green colors, has hardwood floors and views of the pasture and mountains. In addition to the queen-sized bed in a wrought-iron bedstead, there is a twin bed available in this room. An oak desk sits beneath one window; two night-stands with reading lamps and a dresser and mirror complete the simple country furnishings.

The Oak Room, with two sunny windows revealing mountain views, is carpeted in pale blue carpet and has soft pastel colors throughout. The simple furnishings include a desk and queen-sized bed.

Down the hall is the Almond Room, a cozy room looking back toward the pool and gardens. This room has a queen-sized bed and a charming antique sink.

The Willow Room is the largest of the upstairs accommodations, with a king-sized four-poster canopy bed and a twin bed. The light beige carpet and subtle floral wallpaper create a quiet feeling. This room looks northeast to the mountains.

Next door to the main house, nestled between the pool and garden, is the Cottage, featuring a queen-sized bed and a twin bed tucked into a private nook. A sink, microwave and refrigerator are available for fixing a light supper, while a woodstove and sitting area provide a spot to curl up in the evenings.

The last two deluxe accommodations are in the immaculately restored barn. The Hayloft Suite has a snug sitting room downstairs, in front of picture windows looking back over the property, along with a kitchenette and private bath with shower. Up narrow stairs is the loft, a cozy room with skylights above a queen-sized bed.

Next door, with a private entrance, is the Sunrise Suite. This is the honeymooners' choice—a large, open suite with white-washed pine walls and a private deck overlooking the mountains. A sitting area offers a gas fireplace and a table in the sunny bay window, while a grand old fashioned tub-for-two nestles in a second bay window under a large skylight. (The private bath has a double shower, too.) The small kitchenette with sink, microwave and refrigerator and the spacious king-sized bed make this a real hideaway for a special occasion.

The morning we visited dawned sunny and warm, so we joined the other guests on the deck off the dining room for breakfast. Meals at Country Willows are a gourmet affair: each item on the menu was served with a flourish, whether it was a lemon twist in the ice water or the garnish of just-picked mint on the side of the plate. We began with fresh-squeezed orange juice and dark roasted coffee, moving on to delicious pear halves poached in cinnamon and orange rind, accompanied by warm banana bread. Our main entrée was fluffy French toast topped with sliced strawberries. We thoroughly enjoyed all our fellow guests, and spent a leisurely morning in the sun discussing the best towns to ride in the Northwest.

Country Willows was one of the most relaxing spots we visited this summer. It just doesn't get any better than a long ride in the sun, a soak in the pool, a tasty meal at a riverside restaurant and an evening at the outdoor Elizabethan theater—being pampered in such a delightful country inn is just the icing on the cake. You'll find yourself thinking about this vacation long after you've returned home!

BIKING FROM COUNTRY WILLOWS

Terrain

Ashland sits at the southern end of the Rouge River valley. Everything rises slowly up from town as the valley continues up toward Medford. There are rolling hills and high desert-like dry conditions in the summer.

Road Conditions

Roads are in good condition throughout the area, though the bike path has some "whoops" in it.

Traffic

Siskiyou Blvd. has most of the traffic, but also has a good shoulder. E. Main and the streets in town can be busy around showtime, but Main St., Walker and Ashland St. have bike lanes.

Nearest Bike Shop

Ashland Cycle Sport
191 Oak St.
Ashland, OR 97520
(503) 488-0581

Or   Siskiyou Cyclery
1729 Siskiyou Blvd.
Ashland, OR 97520
(503) 482-1997

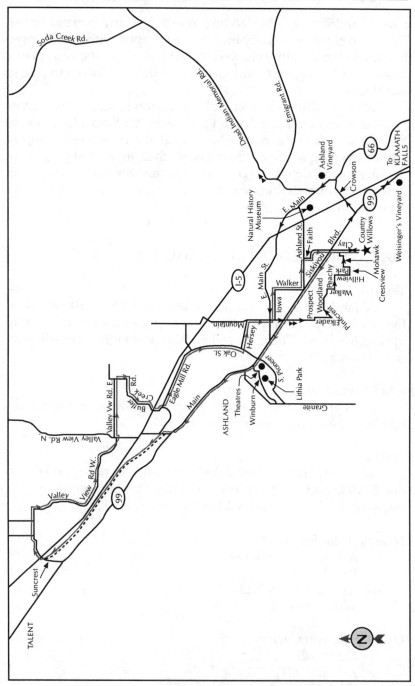

Wine/Museum Circuit ————   Greenway Loop ·············

Best Time to Ride

Early spring through late fall. Shakespeare Festival starts in February.

Mountain Biking Opportunities

There are some great routes starting at Lithia Park and going around the Ashland Watershed (the Lithia Loop). The Siskiyou Crest Ride starts from the Mt. Ashland parking area and goes to Dutchman Peak Lookout. Talk to the helpful gang at Ashland Cycle Sport or Siskiyou Cyclery for information and maps.

WINE/MUSEUM CIRCUIT (8.0 miles)

This route mainly is a way to get to Weisinger's Vineyard-Winery and Ashland Vineyards, with a must-see stop at the Natural History Museum. The rest is to give you a good workout before going back to Country Willows to lounge at the pool. . . and then head out for a local theatre experience. Or this route makes a great start for exploring the town itself; head left on Siskiyous Blvd. till it changes to E. Main and then take a left at South Pioneer. A beautiful place to while away the day.

GREENWAY LOOP (19.8 miles)

There is some wide open country to be seen here. This route follows the valley to the north of Ashland and provides some stunning views of the area. With the exception of the riding in town, most of the route follows low-traffic roads and uses the city bikepath from W Valley View Rd. to Suncrest Rd.

Wine/Museum Circuit (Road)

Pt.-Pt.	Cum.	Dir.	Street/Landmark
			From Country Willows
0.0	0.0	S	Clay
0.4	0.4	R	Siskiyou Blvd.
0.8	1.2	R	Weisinger's Vineyard-Winery
		TA	
0.0	1.2	L	Siskiyou Blvd.
0.4	1.6	R	Crowson Rd.
0.7	2.3	L	Highway 66 (Road CR into E Main)
1.4	3.7	R	Ashland Vineyards
		TA	

0.0	3.7	R	**E Main**
1.1	4.8	–	Natural History Museum on L
0.5	5.3	L	**Mountain Ave.**
0.2	5.5	X	Iowa St.
0.1	5.6	X	Siskiyou Blvd. (major uphill begins)
0.3	5.9	X	Ashland St.
0.2	6.1	L	**Prospect Ave.**
0.1	6.2	R	**Elkader** (short part gravel)
0.2	6.4	L	**Pinecrest**
0.2	6.6	R	**Woodland** (steep downhill)
0.1	6.7	R	**Walker**
0.2	6.9	L	**Peachy** (gravel)
0.2	7.1	R	**Hillview** (uphill)
0.2	7.3	L	**Crestview Dr.**
0.2	7.5	L	**Park St.** (steep downhill)
0.1	7.6	R	**Mohawk**
0.1	7.7	L	**Mary Jane**
0.1	7.8	R	**Clay St.**
0.2	8.0	–	Country Willows at end of road on R

Greenway Loop (Road)

Pt.-Pt.	Cum.	Dir.	Street/Landmark
			From Country Willows
0.0	0.0	S	**Clay St.**
0.4	0.4	L	**Siskiyou Blvd.**
0.9	1.3	X	Ashland St.
0.1	1.4	X	Wightman St.
0.3	1.7	X	Mountain Ave.
0.2	1.9	X	Morse St.
0.5	2.4	CR	Stoplight for fire station, Siskiyou Blvd. changes to **E. Main**
0.2	2.6	X	2nd St.
0.1	2.7	X	Pioneer St.
0.2	2.9	X	Intersection of Siskiyou Blvd. and N Main (stay on Main)
0.2	3.1	X	Laurel St.
1.8	4.9	X-R	**Valley View Rd.**
0.0	4.9	L	Onto **bikepath** (BP Station on R)

0.7	5.6	**CR**	**Follow paved bikepath**
2.0	7.6	–	Under bridge at RV Roundup Camp
0.7	8.3	**R**	**Suncrest Rd.**
0.3	8.6	**R**	**Suncrest Rd.** (changes into Valley View Rd.)
1.2	9.8	**CL**	**Valley View Rd. W**
1.7	11.5	X	Valley View Rd. N and S (follow straight on **Valley View E**)
1.0	12.5	**R**	**Butler Creek Rd.**
0.2	12.7	**R**	**Butler Creek Rd.**
0.9	13.6	X	I-5 overpass
0.1	13.7	**L**	**Eagle Mill Rd.** (no shoulder, light traffic)
1.2	14.9	**CR**	Eagle Mill turns into **Oak St.**
1.0	15.9	**L**	**Hersey** (bike lane)
0.5	16.4	**R**	**Mountain Ave.**
0.7	17.1	X	E Main
0.3	17.4	**L**	**Iowa St.**
0.3	17.7	X	Wightman St.
0.2	17.9	**R**	**Walker Ave.** (bike lane)
0.4	18.3	**L**	**Ashland St.** (bike lane)
0.4	18.7	**R**	**Faith**
0.0	18.7	**L**	**Clay St.**
0.7	19.4	X	Siskiyou Blvd.
0.4	19.8	–	Country Willows at end of road on R

LARA HOUSE B&B
Doug and Bobbye Boger
640 NW Congress
Bend, OR 97701
(503) 388-4064
Rates: $55-75

The Lara House is one of the oldest homes in Bend, built in 1910 by a Bend merchant. The Bogers are the third owners since the inn was extensively remodeled and converted to an inn twelve years ago. The Arts and Crafts-style home is huge, with 5000 square feet covering three stories. Centrally located in a peaceful residential neighborhood, the inn sits just across the street from Drake Park, where swans float by lazily on Mirror Pond. Restaurants and shops in downtown Bend are within easy walking distance of the house.

A huge porch surrounds the house, providing a cool place to relax on a hot day. Crossing the porch to the front entrance, you enter a long living room which extends the length of the house. Dark exposed beams stretch across the ceiling and polished hardwood floors glisten beneath your feet. Several cozy sitting areas are grouped about the room, one in front of the large brick fireplace, another in the window overlooking the garden. Another cluster of armchairs and a cushioned couch provide a spot to curl up and watch television at the far end of the room. Small tables are set out for hot cider and cookies, or for doing a puzzle in by the window. The decor is simple and comfortable, letting the elegant structure of the house speak for itself, with an antique tricycle in one corner and several plants in each window comprising the majority of the decoration. French doors at the far end of the living room open to a small landscaped deck with patio furniture and a luxurious hot tub.

Just off the living room is the winterized sunporch, which now acts as the dining room. This bright solarium has several small tables set for two along the large window overlooking Drake Park. A gorgeous curved wood and glass china hutch stands against the wall, while French doors on either end of the dining room open back into the living room.

Each of the six guest rooms is spacious and offers a private modern bath with shower. The Bachelor Room is the only room downstairs, and offers two twin beds beneath a ceiling fan in a

handsome dark-paneled room. A large armchair and dark print comforters on each bed balance the light beige carpet. A removed hall entrance as well as an outdoor entrance to the front porch make this a very private room.

Four more bedrooms are found on the second floor. Both the Drake and Cascade Rooms were occupied during our visit, but we understand each has a queen bed and a sitting area. The Shevlin Room is a bright, roomy corner room with old-fashioned wallpaper, a ceiling fan and a crocheted spread on the queen-sized bed. Furnishings include two armchairs tucked in an alcove, and a small writing desk.

We stayed in another corner room, the Deschutes Room. The Deschutes looks out through big trees to the park and Mount Bachelor in the distance. This is a cheerful room, with white carpet and pale pink wallpaper, floor-length ivory curtains and a queen-sized bed. An overstuffed armchair and reading lamp in front of one window provide a comfortable spot to review tomorrow's ride route.

The Summit Room is a private attic retreat on the third floor. More like a small apartment than a guest room, the Summit Room has a small bedroom at the top of the stairs with two twin beds, and another larger double bed in the pale pink main room. Floor length windows reveal the tops of trees outside, while the natural alcoves of the roof form cozy nooks throughout the room. A cushioned bent-willow loveseat and matching table sit in one such nook.

Guests select the time they would like to have breakfast when they check in, in order for each group to have personalized attention. We had a cup of coffee and were given a choice of juices to start our meal. Our entrée was fresh apple compote, a stack of piping-hot pancakes and maple syrup, accompanied by a nicely-arranged fruit plate. We enjoyed talking to Doug about his hobby of restoring antique bicycles as he bustled in and out of the kitchen, and appreciated his suggestions for places to ride.

If you've got some time left after your ride, feel free to get a game of volleyball, badminton or croquet going on the wide front lawn, take a stroll through the park or head into town. We enjoyed walking through town and stopping for dinner at the Deschutes Brewery, a microbrewery known throughout the Northwest for its robust Bachelor Bitter and Black Butte Porter. (The food was good, too!) If you're staying a couple of days, you may want to visit The High Desert Museum, six miles from town, which we didn't get a chance to see but have heard wonderful things about.

Whether you stick to the road or take off on the trail, you'll soon come to think of Bend as much more than a ski town—although you may find yourself coming back in the winter, too!

BIKING FROM THE LARA HOUSE

Terrain
Bend is situated in the high desert country to the east of the Southern Cascade Range. Scrub trees and small drought-tolerant plants are seen and the landscape tends toward the open and flat. Neither of the routes has any major hills. The River Trail is a wonderful way to see the lava islands which sit in the Deschutes River and blanket much of the area east of the river. The arid landscape will parch you rapidly, so bring sufficient water.

Road Conditions
Roads are well maintained with a good shoulder on Century Drive. Roads up near Tumalo are narrower but with fairly good surfaces. Trails and Forest Service roads are dirt or gravel and require good tires and bike-handling skills, but there is no real technical off-road riding on these routes.

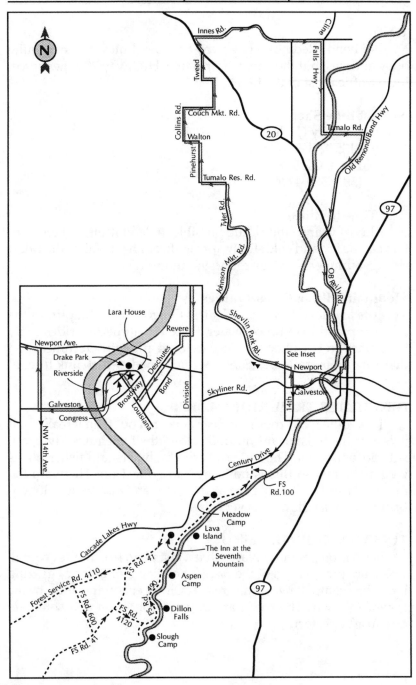

Deschutes Trail Ride ——— Tumalo Loop ———

Traffic

Old Bend/Redmond Highway and Deschutes St. can be quite busy at times, but they are very ridable. Highway 20 is heavy vehicle traffic most of the time.

Nearest Bike Shop

Century Cycles
1135 N. W. Galveston
Bend, OR 97701
(503) 389-4224

Best Time to Ride

Almost year round riding possible in Bend itself, but the winters can be icy and cold. Early spring through late fall is the finest riding. Summers can be around 90° in midday.

Mountain Biking Opportunities

Lots and lots. Pick up a Central Oregon Trails Map from the bike shop and load up on water, there are numerous rides to do here! Shevlin Park Loop is close to town and fairly technical and there are more trails and Forest Service Roads which link from it.

DESCHUTES TRAIL RIDE (24.1 miles)

This route looks more confusing written out than it really is. It is one of the most beautiful trails along the Deschutes River, but still close to town. The trail is shared by hikers and fisherfolk as well as bikers, so this is not a trail to go fast on. There are too many places to sit and gaze at the view anyway, as it is lovely. Bring water, as the area is very dry.

TUMALO LOOP (31.8 miles)

Bend is one of those places that's just plain fun to ride around. There are great views of the Sisters and some of that dry grazing land that characterizes this area. You will encounter little traffic except in town. The roads are in good condition and some are downright perfect.

Deschutes Trail Ride (MTB)

Pt.-Pt.	Cum.	Dir.	Street/Landmark
			From Lara House
0.0	0.0	L	**Louisiana** (changes to **Riverside**)
0.0	0.0	X	Congress
0.3	0.3	R	**Tumalo Ave./Galveston**
0.5	0.8	L	**NW 14th**
1.3	2.1	–	NW 14th changes into **Century Dr.** at Mt Washington Dr. (continue on Century)
5.1	7.2	L	**Forest Service Rd. 41**
1.4	8.6	R	**Forest Service Rd. 4110**
1.2	9.8	L	**Forest Service Rd. 600**
1.0	10.8	L	**Forest Service Rd. 41**
0.7	11.5	R	**Forest Service Rd. 4120** (to Dillon Falls)
0.5	12.0	CL	**Forest Service Rd. 490** (follow signs for Dillon Falls)
0.3	12.3	L	**Fork in road** (straight ahead is boat launch; to R is hiking trail through fence and Slough Camp)
0.1	12.4	S	**Straight on Aspen Trail** (to R of Aspen parking lot; Deschutes River is on R for the remainder of the trail)
0.7	13.1	R	**Sharp R at fork in trail**
0.7	13.8	S	**Straight on Big Eddy Trail** (to R)
1.1	14.9	S	**Lava Island Trail** (to Lava Island Falls)
0.3	15.2	–	Trail briefly enters road then veers off to R
0.8	16.0	S	**Meadow Trail** (trail is across Lava Island Falls parking area; restrooms)
0.8	16.8	R	**At fork** after crossing Vaughn Lake path
0.5	17.3	–	Enter Meadows parking area–follow **Forest Service Rd. 100** out west end of lot
1.3	18.6	R	**Century Dr./Cascade Highway** (changes into **NW 14th**)
4.7	23.3	R	**Galveston/Tumalo**
0.5	23.8	L	**Riverside** (stay R)
0.3	24.1	X	Congress
0.0	24.1	–	Lara House on L

Tumalo Loop (Road)

Pt.-Pt.	Cum.	Dir.	Street/Landmark
			From Lara House
0.0	0.0	L	**Louisiana** (changes to **Riverside**)
0.0	0.0	X	Congress
0.4	0.4	R	**Tumalo Ave./Galveston**
0.4	0.8	R	**NW 14th**
0.4	1.2	L	**NW Newport Ave.**
0.3	1.5	–	Newport changes to **Shevlin Park Rd.** at College Way (continue S; great downhill)
2.7	4.2	R	**Johnson Market Rd.**
2.5	6.7	R	**Tyler Rd.** (awesome view of Sisters at turn)
2.0	8.7	L	**Tumalo Res. Rd.**
0.8	9.5	R	**Pinehurst**
0.9	10.4	L	**Walton Rd.**
0.5	10.9	R	**Collins Rd.**
1.0	11.9	R	**Couch Market Rd.**
0.7	12.6	L	**Tweed Rd.**
1.9	14.5	L	**Highway 20** (high traffic, 55 MPH)
0.4	14.9	R	**Innes Market Rd.** (farmland, no shoulder)
4.0	18.9	R	**Cline Falls Highway**
3.2	22.1	L	**Tumalo Rd.** (Ivy Store is S ahead 0.2 miles)
1.8	23.9	R	**Old Redmond/Bend Highway** (rolling, narrow shoulder)
3.1	27.0	X	Highway 20
0.2	27.2	L	**O. B. Reily Rd.** (good shoulder; bike lane)
2.7	29.9	R	**Highway 20/97** (bike lane)
0.2	30.1	CR	**Division**
0.7	30.8	R	**Revere**
0.1	30.9	L	**Deschutes** (high traffic)
0.2	31.1	X	Portland Ave. (Deschutes changes to **Wall**)
0.3	31.4	X	Newport
0.0	31.4	X	Oregon
0.2	31.6	X	Franklin
0.1	31.7	R	**Louisiana**
0.0	31.7	X	Broadway St.
0.1	31.8	–	Lara House on R

STATE STREET INN
Mac and Amy Lee
1005 State Street
Hood River, OR 97031
(503) 386-1899
Rates: $55-75

The drive to the State Street Inn along either the Washington or Oregon side of the Columbia River is breathtaking. Once in Hood River, the sight of colorful windsurfers sailing along the river, Mount Adams to the north and Mount Hood to the south is equally spectacular. The inn is positioned on the steep hillside just a few blocks west of town, with views of snow-capped Mount Adams and the river below.

Mac and Amy Lee are energetic, friendly innkeepers who are raising a toddler in addition to running a great B&B. Mac is also an operations manager at the Full Sail Brewing Company just down the street. During our visit we were invited along on a family trip to the annual Hood River Valley Harvest Fest, where we got a thoroughly enjoyable glimpse at this fun little town.

The inn is an unpretentious English-style home built in 1932, with a gabled roof and pitched ceilings. Tastefully restored, the home combines timeless craftsmanship with cheerful contemporary decor. Original oak floors and leaded glass remain throughout the house, while large picture windows in the living and dining rooms have been added to take advantage of the stunning view.

The living room has two comfortable seating areas, one oriented to the picture window, the other in front of a large cozy fireplace, both furnished with wicker couches and armchairs covered in forest green cushions. At the far end of the room a window seat tucks in a window overlooking an ivy-covered retaining wall and a tall maple. The room is simply decorated, with Amy's matted and framed nature photos of Alaska and the Yukon colorfully covering one wall.

A small den just off the living room has a table and chairs, games, puzzles and a phone for guests' use, all overlooking the view through multipaned leaded glass windows. An old church pew provides additional seating for a heated game of Scrabble.

Each of the five guest rooms, which all share two full baths upstairs and one down, are named for a state the Lees have lived in, and decorated accordingly. While not listed in the brochure as

a room choice, the downstairs Oregon Room is used for extra guests in the peak summer months. This room faces the back side of the property, with a view of the ivy wall just outside. White walls, light oak floors and a pink and white spread on the full bed brighten the room. A wicker armchair with green trim, two nightstands with stained glass lamps and a pine headboard with carved pineapple knobs complete the furnishings.

The remaining rooms are all upstairs. The Maryland Room is a spacious, light room with a view of the river and an air of Southern grace. Both the queen-sized and twin-sized day beds are covered in white spreads, complementing the white floral print wallpaper, while cushioned white wicker chairs and a low table sit in an salmon-colored alcove with a large bay window. A pretty cream and pale pink rug sits atop the polished oak floors.

The Massachusetts Room is just down the hall, a quiet room with dappled sun coming in through the maples outside. Decorated with a Colonial touch, an antique rocking chair, nightstand and old chest add authenticity. The queen-sized bed has a mahogany headboard, dark patterned spread and is topped with white lace pillows to match the linen and lace curtains. Two walls are a soft beige, while the other two are papered with a subtle navy and white print.

At the far end of the hall is the Colorado Room, decorated with a decidedly Southwest flair from the raw aspen armchair to the brightly patterned Navajo rug. This smaller room, which gets flooded with morning sun, has a cozy double bed in a white wrought-iron bedstead and a built in dresser and vanity.

We stayed in the California Room, which has fabulous mountain and river views through a wonderful coved window. Pale peach walls, a peach, blue and mint-colored dhurri rug on the light oak floor and two directors chairs with brightly colored pink and blue seat covers make this room sunny on even the darkest day. The tropical bedspread in pink, yellow and green on the queen-sized bed fits right in with the papier-mâché parrot hanging from a hoop in the corner. You can watch the sun rise over Mount Adams from the comfortable cushioned wicker armchair or propped up on the bright pillows on the bed.

Breakfast is served downstairs just across the foyer from the living room. The dining room features built-in china cabinets, an impressive sideboard and a long table which comfortably seats eight, but the most outstanding feature is the view. This room has another enormous picture window offering views of Mount Adams; fortunately guests don't have to vie for the view side of the table since the Lees have hung an equally large mirror on the opposite wall! Breakfast starts around 8 a.m., or earlier in the summer when the windsurfers are eager to get going. The fare is healthy and filling here: we had juice and coffee with our hot orange muffins before diving into a stack of banana-nut pancakes drizzled with syrup.

Visitors to State Street Inn tend to be a fairly active lot, since Hood River's proximity to outdoor activities doesn't end with windsurfing. If you tire of the riding here (which doesn't seem possible!), you're within moments of some excellent spots to go white-water rafting, hiking or flyfishing. For the less athletically inclined, Hood River also boasts many cute shops and several nearby museums and wineries. Whatever you choose to do during your stay, make reservations well in advance in the summer, since this inn is an understandably popular spot!

BIKING FROM THE STATE STREET INN

Terrain

There's an amazing amount of variety on these rides: One explores the Hood River Valley and it's orchards and farms, all very lush and green, while the other dips into the drier regions toward The Dalles. Pedaling along the Columbia River on the Historical

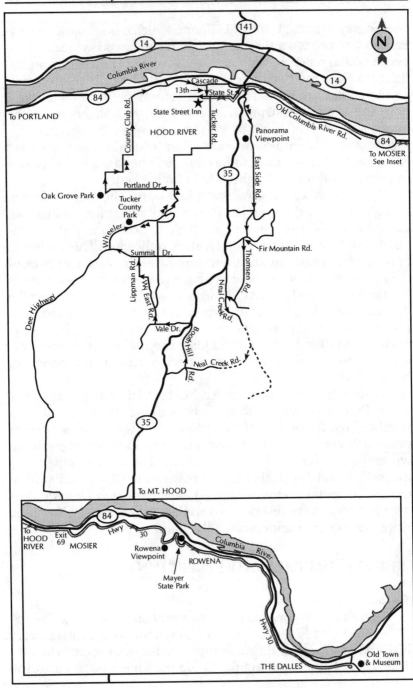

Sam Hill O & B ———   Valley Loop ———

Columbia River Highway is more than exhilarating as you first climb and then descend on this beautiful road. It was built by Sam Hill and features some great stonework bridges.

Road Conditions

Roads in the valley are variable; Neal Creek Road is partially gravel and there is one very rickety bridge to cross (easy for bicycles). The stretch on I-84 isn't too bad–there is a good shoulder the whole way. Watch for the railroad tracks before Lippman Road, they are in bad shape and there are dogs just before it. Cascade Ave. is in poor condition, watch for potholes and glass.

Traffic

Cascade Ave. is very busy, as is most of I-84. Be careful when taking the left onto Portland from Summit/Wy East Drive, the climb is strenuous and the traffic can be heavy.

Nearest Bike Shop

Discover Bikes
1020 Wasco St. (Dill Bldg.)
Hood River, OR 97031
(503) 386-4820

Best Time to Ride

Temperatures are fairly mild year around, but early spring through late fall is wonderful. The best windsurfing in the Gorge is in the winter, but the wind does blow pretty steady all the time.

Mountain Biking Opportunities

The Hood River Valley is surrounded on three sides by National Forest land and offers some great off-road riding. Surveyors Ridge off Pinemont Dr. is one good one, Lost Lake is another, though further away. Talk to the folks at Discover Bikes, they lead rides all over the area.

SAM HILL OUT & BACK (31.1 miles)

Even with the stretch on I-84, this ride is wonderful, as it includes probably the finest views of the Columbia Valley from a bike. The terrain visibly changes as you go from the greens of Hood River to the browns of the Dalles area. It is really stunning. Rowena View Point will take your breath away.

*Optional route continues to The Dalles 9 miles beyond Mayer State Park and then turns around and returns same way to Hood River. The Dalles Old Town has a museum and is the end of the Lewis and Clark Trail. The Dalles is also very busy with many car dealers, restaurants and shops. Traffic is very heavy. Only go if you need the extra 18 miles.

VALLEY LOOP (30.5 miles)

This is just one fun loop as far as variety goes. There's a little of everything here with even some gravel thrown in. The route follows the perimeter of the Hood River Valley and gives you a great sense of how much else is here beyond the much publicized sail-boarding. There are many farms with fruit, hops and other crops. Road surfaces vary greatly and are generally good, but watch out for the dogs in some spots.

Sam Hill Out & Back (Road)

Pt.-Pt.	Cum.	Dir.	Street/Landmark
			From the State Street Inn
0.0	0.0	R	**State St.**
0.1	0.1	X	9th
0.4	0.5	X	Front St. (bridge over Hood River)
0.4	0.9	L	**Highway 35**
0.3	1.2	CR	**I-84/30** (55 MPH; wide shoulder)
5.2	6.4	R	**Exit 69**
0.2	6.6	R	**Highway 30/Historical Columbia River Highway** into Mosier, incredible views; rolling uphill and flat stretches)
6.8	13.4	–	Rowena View Point
1.9	15.3	–	Mayer State Park on L
		TA*	**Or continue to The Dalles (18 miles round-trip—see above)**
1.9	17.2	–	Rowena View Point
6.8	24.0	–	Mosier
0.2	24.2	L	**I-84/30 entrance ramp**
5.3	29.5	R	**Exit 64**
0.3	29.8	L	**Highway 35 S/West 30**
0.1	29.9	R	**Highway 35 S/West 30** (over bridge)
0.3	30.2	R	**Highway 30**

0.3	30.5	X	Front St. (Hwy. 30 changes to **State St.**)
0.5	31.0	X	9th
0.1	31.1	–	State Street Inn on L

Valley Loop (Road)

Pt.-Pt.	Cum.	Dir.	Street/Landmark
			From the State Street Inn
0.0	0.0	**R**	**State St.**
0.1	0.1	X	9th
0.4	0.5	X	Front St. (bridge over Hood River)
0.4	0.9	**CR**	**Highway 35**
0.3	1.2	**L**	**Eastside Rd.** (cross with caution—Hwy 35 is 55 MPH; uphill)
1.5	2.7	–	Panorama Point on R (good view of valley and Mt. Hood)
2.4	5.1	**L**	**Eastside Rd.** (Pine Grove School on L; hop field on R; Pine Grove Methodist Church 1907 on L)
0.9	6.0	**R**	**Fir Mountain Rd.**
0.1	6.1	**L**	**Thomsen Rd.**
2.0	8.1	**L**	**Neal Creek Rd.**
0.4	8.5	**CL**	**Neal Creek Rd.**
1.2	9.7	–	Cross old bridge over Neil Creek; gravel
0.3	10.0	**CR**	**Neal Creek Rd.** (not L)
2.3	12.3	**R**	**Booth Hill Rd.**
1.6	13.9	X	Highway 35 (Booth Hill changes to **Central Vale Rd.**)
1.0	14.9	**R**	**Wy' East Rd.**
1.5	16.4	**L**	**Lippman Rd.**
0.1	16.5	**CR**	**Lippman Rd.** (not Canyon Rd.)
0.8	17.3	X	Railroad tracks (watch for dogs—both sides of road)
0.4	17.7	**L**	**Summit Dr.**
1.0	18.7	**R**	**Wheeler/Dee Highway**
0.1	18.8	**CL**	**Dee Highway**
1.8	20.6	–	Tucker County Park on L

0.4	21.0	CL	**Summit Dr./Wy' East Rd.** (downhill; moderate traffic; then uphill)
1.0	22.0	L	**Portland Dr.**
2.1	24.1	R	**Country Club Rd.** (Oak Grove Park, restroom to L)
1.9	26.0	L	**Country Club Rd.** (great downhill)
3.1	29.1	R	**Cascade Ave.** (heavy traffic)
1.2	30.3	R	**13th**
0.1	30.4	L	**State St.**
0.1	30.5	–	State Street Inn on R

YOUNGBERG HILL FARM INN
Eve and Norman Barnett
10660 Youngberg Hill Road
McMinnville, OR 97128
(503) 472-2727
Rates: $110-125

Driving through McMinnville, one certainly wouldn't expect to find a gracious inn *anywhere* nearby, much less just a few miles from town. Get through the downtown strip, however, and the countryside opens up to reveal rolling farms and vineyards dotted by stands of deciduous forest. While just an hour from both Portland and Salem, the area outlying McMinnville is so peaceful and bucolic it may as well be the middle of nowhere.

High on a hilltop, the 500 acre Youngberg Hill Farm has almost 360° views of the Willamette Valley, the Cascades and the Coast Range. Surrounded by a working vineyard and farm, it isn't uncommon to see lambs frolicking in the meadow or deer strolling through the rows of pinot noir grapes. You'll fall asleep looking at a sky full of stars, and wake to the sound of roosters crowing.

This is no ordinary country inn, however. The Barnetts built the home in 1989 with the intention of creating an elegant B&B, and although the architectural style and turn-of-the-century antiques throughout the inn recall an earlier era, no expense was spared in providing a luxurious modern retreat.

The downstairs sitting area and adjacent dining room take full advantage of the sweeping panorama outside the window. Both rooms have tall picture windows and glass doors opening to the wrap-around deck. Two overstuffed couches, a matching easy chair and two antique armchairs provide plenty of spots to admire the view or curl up beside the woodstove in the sitting room. The room is decorated simply, with white walls and deep blue carpet creating an open but warm ambiance. Cheese and crackers are set out in the evening, along with an honor bar featuring wines from Youngberg Hill and other Yamhill County wineries.

The dining room has hardwood floors and a long table which seats eight to ten guests. The table is set with fine china and nice linens, with a bouquet of fresh flowers in the middle.

Each guest room at the inn offers a full private bath, wonderful views and a queen-sized bed with a delightfully soft comforter. The only downstairs room, the Garden Room, has a fireplace and

private porch. Refined dark wood antiques lend an elegant air to this spacious room.

The upstairs rooms have white walls and soft mauve carpeting, complementing the maroon comforters on each bed. Wadenswil Room (named after a variety of grape), just above the Garden Room, also has a fireplace, with two large armchairs arranged before it. Antique nightstands and a large dresser and mirror highlights this corner room, which looks back over the property to the southwest.

Down the hall is the Pommard Room, with marble-topped nightstands and two antique armchairs in a bay with three tall windows. A handsome dresser/desk and carved headboard add to the furnishings.

We stayed in the Mount Jefferson Room, a corner room with views of Mount Hood and Jefferson out over the vineyard. Two dark wood cushioned armchairs sit on either side of a handsome coffee table between large windows.

The Mount Hood Room at the end of the hall looks southeast to the mountains through five tall windows. Marble-topped nightstands, a tall narrow dresser and elegant bedstead complete the refined decor.

Breakfast is served between 8:30 and 9:30 a.m. in the dining room. The morning we visited our fellow guests had left early to catch a plane, so we had the place to ourselves. We started our meal with coffee and a fruit plate, then were treated to Austrian pancakes with boysenberry syrup, accompanied by Canadian bacon, a poached apple and fresh blackberries. Both Eve and Norman have jobs in addition to running the inn, so breakfast was served by their outgoing and cheerful assistant Teri.

While you're exploring the area around the Youngberg Hill Farm, don't miss a stop at the Lawrence Gallery, Oregon Wine Tasting Room and Augustine's Restaurant, all housed in the same building (noted on the cue sheet for Amity Loop). McMinnville also boasts a well known restaurant—Nick's—which we weren't able to get into, but have heard rave reviews about. For an alternative, the Golden Valley Brewery and Pub offers good food, a great selection of local wines and several varieties of their own microbrew.

For a quick weekend getaway, you can't beat the location of Youngberg Hill Farm. The pastoral setting and appealing accommodations will leave you feeling as though you've truly gotten away.

BIKING FROM THE YOUNGBERG HILL FARM

Terrain
McMinville is comprised of farmland which spreads out from the hills of the Coast Range. As you go nearer the range the hills increase, but toward the west the land flattens out considerably. There are some serious hills around Powerhouse Hill Rd., but the views below are worth it.

Road Conditions
Roads are usually two lane, with some just wide enough for you and the tractor you may meet. 99W is and Highway 18 have moderate shoulders. Powerhouse Hill Rd. is gravel and steep, so take care when descending.

Traffic
Traffic is light except on Highway 99W.

Nearest Bike Shop
Tommy's Bike Shop
624 3rd St.
McMinville, OR 97128
(800) 924-2925/(503) 472-2010

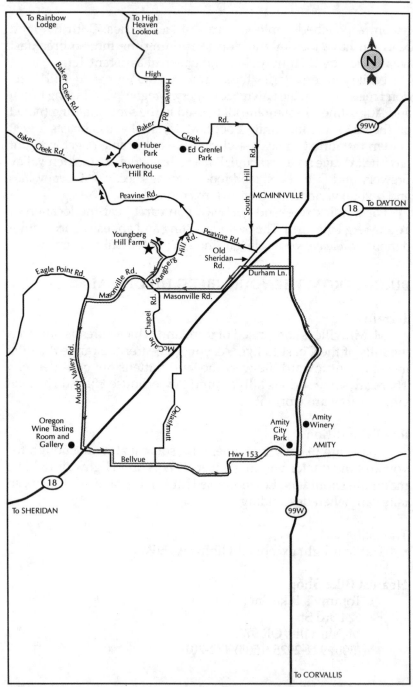

Powerhouse Loop ————   Amity Loop ————

Best Time to Ride
From early May through late October, the weather is very pleasant and it's a good time to ride in this area.

Mountain Biking Opportunities
There is good off-road riding near Rainbow Lodge off of Baker Creek Rd. The crew at Tommy's can tell you where to get dirty.

POWERHOUSE LOOP (20.2 miles)
Hills abound on this route but the real challenge is coming down Powerhouse Hill Road. The only serious climb would be if you decided to ride up to High Heaven Lookout. Peavine Road is beautiful and allows vistas of the countryside to your left.

AMITY LOOP (24.0 miles)
This is a pleasant ride through the agricultural area around Youngberg Hill Farm. The Oregon Wine Tasting Room and Gallery is filled with local art of all kinds; the quality of the art is outstanding. Make sure you go out and see the garden which surrounds the back of the Gallery: The water ponds and outdoor sculptures are wonderful. Amity is a farm town but Highway 99W can be busy.

Powerhouse Loop (Road)

Pt.-Pt.	Cum.	Dir.	Street/Landmark
			From Youngberg Hill Farm
0.0	0.0	S	**Gravel driveway** (downhill)
1.0	1.0	L	**Youngberg Hill Rd.**
1.1	2.1	L	**Peavine Rd.**
5.1	7.2	R	**Powerhouse Hill Rd.** (gravel; steep downhill)
1.5	8.7	R	**Baker Creek Rd.** (paved)
0.6	9.3	–	Huber Park on R (restrooms, picnic spot, pretty creek)
1.4	10.7	–	High Heaven Rd. on L (goes up to lookout—3 to 4 miles up)
0.2	10.9	–	Ed Grenfel Park to R
2.7	13.6	R	**South Hill Rd.**
1.3	14.9	S	**Hill Rd.**

1.6	16.5	R	**Peavine Rd.**
1.6	18.1	L	**Youngberg Hill Rd.**
1.1	19.2	R	**Gravel driveway** (steep uphill)
1.0	20.2	–	Youngberg Hill Farm

Amity Loop (Road)

Pt.-Pt.	Cum.	Dir.	Street/Landmark
			From Youngberg Hill Farm
0.0	0.0	S	**Gravel driveway** (downhill)
1.0	1.0	R	**Youngberg Hill Rd.**
0.7	1.7	R	**Masonville Rd.**
1.1	2.8	L	**Muddy Valley Rd.**
4.0	6.8	X	Highway 18 (Muddy Valley changes to **Bellvue**; Oregon Wine Tasting Room and Lawrence Gallery on R—must see)
2.1	8.9	–	Pass Delashmutt on L (Bellvue changes to **Highway 153**—continue straight)
3.9	12.8	–	Amity City Park on L (restrooms; picnic area)
0.2	13.0	L	**Highway 99W**
0.4	13.4	–	Amity Winery on R
4.3	17.7	L	**Durham Lane**
1.1	18.8	X	Highway 18
0.1	18.9	L	**Old Sheridan Rd.**
0.7	19.6	R	**Masonville Rd.**
2.7	22.3	R	**Youngberg Hill Rd.**
0.7	23.0	L	**Gravel driveway** (steep uphill)
1.0	24.0	–	Youngberg Hill Farm

CENTRAL WASHINGTON INNS AND RIDES

The inns in this chapter technically cover Eastern Washington and the Cascades, which vary tremendously in climate and terrain. These are summer-only riding destinations, as all the areas in this chapter get snow in the winter. (However, if you're a skier you'll enjoy a winter visit to many of these spots.)

Eastern Washington can get unbelievably hot in the summer, so you may want to plan a spring or fall trip. If you ride in the summer, try to get an early start so you can be back in the shade by the time the thermometer hits the 100° mark. Trust us—we didn't get out early enough one day and rode in 107° heat! Bring extra water on these rides.

Eastern Washington tends to be fairly flat, with miles and miles of irrigated farmland, orchards and vineyards. Wineries and roadside fruit stands abound here, so there are plenty of places to stop along your ride.

A note of caution about riding in Eastern Washington: almost every farm we rode by had at least one dog, and we're not talking about Chihuahuas here. The dogs are large, loose and bored; chasing after a cyclist is their idea of a really good time. Your best defense is to be aware of them before they spot you, but if they come after you with serious intent, get off your bike and place it between you and the dog. Look the dog in the eye and shout "No" firmly. Remarkably enough, the dog will likely slink off and leave you alone.

The crisp mountain air and cool evenings in the Cascades make this a pleasant place to ride all summer, although temperatures can be in the 90s during the day. The terrain is *not* flat—you're in the mountains, after all—but you'll find magnificent views surrounding you at these higher altitudes.

Our first inn in this chapter is at the base of Mount Rainier, a landmark of the Northwest. This volcanic peak is a designated National Park of unrivaled alpine beauty, with abundant wildlife and a glorious display of wildflowers throughout the summer. The Nisqually Loop from **Alexander's Country Inn** will let you glimpse the mountain from several vantage points while sticking to relatively level terrain, but the formidable climb up to aptly-named Paradise provides a simply awe-inspiring vista. It's more than worth the effort.

After all the huffing and puffing up Rainier, you'll want to head over to the **Green Gables Inn** in Walla Walla for more level terrain. Largely agricultural, Walla Walla is a charming mid-sized town with a Midwestern feel. Our rides in Walla Walla meandered through rolling wheat fields and along a lush river. The inn itself is in a lovely treed neighborhood of stately old homes.

Back up in the mountains, the Methow Valley is a mountain bikers paradise. Miles of gravel forest roads and singletrack await you just outside the back door at **North Cascades Basecamp**. The Upper Valley Tour ride sticks to the road (although the road through the forest requires fatter tires), taking you from Mazama almost into the charmingly restored Old West town of Winthrop.

You'll think you've wound up in the Alps when you arrive in Leavenworth, a picture-perfect Bavarian town in the central Cascades. Nestled at the bottom of a confluence of canyons to one side and surrounded by orchards to the other, **Run of the River** offers splendid rides in any direction. Heading up into the canyon on a mountain bike allows you to experience the views from the high ridges, while sticking to the road on the southern loop presents opportunities to sample just-picked peaches, plums, apricots pears and a number of other delights at one of the many roadside fruit stands.

In addition to a plentiful number of fruit stands, in Sunnyside you can sample the fruit of the vine in one of the many nationally-acclaimed wineries that dot the Yakima Valley. From the **Sunnyside Inn** you can choose the Valley Vista Loop up along the ridge above the wide Yakima River, or the Fruit Loop, which rambles through the valley, pausing at up to six different wineries.

The inns in this chapter offer a wide variety of terrain and a number of different attractions. Whether you want to visit one of the nation's most beautiful parks in Ashford, marvel at the wheat fields in Walla Walla, do some strenuous off-road riding in Mazama, climb your way up a canyon in Leavenworth or take a leisurely wine-tasting tour in Sunnyside, you're sure to find something to suit you at one of these inns.

ALEXANDER'S COUNTRY INN
Jerry Harnish & Bernadette Ronan
37515 SR 706 East
Ashford, WA 98304
800-654-7615
Rates: $65-138 per night, off-season rates apply November-April

Alexander's is just one short mile from the entrance of Mount Rainier National Park, which features one of the most challenging rides we did all summer. At 14,410 feet above sea level, Mount Rainier is the largest mountain in the lower 48 states; consequently, views from just about any point on the road up are magnificent, but one must ride to aptly-named Paradise for the full effect.

The inn is the oldest historical building in the Mount Rainier area; built as an inn in 1912 by the Mesler family, Alexander's once hosted Presidents Theodore Roosevelt and William Howard Taft. Photos of the Mesler family and other vacationers, hikers, mountain climbers and skiers from the turn-of-the-century line the hallways.

The three-story building is right off the road, backed up against enormous pines and a glacier-fed trout pond. A striking four-story octagonal tower rises from the southeast corner of the building, overlooking the duck pond in front of the inn.

With twelve rooms, it was the largest establishment we visited. The rooms are simply decorated, with names reflecting the surrounding views, such as Eagle Rock & Mt. Beljica, Pyramid Peak, Glacier View, Plummer Peak & High Rock. Rooms are reserved by their corresponding number now, although the names still appear on calligraphed signs outside each door.

Rooms 7 and 13 are the rooms to ask for, though you'll have to do it in advance since everyone who has been to the inn knows this secret. Room 13 is a suite on the second floor, with its bedroom in the lower half of the octagonal tower. The sitting room has cheerful wicker furniture and a door leading onto the small east-facing private deck, but the bedroom is the real gem. Six tall windows, surrounded by wood paneling, look out in slightly different directions, making the room seem round. A queen bed with floral spread is positioned to take advantage of the views; it might be tempting to just stay in bed and watch the sun spreading across the mountains.

Room 7 is just above room 13, in the upper half of the octagonal tower, but this room has a sitting room on the third floor and stairs up to the bedroom on the fourth—both rooms are in the tower. The bedroom is the highest point in the inn, and has uninterrupted views of all angles.

Most of the other rooms in the inn have good views. All but three of the rooms share the designated men's or women's bathrooms, which have showers in the men's rooms and a tub and shower in the women's. The rooms are decorated with simple antiques like large armoires and delicate end tables. Most rooms have queen-size beds with antique headboards. Gentle pastel colors and quilts or floral bedspreads and curtains add a bright sunny feeling to each room.

The sitting room on the second floor is spacious, with high ceilings, a brass chandelier, European stained-glass windows, and several plush couches and armchairs arranged in conversational groupings. Soft pink walls with paneled wood wainscoting make the room at once bright and inviting. Wine is set out between 5:30 and 6 p.m., and on chilly evenings a fire is lit. Browse through the "Things to do in the area" scrapbooks, peruse the guest books with entries from several Mesler family relatives, and be sure to see the original blueprints for the inn, framed at the far end of the room.

After a tough (but infinitely rewarding) ride, a glass of wine by the fire, and a full dinner, you'll want to be sure and hit the hot tub before bed. Perched on a deck overlooking the trout pond, the tub is private and peaceful.

In keeping with the country inn tradition, the dining room is open to the public, so you'll be asked to sign up in advance for a specific breakfast time. You may also want to have dinner at the inn, since restaurants in the area are somewhat scarce. The dining room has about twelve intimate booths and small tables, each covered with a bright floral-print tablecloth. Breakfast is a lavish affair, with juice and coffee, an assortment of breakfast bread (we sampled the zucchini and applesauce spice breads), seasonal fruit and a choice of entrées. We tried the blackberry blintzes and the blueberry pancakes.

The number of friendly and helpful staff at the inn ranges from twelve in the winter to thirty-five in the summer. The manager, Melinda Simpson, was particularly enthusiastic; having worked at Mount Rainier for 18 years prior to managing the inn, she is also a wealth of information on the area.

If you're traveling with a group or family, you may want to consider renting one of the 3-bedroom houses next door. Both have fully equipped kitchens. The Forest House is a perfect family retreat, with a big dining room and a fireplace in the living room. The back of the house looks out into the woods, while sliding glass doors from the kitchen open onto a deck and sunny yard. The Chalet is a two-story, new building, with a huge master bedroom downstairs and two snug bedrooms in the upstairs loft. High ceilings and modern amenities such as a CD player make this a luxurious getaway.

Regardless of which accommodations you take advantage of, the tranquil mountain setting, the history of the inn and the challenging riding nearby make Alexander's a bicycling destination you don't want to miss.

BIKING FROM ALEXANDER'S COUNTRY INN

Terrain

The Nisqually Valley floor is flat and fairly wide, with Highway 706 following the river almost to its source at the Nisqually Glacier. The Tatoosh Range to the south is very dramatic, the destination of many backcountry skiers. The Nisqually entrance sits at 2003 feet, Paradise is at 5400 feet, and Round Pass on the Westside Road is at 3900 feet. To the north and east is Mount Rainier National Park with major elevation gains, to the south and west is Mount Baker-Snoqualmie National Forest with less severe elevation gains.

Road Conditions

Road surfaces are good on Highway 706, but the shoulder varies from narrow to nonexistent. Forest Service Road 52 is rough in spots but very ridable. At higher elevations watch for ice in the early mornings.

Traffic

Highway 706 is a main paved thoroughfare going west to east across the National Park, so it can be fairly busy, especially in the summer. The road is also narrow and drivers are watching the sights, not you, so ride defensively. Forest Service Road 52 is paved and almost traffic-free.

Nearest Bike Shop

Northwest Mountain Bike
6304 6th Ave.
Tacoma, WA 98406
(206) 565-9050
(1 hour away)

Best Time to Ride

September. The leaves are changing and the summer tourists in their RV's are migrating south, the weather is fairly predictable, cool in the mornings and warm at midday. June is the first month where the roads are becoming clear of snow, and skiers are still making their way to Paradise for some spring skiing, but by July the crowds have come. FSR 52 has little traffic even in the peak summer.

Mountain Biking Opportunities

The Mount Tahoma Trails Association has a central and south unit on either side of Highway 706. To access the north unit take FS Rd. 59, which is a mile west of Alexander's on the right and leads up to Glacier Vista. The south unit access is in Ashford. Most of the system follows logging roads, with much climbing. You

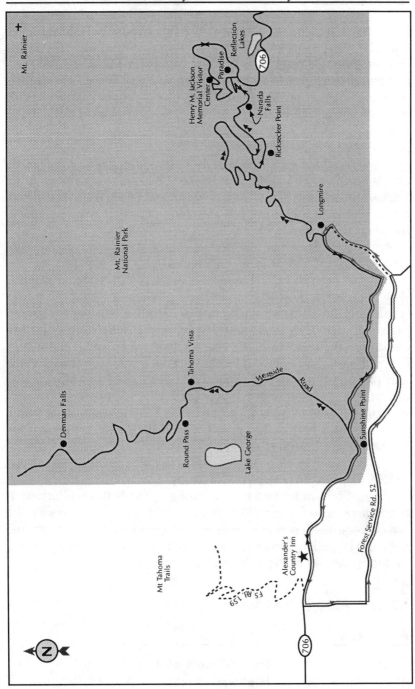

Nisqually Loop ———   Paradise O & B ———

need a map, which is available at The Bunkhouse in Ashford, and a local county map is available at the gas station near the Scale Burger shop. Or use USGS 7.5 min. quads for Mt. Wow, Ashford (central district), and Sawtooth Ridge and Anderson Lake (south district). There is *no* mountain biking allowed in the National Park or Wilderness areas.

NISQUALLY LOOP (21.4 miles)

This ride follows the Nisqually River valley on first the south and then the north sides. The FS Rd. 52 is an alternate route to Packwood and the White Pass area. There is very little traffic and a few places to hike down to the river's edge. It would make a nice morning ride after breakfast. The overall route is fairly flat.

PARADISE OUT & BACK (38.2 miles)

This trek is not for the faint of heart if you decide to go all the way to Paradise. Best to go as early as possible to avoid the traffic (especially on summer weekends)—Paradise is a very popular place because of its views and hiking and as a starting point for climbing "the mountain." If you really want to avoid the traffic and still get some incredible views, take a left on Westside Rd. and pass by the gate. This road has been closed to automobiles and leaves a very serene passage for the bicyclist—the Park Service only wants cyclists to go as far as Klapatche. At that point there are trails to hike, but no off-road riding—this area is within National Park boundaries.

WEST SIDE ROAD (Up to 24.4 miles)

In just two miles you can be riding in the National Park on a road that's closed to cars! Yes, that's right, the route follows a road which requires too much maintenance for vehicular traffic, but suits the bicyclist perfectly. It's one of the few places that provide incredible views of the Tahoma Glacier close up.

Nisqually Loop (Road/MTB)

Pt.-Pt.	Cum.	Dir	Street/Landmark
			From Alexander's Country Inn
0.0	0.0	**R**	**Highway 706 W**
2.2	2.2	**L**	**Forest Service Rd. 52**

1.2	3.4	**CL**	**Forest Service Rd. 52**
7.8	11.2	**L**	**Forest Service Rd. 5230** (gravel)
0.2	11.4	**L**	**unmarked gravel road**
0.8	12.2	–	Park boundary gate (go around and follow paved service road through campground and over bridge into Longmire)
1.5	13.7	**L**	**Highway 706 E**
7.7	21.4	–	Alexander's Country Inn on R

Paradise Out & Back (Road)

Pt.-Pt.	Cum.	Dir	Street/Landmark
			From Alexander's Country Inn
0.0	0.0	**L**	**Highway 706E**
1.3	1.3	–	Mt. Rainier National Park entrance ($3 for bicyclists)
0.9	2.2	–	Westside Rd. to L (closed to autos)
5.5	7.7	–	Longmire (restaurant, gift shops, restrooms, museum; begin uphill climb)
5.9	13.6	**R**	**View Point–one way turnoff** to Paradise (awesome views of the Tatoosh Range from Ricksecker Point)
1.3	14.9	**R**	**Highway 706** (to Paradise)
1.5	16.4	–	Narada Falls to R
0.9	17.3	**CL**	**Stay L to Paradise**
1.8	19.1	–	Paradise Visitors Center to L
0.3	19.4	–	Paradise parking lot and Lodge (get ready for a very long downhill back to Alexander's Country Inn)
		TA	
11.2	30.6	–	Longmire
7.6	38.2	–	Alexander's Country Inn on R

GREEN GABLES INN
Jim and Margaret Buchan
922 Bonsella
Walla Walla, WA 99362
(509) 525-5501
Rates: $75-160

Surrounded by waving wheat fields, Walla Walla is one of the oldest settled communities between the Rockies and Cascades. Home of the first institute of higher learning in the Northwest, Whitman College, as well as one of the oldest newspapers west of the Missouri River, the first bank in the state, and the area's oldest railroad line, Walla Walla retains a simple hometown charm and the refined demeanor of days gone by.

The Green Gables Inn resides in a neighborhood of stately older homes on wide streets lined with mature shade trees. Built in 1909 for the daughter of William and Mary Green, among Walla Walla's earliest residents, this venerable Arts and Crafts-style mansion has been impeccably restored to its original character (in fact, in 1990 the inn won an architectural award for restoration and renovation).

The house was built with entertaining in mind, with spacious guest rooms, a good sized dining room, and fireplaces at either end of the long living room. A carved mantle atop one fireplace is inscribed, "The Ornaments of a House are the Friends Who Frequent It", a creed reflected in the simple but welcoming decor of the living room. Exposed beam ceilings, a bank of low windows and light oak floors reflect the Craftsman era's simplicity, while built-in bookshelves and a built-in settee show its creative side. The room is furnished with a few select antique pieces, such as a coal scuttle, old clocks, first-edition books and original light fixtures, an assortment of mahogany chairs and coffee tables, and couple of more contemporary couches and armchairs. Either end of the living room forms a cozy spot to sit by the fire or look out at the park-like college campus just across the street.

A substantial dining area opens from the living room, with a massive built-in sideboard, complete with drawers and cabinets, stretching across one end. Lace-covered French doors lead to the back porch at the other end, letting in plenty of morning light. A silver tea set is set out on a mahogany tea cart, while the table for up to ten guests is set with nice china and fresh flowers.

Back in the foyer, a wide dark wood staircase leads to the up-stairs guest rooms. Each room has a private bath, cable television and a mini refrigerator, as well as access to a large book and game library in the hall.

We stayed in Idlewild, the master suite at the far end of the hall. This gracious room has a lovely antique mahogany bedroom set, a king-sized bed and a spacious sitting area with a comfort-able couch and built-in cushioned window seat in front of a white-mantled fireplace. Ornate floral wallpaper in green, pale blue and rose hues complements dark green carpeting. A large window looks out over the green trees and lawn below, while a set of French doors leads to a sizable private porch. A large walk-in closet with a window holds the mini refrigerator and ample space for hanging clothes. The private bath has a Jacuzzi tub and shower.

Just around the corner is the Mayflowers room (all the room names were adopted from the "Anne of Green Gables" book). This is a snug, quiet room with a queen-sized bed in an ornate iron and brass bedstead, covered with an antique quilt. The decor is more Victorian, and the bathroom has a wonderful clawfoot tub and shower.

The Willowmere and Birchpath rooms are next door to each other, with a door between them. Willowmere has a king-sized bed with estate furnishings and original turn-of-the-century paint-ings. Its private bath has a clawfoot tub and shower. Birchpath has two twin beds (which can be converted to a king-sized bed) covered in white comforters, a mahogany bedroom set, and a large window overlooking the neighborhood. The soft peach bathroom has a modern tub and shower.

Dryad's Bubble is a fun room, decorated with bolder colors and Maxfield Parrish prints. The king-sized bed is covered with a navy and white striped comforter. Well-crafted Arts and Crafts-period birdseye maple pieces, including a dresser, vanity, desk and rocking chair, furnish the room. A deep blue overstuffed armchair and footstool sit in the corner by a large window looking out through the trees to the Carriage House. The cheerful blue and white private bath has a clawfoot tub and shower.

In back of the main house is the Carriage House, a spacious cottage with a large bedroom, one-and-a-half baths, living room and fully equipped kitchen downstairs, and an enormous screened sleeping porch upstairs. The living room has a queen-sized hide-a-bed couch and daybed. This is a perfect choice for two couples traveling together or a family with younger children (children over twelve are welcome in the main house).

In the morning we found a coffee thermos set outside our room door, and sat out on the balcony enjoying the crisp fall morning and a cup of coffee as we watched the neighborhood wake up. We joined our fellow guests for a candlelit breakfast in the dining room around 8:30 a.m. We started out with a delicious blended mango and tangerine juice, a piece lemon biscotti and a slice of sour cream brunch cake. Croissants and homemade jams were brought out with our main course, a fluffy vegetable omelet with a bunch of fresh grapes on the side. Guests at the inn are often associated with nearby Whitman College, so at breakfast you'll likely meet interesting folks from all over the country.

Having both been raised in the Midwest, Walla Walla held a certain nostalgic charm for us. The acres of wheat fields surrounding the brick downtown area, the bike path along a lazy river and the old neighborhoods with noble homes and tall shade trees don't represent what we think of as the Northwest. Yet the history in this area clearly illustrates it has played a very important part in shaping the character of the Northwest. For a completely different look at our region, try a trip to Walla Walla. Whether you're a history buff or just enjoy bicycling in level terrain, you're sure to delight in this friendly town and the amiable accommodations at the Green Gables Inn.

BIKING FROM GREEN GABLES INN

Terrain
This is a road bicyclist's dream. Slight, rolling hills, and wide open views. Farms dot most of the landscape and grain elevators tower overhead. The Blue Mountains make up the backdrop.

Road Conditions
All are in good condition, with few shoulders but smooth roads.

Traffic
Except for State Route 12, where traffic can be heavy, there's none to speak of. Crossing the highway involves good judgement and a quick traverse. Watch for farm machinery around the fields and farms.

Nearest Bike Shop
Bicycle Barn
1503 E. Isaacs
Walla Walla, WA 99362
(509) 529-7860

Best Time to Ride
Mid-spring to late fall, depending on if you want to see the planting or the harvesting.

Mountain Biking Opportunities
There are short trails at Vista Terrace Park, Eastgate Lions Park, and Fort Walla Walla Park. Talk to the Bicycle Barn people about where to go in the Blue Mountains, or try to get in on a Saturday ride.

SUDBURY LOOP (25.0 miles)
For the sheer fun of riding, this is a great place. The wheat fields are almost endless and the riding nearly effortless on this route where you should watch for tractors and combines rather than cars (except State Route 12).

COTTONWOOD LOOP (20.0 miles)
Another ride purely for the joy of bicycling. The expansiveness of the fields here is mind-boggling, and they are laced with rolling, nearly empty roads. On the way back, take a spin through the Oddfellows Cemetery for an interesting look at the area's history.

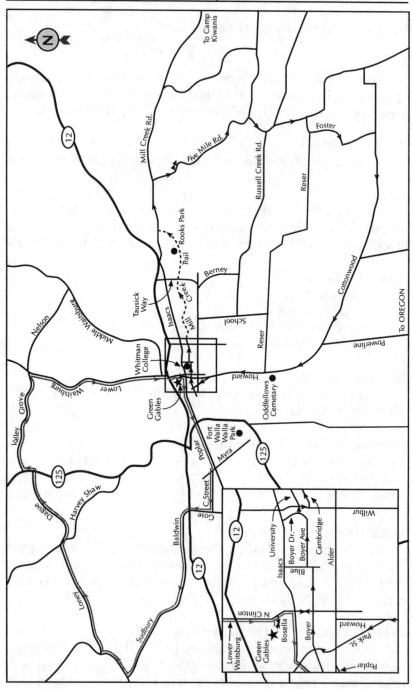

Sudbury Loop ⎯⎯⎯⎯⎯   Cottonwood Loop ⎯⎯⎯⎯⎯

Sudbury Loop (Road)

Pt.-Pt.	Cum.	Dir	Street/Landmark
			From Green Gables Inn
0.0	0.0	–	Corner of Estella St. and Bonsella St.
0.0	0.0	R	**Bonsella St.**
0.0	0.0	R	**N Clinton St.**
0.2	0.2	X	Isaacs Ave.
0.2	0.4	X	Boyer Ave.
0.2	0.6	R	**E Alder St.** (bike lane)
0.4	1.0	CL	**E Poplar**
0.3	1.3	X	First Ave.
0.0	1.3	X	2nd Ave.
0.1	1.4	X	3rd Ave.
0.1	1.5	X	4th Ave.
0.3	1.8	X	9th Ave.
1.3	3.1	R	**Myra Rd.**
0.0	3.1	L	**C Street NE** (immediate L)
0.4	3.5	–	Continue straight on C Street
0.5	4.0	R	**College Ave. N**
0.1	4.1	X	Rose (from center lane, cross on N College)
0.1	4.2	L	**Wallula**
0.0	4.2	R	**Gose** (immediate R)
0.4	4.6	X	Electric/Finch
0.4	5.0	X	SR 12 (be careful!—cross traffic does not stop)
0.2	5.2	L	**Baldwin Rd.**
0.7	5.9	R	**Sudbury**
4.9	10.8	R	**Loney Rd.** (at grain elevators)
3.1	13.9	R	**Harvey Shan Rd.**
0.1	14.0	L	**Dague Rd.**
2.6	16.6	L	**Hwy 125** (high speed auto traffic)
0.3	16.9	CR	**Valley Grove Rd.** (under railroad trestle)
2.7	19.6	R	**Lower Waitsburg**
4.9	24.5	X	SR 12 (be even more careful here—Waitsburg changes to **N Clinton**)
0.4	24.9	R	**Bonsella**
0.1	25.0	–	Green Gables on L

Cottonwood Loop (Road/MTB)

Pt.-Pt.	Cum.	Dir	Street/Landmark
			From Green Gables Inn
0.0	0.0	–	Corner of Estella St. and Bonsella St.
0.0	0.0	R	**Bonsella St.**
0.0	0.0	R	**N Clinton St.**
0.2	0.2	X	Isaacs Ave.
0.2	0.4	L	**Boyer Ave.**
0.4	0.8	L	**Blue St.**
0.0	0.8	R	**Boyer St.** (immediate R)
0.1	0.9	X	Roosevelt St. (Boyer curves left)
0.5	1.4	R	**University Drive**
0.0	1.4	R	**Wilbur**
0.1	1.5	L	**Cambridge Dr.**
0.1	1.6	–	Mill Creek Recreation Trail at dead end (paved—go straight onto trail)
0.9	2.5	X	Tausick Way
1.4	3.9	–	Rooks Park on L (restrooms & picnic areas)
0.3	4.2	R	**Park road** out of Rooks Park (path ends)
0.3	4.5	R	**Mill Creek Rd.**
1.0	5.5	CR	**5 Mile Rd.** (incredible views—road changes to **Russell Creek Rd.** at Scenic Loop Rd.)
3.6	9.1	L	**Foster Rd.**
2.9	12.0	R	**Cottonwood Rd.**
4.0	16.0	R	**Cottonwood Rd.**
1.1	17.1	X	Reser Rd.
0.3	17.4	–	On L is Abbot Rd. (for exploring the Oddfellows Cemetery)
0.3	17.7	X	Tietan Rd.
0.8	18.5	CL	**S Park St.**
0.5	19.0	X	East Alder St.
0.2	19.2	R	**Boyer St.**
0.4	19.6	L	**N Clinton St.**
0.2	19.8	X	Isaacs Ave.
0.1	19.9	L	**Bonsella**
0.1	20.0	–	Green Gables on L

NORTH CASCADES BASECAMP
Dick and Sue Roberts
255 Lost River Road
Mazama, WA 98833
(509) 996-2334
Rates: $70 for bed & breakfast, $110-120 full meals (only in winter)

The Methow Valley is a sparsely populated, ruggedly beautiful spot in the middle of the northern Cascades. Three small towns, Mazama, Winthrop and Twisp, are interspersed through the sunny valley, surrounded on either side by stalwart snow-capped peaks. This is a mountain bikers delight in the summer, and one of the most popular cross-country skiing spots in the region in the winter.

North Cascades Basecamp provides a casual and affordable spot to call home while you explore this fabulous wilderness. Goat Wall rises dramatically behind the raw cedar inn, which sits on 20 acres encompassing a swimming pond and a series of hiking trails. You enter the inn through a large, enclosed, two-story passive solar deck which runs the length of the house. Just outside the door a separate staircase entrance leads to the upstairs rooms. The dining room, open kitchen and sunken living room comprise the front half of the downstairs. The dining room is simple, with a sideboard and long table where meals are served three times a day upon request in the summer. (Winter rates include breakfast, lunch fixings and dinner, while summer rates include breakfast only unless prior arrangements have been made.)

The sunken living room looks out to the woods through large windows along one wall. A cozy woodstove, casual couches, shag carpet and stacks of books, games and children's toys make this a comfortable spot to unwind after a long ride. Families are more than welcome at this B&B, and several special spots have been set aside just for kids, which creates a relaxed atmosphere throughout the inn. Just off the living room a hexagonal deck nestled under the trees hosts a large hot tub, which you'll want to take advantage of in the evenings!

All six of the bedrooms in the main house are carpeted and share baths. The decor throughout the house leans toward "rec room", with neutral carpeting, functional furniture, and plenty of room to get comfortable. There are three bedrooms downstairs, two with queen-sized or double beds, and the third with a double

bed and two twin beds. This "family suite" has pine ceilings and a ladder up to a small loft with the double bed, allowing parents a little privacy. All the rooms have views of the woods, with dappled sunlight coming in through large windows. A ladder in the main hallway leads up to a carpeted, kid-sized, open alcove.

There are three more bedrooms upstairs, reached via a staircase from the dining room or the separate outdoor stairway. The spacious landing between the guest rooms has a sitting area with a piano. The rooms upstairs each have a double or queen-sized bed; two rooms have an additional bunk bed. The rooms are so quiet and well-insulated we had a crying baby next to us all night and never knew it!

The special accommodations at this inn are in the cabin next door. When the Roberts were building the main house 13 years ago their family of four lived in this pretty two story cabin. Hexagonal shaped right down to the deck outside, the cabin has clever angles and an interesting floor plan. The cabin is light and open, with white walls and soft green carpeting. Downstairs there are two bedrooms, one with a double bed and a bunk bed, separated by a low wall, the other with a queen-sized bed and a private bath. The larger second bedroom has a skylight and a spacious closet.

The sitting area and dining room downstairs have a table and chairs, a hide-a-bed couch, a woodstove and tall windows looking out over the property to the mountains across the valley. A full kitchen sits just off the dining area.

A narrow staircase leads to the upstairs sitting area, which has an additional couch that can serve as a twin bed. With a high ceiling and windows all the way around the room, this little loft feels almost like the top of a lighthouse, except for the forest and mountain view. A television and VCR are available on one of the built-in shelves.

Breakfast is an informal gathering, with people grouped around the table in their pajamas and kids wandering in and out of the room. We had hot oatmeal with milk and brown sugar, scrambled eggs, bacon and toast. Plenty of juice, coffee and cold cereals are available. After breakfast Sue sets out lunch fixings for full-board guests, allowing people to make their own lunches to eat out on the trail later in the day.

The atmosphere here is very welcoming and low-key. We felt more like we'd spent a weekend with friends than a night at an inn. Both Sue and Dick are enthusiastic outdoors people, and Dick supplied us with a ton of route suggestions and good maps for nearby road and off-road rides. This remote spot is located in one of the most beautiful regions of the Northwest, and the ambiance at North Cascades Basecamp will let you truly relax and enjoy it to its fullest.

BIKING FROM NORTH CASCADES BASECAMP

Terrain

Mazama is in the heart of the North Cascades and offers both outstanding beauty and exhilarating riding. Climbing is almost mandatory outside of the Methow Valley itself, as most of the land rises abruptly from the valley bottom. The Goat Wall Loop allows a wonderful glimpse into the Blackpine Basin and 3500 feet of vertical climbing to get there. The Methow Valley Tour cruises the lower elevations and meanders close to the town of Winthrop. Views of Mt. Gardener are just one of the treats on this ride!

Road Conditions

Both routes traverse gravel road, pavement and trail sections, so conditions are variable. All paved sections are well-maintained and Highway 20 has a wide shoulder for most of its length. Wolf Creek Rd. is dirt and rough in places. Forest Service Rd. 5227-100 is rough and technical in spots, but very exciting!

Traffic

Highway 20 has the only real traffic, but offers a wide shoulder. Watch out for open-grazing cows on your descents from the Goat Wall.

Nearest Bike Shop

Winthrop Mountain Sports
257 Riverside Ave.
P. O. Box 639
Winthrop, WA 98862
(509) 996-2886/Fax (509) 996-3388

Best Time to Ride

June through early October is best, with mid-summer getting rather dry. Snow hangs in the higher elevations till June or so.

Mountain Biking Opportunities

Everywhere. This place has a gargantuan number of mountain-biking opportunities. Pick up the Forest Service booklet on Mountain Bike Routes and go exploring! The Sun Mountain Trails are well marked and fun, Pipestone Canyon is beautiful. Bring water and flat-fixing gear as many trails can be remote and fairly dry.

UPPER VALLEY TOUR (34.2 miles)

This is a combination of gravel and pavement with a good section of the upper Methow Valley taken in. This is a beautiful place, with great vistas of the mountains and the Methow River. Traffic is fast on Highway 20 but the shoulder is good. Visit Winthrop before you head back to Mazama, as there are wonderful restaurants and many sights to see. An optional route back is to take a right at Goat Creek Rd. instead of following Hwy. 20 to Lost River Rd. It cuts out some of the highway riding.

GOAT WALL (28.7 miles)

This is a more strenuous route, but rewards you with awesome views and a wonderful off-road section. Only Goat Creek Rd. and Lost River Rd. are paved, the remainder are gravel and dirt track. It is open grazing land, so watch out for cows (as in, don't run into them). It is one of the best rides in the upper valley.

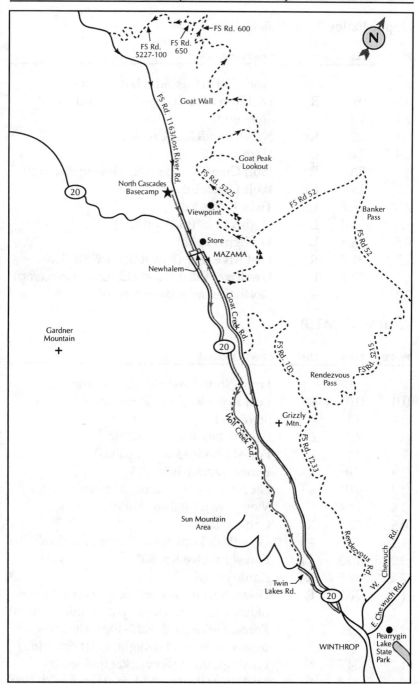

Upper Valley Tour ----------   Goat Wall ----------

Upper Valley Tour (Road/MTB)

Pt.-Pt.	Cum.	Dir	Street/Landmark
			From North Cascades Base Camp
0.0	0.0	**R**	**Lost River Rd.** (Forest Service Rd. 1163)
2.1	2.1	–	Store on L
0.1	2.2	**R**	**Newhalem/Goat Creek Rd.**
0.4	2.6	**L**	**Highway 20**
4.5	7.1	**R**	**Wolf Creek Rd.** (gravel, sometimes rough)
6.7	13.8	**CL**	**Wolf Creek Rd.**
2.9	16.7	**L**	**Twin Lakes Rd.**
1.3	18.0	**L**	**Highway 20** (to Winthrop)
0.5	18.5	**L**	**W Highway 20**
13.2	31.7	**R**	**Lost River Rd.** (Forest Service Rd. 1163)
0.4	32.1	**L**	**Lost River Rd.** (to North Cascades Basecamp)
2.1	34.2	–	North Cascades Basecamp on L

Goat Wall (MTB)

Pt.-Pt.	Cum.	Dir	Street/Landmark
			From North Cascades Base Camp
0.0	0.0	**R**	**Lost River Rd.** (Forest Service Rd. 1163)
2.1	2.1	–	Store on L
0.1	2.2	**L**	**Goat Creek Rd.**
1.9	4.1	**L**	**Forest Service Rd. 52** (gravel)
2.9	7.0	**L**	**Forest Service Rd. 5225**
2.0	9.0	–	Great view of Gardener Mountain
2.4	11.4	–	View down Methow Valley
0.8	12.2	X	Cattle guard
1.1	13.3	–	Goat Peak Lookout to R (optional climb up)
3.0	16.3	**CR**	**Forest Service Rd. 600**
2.2	18.5	X	Cattle guard
1.7	20.2	**R**	**Forest Service Rd. 650** (jeep road at bottom of hill, easy to miss; steep downhill portion)
2.6	22.8	**S**	**Forest Service Rd. 5227-100** (at clearing follow main road straight; great downhill)
1.7	24.5	X	Cattle guard (Yellowjacket trailhead)
0.1	24.6	**L**	**Lost River Rd.** (paved-Forest Service Rd. 1163)
4.1	28.7	–	North Cascades Basecamp on R

RUN OF THE RIVER
Monty and Karen Turner
P.O. Box 285
9308 E. Leavenworth Road
Leavenworth, WA 98826
(509) 548-7171 or 1-800-288-6491
Rates: $90-140

Leavenworth is featured in just about every pictorial collage of the Northwest that's ever been published. This picturesque locale nestled in the mountains was formerly a declining timber town, but decided years ago to revitalize the downtown area and focus on tourism. They remodeled existing structures to create the appearance of a small Bavarian town, and today tourists come from all over to poke about the quaint village, enjoying a profusion of unique shops and restaurants.

The real glory of this area is still its geographic location, however. Mountains tower above half the town, while fruit orchards extend for miles in the other direction. Just a short distance from town, Run of the River perches on the bank of the Icicle River, a tributary of the larger Wenatchee River, with commanding views up the Icicle and Tumwater Canyons. Across the slow-moving river lies a bird refuge island, where we spotted eagles, kingfishers, blue herons and a variety of other birds, in addition to several deer. One couple reported seeing an elk at the water's edge early on the morning we visited.

The entrance to Run of the River is oriented toward the pastoral land surrounding the front of the inn, where roosters crow from neighboring farms and wildflowers sway in the meadow in front of the house. An arbor and a few secluded benches appear in the more formal rose gardens blooming along either side of the inn.

Once inside, a stone-floored foyer at the entrance has a handhewn curved stairway leading upstairs to the left and wide hallway to the dining and sitting area straight ahead. To the left in the hall, a small store offers tasteful gifts, local crafts and guide books. Once in the open dining and sitting area, the focus turns to the river and forest behind the lodge, with the rough-hewn log walls and high ceilings opening to the woodsy view through huge picture windows. French doors lead out to a large porch stretching the length of the inn, divided into private areas for The Aspens

and Pinnacles rooms with rough-hewn log railings. The dining room table, set with cheerful stoneware and fresh flowers, seats ten people comfortably. This open room has several couches and armchairs along the windows, arranged to take full advantage of the view.

All six of the log-walled guest rooms in the inn feature hand-hewn log furniture built by a local artist, as well as forest green duvets, lots of pillows, private baths and unique extra touches throughout the room. The rooms are spotlessly clean, at once rustic and elegant, with tremendous views. Bouquets of flowers grace each room, as do binoculars and field guides for bird watching on the porch, and beribboned jars of bubble solution, for whiling away an afternoon by the river. Small refrigerators, a television and wine glasses for two are also available.

Up the spiral log staircase are three guest rooms and a sunny sitting area, with beautifully calligraphed quotes adorning the walls, a comfortable couch and a desk with a phone for guests' use. Two of the three rooms face the river, while the third looks east over the wildflower meadow. The River has a spectacular window looking out on the river, the Tumwater and Icicle Canyons and the Enchantments. The corner room, The Rose, has views of the meadow and the river, as well as a Jacuzzi tub in the private bath. The Meadows gets wonderful morning sun.

The doorway to the Tumwater Suite is downstairs, at the north end of the sitting area. This is the most luxurious of the available rooms, with a loft, a Jacuzzi, two woodstoves and a private deck.

A door marked "The Enchantments" at the opposite end of the sitting area leads to The Aspens and The Pinnacles. The Aspens features a woodstove surrounded by river rock, a private walkway off the porch down to the river and a delightful log swing for two on the deck.

We stayed in The Pinnacles, a deluxe corner room with a private entrance through the sliding glass door to the porch and another wonderful log swing. Both the cozy glass-paneled woodstove in the bedroom and the lavish Jacuzzi in the bathroom were surrounded by smooth river rock. A few country antiques added to the decor, including a refinished dresser converted to an in-room sink with the addition of an attractive ceramic bowl.

The next day we headed down to the riverside hot tub before breakfast, enjoying the first morning sun and the sound of birds twittering in the trees in the refuge just across the river.

We joined three other couples for breakfast in the dining room, where we were treated to a extravagant repast. We began with blueberry yogurt served with fresh cherries on top, fresh-squeezed orange juice, dark-roasted coffee and hot apple-bran muffins. After pausing to catch our breath, we dove into a spicy "South of the Border" quiche, accompanied by potatoes topped with fresh cilantro, and a tropical fruit plate that included kiwi, pineapple, oranges and grapefruit.

After breakfast we enjoyed chatting with Monty about bicycling in the area and seeing his impressive collection of antique bikes, some of which are exceptionally rare and in great condition. Monty and Karen are enthusiastic cyclists who take bike vacations whenever they can, so they had great suggestions for rides in the area. They have prepared three different well-written brochures for driving, hiking, and biking tours, complete with maps and commentary on nearby attractions. You'll have no trouble coming up with places to ride with this wealth of information at your fingertips!

Monty mentioned that often people come with bikes on top of the car, but they end up sitting on the deck the whole weekend and never take their bikes off the car! With the tranquil surroundings, friendly hosts and abundant wildlife just a few feet from the door, we could see how you could just lie back in the swing, put your feet up on the porch rail, and accidentally forget to go riding. . . Do make yourself get out for at least a brief ride, though, as this area offers some truly magnificent scenery.

BIKING FROM RUN OF THE RIVER

Terrain

Most of the land rises up from the Wenatchee River valley and roads follow the many canyons which intersect it. There is an interesting blend of the green forested slopes above and the fruit orchards along the river, with an occasional snow-covered peak overlooking it all. This is a beautiful area and both routes give you very differing perspectives of it.

Road Conditions

Highway 2 is wide and smooth, but roads that lead in and around the orchards are rough, winding and narrow, but nonetheless are a pleasure to ride. Mountain Home Rd. is all gravel and dirt track with trails lading off from the top.

Traffic

The town of Leavenworth can be busy during the peak summer months, but both routes here should give you some escape from that. Highway 2 has quite a bit of traffic but a nice wide shoulder and smooth pavement. Watch out on blind curves on Deadman's Hill Rd.

Nearest Bike Shop

Der Sportsman
837 Front St.
Leavenworth, WA 98826
(509) 548-5623

Best Time to Ride

May through early October is best. Snow hangs in the higher elevations till late spring.

Mountain Biking Opportunities

Mountain Home Rd., Boundary Butte and Ranger Rd. to Tumwater Mountain offer the closest mountain biking. Ask the innkeepers or the bike shop for directions and bring plenty of water.

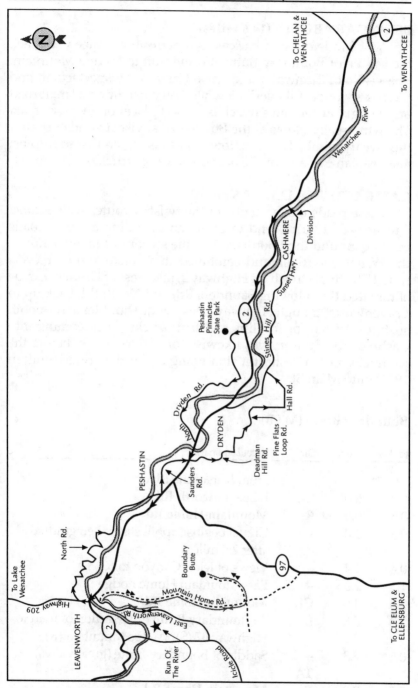

Boundary Butte ----- Cashmere Roller -----

BOUNDARY BUTTE (14.6 miles)

A 14.6 mile out and back with other options once you reach the saddle of Boundary Butte and the trail to Wedge Mountain. The views of Tumwater and Icicle Canyon are spectacular, and there is a wonderful overlook when you come upon a small road on the right at 1.4 miles which is a good place for a water break. The wind really blows at the Butte—we advise a windshirt after the sweaty climb. The ride down is as fast as you want it to be, just keep an eye out for the occasional car or truck.

CASHMERE ROLLER (30.6 miles)

These roads make up one of the twistier routes we've done! Orchards and farms tend to create an unending array of roads curving around their borders. Add the swoops of many bends in the Wenatchee River, and combined they make a great bicycle route! The final stretch on Highway 2, just west of Dryden, can be eliminated by following Saunders Rd. and North Rd. back up to Leavenworth, though Highway 2 has a wide shoulder and smooth surfaces. Watch for forklifts and fruit trucks when coming into Cashmere on Sunset Ave., likewise for N. Dryden St. before the RR tracks and in Peshastin after going under the bridge (built in 1927) onto Main St.

Boundary Butte (MTB)

Pt.-Pt.	Cum.	Dir	Street/Landmark
			From Run of the River
0.0	0.0	L	**E Leavenworth Rd.**
0.5	0.5	R	**Mountain Home Rd.**
0.5	1.0	–	Gravel begins (uphill steep then gradual after 2.0 miles)
0.4	1.4	–	Views of Icicle Canyon to R
1.1	2.5	–	Pass Mountain Home Lodge
2.0	4.5	CL	**Mountain Home Rd.**
2.3	6.8	L	**To Boundary Butte** (intersection of road to Highway 97 (S), Wedge Mountain (R)
0.5	7.3	– TA	Saddle of Boundary Butte (great views)
0.5	7.8	R	**Mountain Home Rd.**

| 6.3 | 14.1 | L | **E Leavenworth Rd.** |
| 0.5 | 14.6 | – | Run of the River on R |

Cashmere Roller (Road)

Pt.-Pt.	Cum.	Dir	Street/Landmark
			From Run of the River
0.0	0.0	L	**E Leavenworth Rd.**
1.0	1.0	L	**Highway 2** (over Wenatchee River)
0.2	1.2	R	**Highway 209**
0.5	1.7	R	**North Rd.** (to Peshastin)
4.1	5.8	R	**Under bridge onto Main St.** (in Peshastin)
0.2	6.0	L	**Highway 2**
0.4	6.4	L	**Saunders Rd.**
0.1	6.5	CL	**Saunders Rd.**
1.3	7.8	–	Narrow bridge
0.3	8.1	X	Highway 2
0.0	8.1	S	**Deadman Hill Rd.** (very rolling & narrow)
1.9	10.0	S	**Pine Flats Loop Rd.** (rough pavement)
0.6	10.6	CR	**Pine Flats Loop**
0.7	11.3	L	**Hall Rd.**
0.9	12.2	R	**Stines Hill Rd.**
2.3	14.5	–	Stines Hill Rd. changes to **Sunset Hwy.**
0.8	15.3	–	Sunset Hwy. changes to **Sunset Ave.**
0.3	15.6	L	**Division St.**
0.1	15.7	–	Cross RR tracks
0.0	15.7	X	Cottage Ave.
0.3	16.0	L	**Highway 2**
2.2	18.2	R	**N. Dryden Rd.**
0.4	18.6	–	Peshastin Pinnacles State Park on R
1.6	20.2	CR	**N. Dryden Rd.**
1.7	21.9	–	Cross RR tracks
0.0	21.9	S	**N. Dryden Rd.**
0.5	22.4	X	School St. (Dryden changes to **Main St.**)
1.4	23.8	L	**Stop sign** (near Hwy. 2)
0.0	23.8	R	**Highway 2**
5.9	29.7	L	**E Leavenworth Rd.**
0.9	30.6	–	Run of the River driveway on R

SUNNYSIDE INN B&B
Jim and Jeri Graves
804 E. Edison Avenue
Sunnyside, WA 98944
1-800-221-4195
Rates: $49-89

The Yakima Valley has gained national acclaim in the past few years for producing top-quality wines from several of the dozens of wineries which abound in this area. This valley is also the largest apple-producer in the nation. The land here is rolling and dry, with irrigated fruit orchards and vineyards blanketing the countryside. Yakima Valley receives an average of 300 sunny days a year, so you're almost guaranteed a sunny vacation.

The Sunnyside Inn was built in 1919 by a doctor and his wife to serve as his office and their residence. Today the expansive home has been converted to a comfortable B&B, close to town and the surrounding attractions. The Graves, who live in the smaller house next door, have been running the inn since 1990.

Most of the house has been devoted to spacious guest rooms; the kitchen and several dining areas serve as the common areas for guests. One small dining room, located in the foyer leading to the upstairs rooms, is simply furnished with a table for two in the window and a comfortable scalloped couch and armchair along one wall. Another "breakfast nook" is accessed through the modern kitchen, in which guests can help themselves to ice cream, popcorn, coffee and tea, as well as use the refrigerator and microwave. The breakfast nook has a table for four with high-backed benches looking out over the back patio. The furthest dining room, a sunny white room with a country-kitchen decor, is used primarily by guests in the Helen and Jean rooms and seats six at a long table.

There are eight guest rooms available in the main house, with two additional rooms in the Graves' house next door used for extra guests. The rooms are furnished simply, with country antiques and heirloom quilts in many of the rooms. Lace curtains and plenty of sunshine in all the second and third floor rooms make each room cheerful and homey. All the rooms have private baths (seven of the rooms have "double occupancy" Jacuzzi tubs, as well), phones and cable television.

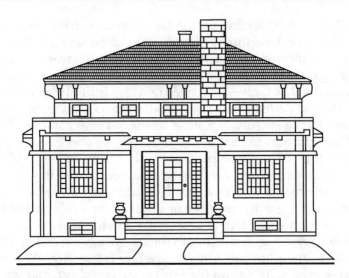

The two largest rooms, Alice and Lillian, are in the daylight basement. Alice is the most spacious of the two, with a king-sized bed and separate sitting area. Light walls and a pale green bedspread make this a cool, tranquil room. Lillian, just across the hall, is a bit sunnier and features a woodstove on a red brick hearth in addition to a king-sized bed. Both rooms have ample Jacuzzi tubs.

The bedrooms on the main floor have carpeting over light polished-wood floors. Karen and Jean have king-sized beds, while Helen has a double bed and a twin day bed. We stayed in Karen, which was formerly the front parlor and is now an enormous room with high ceilings and a private entrance (once the front door, in fact). All three of the rooms on this floor have luxurious Jacuzzi tubs in the private baths.

The third floor rooms are slightly smaller, but equally bright and sunny. Lola has a queen-sized bed and a daybed, as well as a glassed in sun porch. Mary Ann features a queen-sized bed with a blue and white coverlet, a ceiling fan, and a small hallway to the private bath.

Viola is a corner room with a pine four-poster bed and a small sitting area. Floral print wallpaper and a coordinating bedspread further brighten this cheerful room.

Hannah, one of the two "overflow" rooms in the house next door, has a double and a single bed, while Christy, the other next door room, has a queen-sized bed.

Many of the guests to the inn are on business trips to the nearby Del Monte or Tree Top operations, and often stay a full week or more. The morning we visited our fellow guests were off to work before we ate breakfast, so we dined alone in the sunny window downstairs. The Graves' son fixed us a nice fruit plate and brought us juice and coffee to start our meal. We each had an apple muffin, and then were served plate of scrambled eggs and French toast.

Geri came in to chat as we finished up, and gave us lots of good information about places to visit during our stay. She also told us about the peculiar tree which drops sharp thorns on the side of the road all summer throughout the area. We thought she must be exaggerating until we headed out for a ride and changed two tires in the first two hours! (Bring a patch kit.)

We visited Sunnyside Inn in the fall, when the orchards were winding down but the wineries were in full swing. We've indicated several wineries on the Fruit Loop cue sheet, and whether you choose to sample the wine or not, they are fun places to stop for a picnic or stretch your legs. Sunshine, relatively easy terrain and interesting stops along the way make Sunnyside a great destination for a cycling weekend.

BIKING FROM THE SUNNYSIDE INN

Terrain

Generally the land is flat to slightly rolling, with wonderful views of the Yakima River from Emerald Rd. Routes are longer here to take advantage of the level landscape.

Road Conditions

Orchard roads tend to be somewhat rough, even when paved. Parts of Houghton Rd. are gravel, as are the entrances to most of the vineyards. Be aware that the area is rife with tiny very sharp thorns that puncture tires easily. Bring a patch kit, pump and tube and know how to use them!

Traffic

There is very little traffic on most of the roads here, with the Yakima Valley Highway being the exception. Watch out for tractors that haul fruit, which have big fruit crates making them wider than they first appear on these narrow roads.

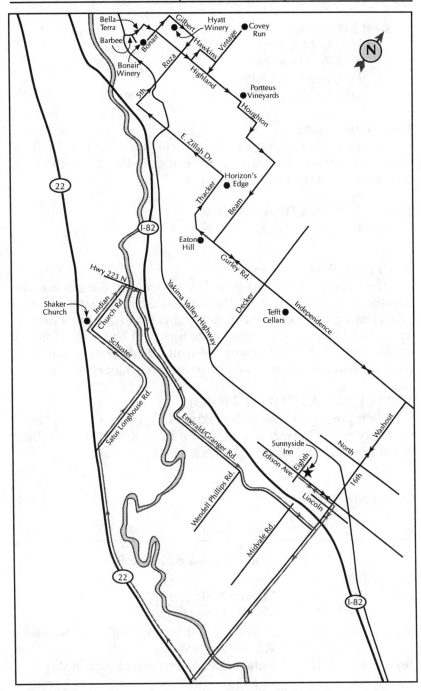

Valley Vista Loop ———— Fruit Loop ————

Nearest Bike Shop
Schwinn Cyclery
1012 East Lincoln
Sunnyside, WA 98944
(509) 837-7877

Best Time to Ride
It is possible to ride year-round here, but spring and fall are the better seasons. If possible, ride earlier in the day because afternoons can become quite warm.

Mountain Biking Opportunities
No designated areas.

FRUIT LOOP (48.3 miles)
The Fruit Loop is part of a driving loop by the same name that the area uses to promote its wine industry. It is a great way to wind through all the wine country and visit most of the wineries. You would be hard pressed to taste them all! The countryside is lovely and filled with the smell of fruit. In addition to watching for dogs here, keep your eye out for farm machinery on the road.

VALLEY VISTA LOOP (36.4 miles)
There are great views of the Yakima Valley from Emerald Road; probably one of the nicest roads in the area, smooth and winding. It can get hot here, so an earlier ride would be best.

Fruit Loop (Road)

Pt.-Pt.	Cum.	Dir	Street/Landmark
			From Sunnyside Inn B & B
0.0	0.0	L	**Edison**
0.5	0.5	L	**Sixteenth St.**
0.3	0.8	X	Yakima Valley Highway
0.2	1.0	X	North Ave. (Sixteenth changes to **Washout Rd.**; narrow; moderate traffic)
3.0	4.0	L	**Independence** (not signed, turn at stop sign)
4.7	8.7	–	Tefft Cellars on L

1.4	10.1	X	Decker (Independence changes to **Gurley Rd.**—watch for farm machinery. Eaton Hill Winery to L)
2.9	13.0	**R**	**Thacker Rd.** (view of Mt. Rainier near irrigation canal)
2.0	15.0	**L**	**E Zillah Dr.** (changes to **2nd Ave.**; Horizon's Edge Winery to R)
2.5	17.5	X	Yakima Valley Highway
1.1	18.6	**R**	**5th**
1.0	19.6	**L**	**Yakima Valley Highway**
2.3	21.9	**R**	**Barbee Rd.**
0.2	22.1	**L**	**Bella Terra Rd.**
0.7	22.8	**R**	**Highland Dr.**
0.6	23.4	**L**	**N Bonair** (Bonair Winery to R)
1.0	24.4	**R**	**Gilbert Rd.**
0.5	24.9	–	Hyatt Winery on R
1.0	25.9	**R**	**Roza Dr.**
1.0	26.9	**L**	**Highland Dr.**
0.5	27.4	**L**	**Hawkins Rd.** (gravel)
1.0	28.4	**R**	**Vintage Rd.** (Covey Run Vineyards to L; 1 mile)
0.5	28.9	**L**	**Highland Dr.**
0.6	29.5	–	Highland turns to gravel
0.7	30.2	**R**	**Houghton Rd.** (gravel; Portteus Vineyards to L)
0.3	30.5	**CL**	**Houghton Rd.**
0.7	31.2	**CR**	**Houghton Rd.** (paved)
0.5	31.7	**CL**	**Houghton Rd.**
1.3	33.0	**R**	**Beam Rd.**
3.2	36.2	**L**	**Gurley Rd.**
2.0	38.2	X	Decker (Gurley changes to **Independence**)
6.1	44.3	**R**	**Washout**
3.0	47.3	X	North (Washout changes to **16th**)
0.2	47.5	X	Yakima Highway
0.3	47.8	**R**	**Edison Ave.**
0.5	48.3	–	Sunnyside Inn B & B on R

Valley Vista Loop (Road)

PtPt.	Cum.	Dir	Street/Landmark
			From Sunnyside Inn B & B
0.0	0.0	L	**Edison**
0.5	0.5	R	**Sixteenth St.**
0.5	1.0	X	Lincoln Ave.
0.7	1.7	–	Cross bridge over I-82
5.1	6.8	–	Cross bridge over Yakima River
1.0	7.8	–	Enter Mabton
0.4	8.2	R	**State Route 22** (good shoulder; minimal traffic; great views)
8.2	16.4	R	**Satus Longhouse Rd.** (look for hawks flying above)
2.7	19.1	CL	Satus changes to **Schuster Rd.**
2.6	21.7	R	**Indian Church Rd.** (on L is Satus Shaker Church built in 1910)
1.4	23.1	R	**Highway 223 N**
0.6	23.7	–	Granger dinosaurs on L
0.3	24.0	R	**Emerald Rd.** (beautiful views of valley; changes to **Wendell Phillips Rd.**)
7.3	31.3	L	**Emerald Rd.**
2.1	33.4	X	Midvale Rd.
1.0	34.4	L	**SS Mabton Rd.**
1.0	35.4	X	Lincoln
0.5	35.9	L	**Edison Ave.**
0.5	36.4	R	**Eighth**
0.0	36.4	–	Sunnyside Inn B & B on R

COASTAL WASHINGTON AND OREGON INNS AND RIDES

The Pacific coast between Northern Washington and Southern Oregon ranges from wild rocky beaches to endless stretches of white sand. South of the Olympic National Park beaches, the Washington coast tends to be more developed and populated, while the Oregon Coast has maintained a more untamed feel, despite the fact that there are many more towns along its coast.

Two of the joys of cycling the coast are the relatively flat terrain and the terrific ocean views. The only real drawback, in fact, is the sometimes-fierce headwinds which blow from the north in the summer and reverse direction in the winter. We planned our routes for summer riding, and tried to ride south in the open stretches and north in the more protected areas, but you could easily reverse the routes if you find yourself taking a late fall or early spring trip.

Because the seashore is the main attraction, there aren't too many roads that lead away from the water, which means several of the rides included in this chapter are out-and-back rides rather than loops. The advantage to out-and-back rides is the ability to bail out early if conditions (yours or the weather's) are less than ideal.

Several of the rides in Oregon utilize parts of Highway 101; as mentioned in the Bicycling in the Pacific Northwest chapter, this is nothing to dread. The shoulders are wide and in excellent condition, and the views are stunning along much of the way. Yes, big trucks come by at high speeds, but they know you're there and provided you stick to your side of the road, you won't have any trouble.

Cycling north from **Boreas B&B** in Long Beach is fairly quiet, as the community is quite a distance up a narrow peninsula and not on a main thoroughfare. Heading south you'll meander through the tiny town of Seaview, really an extension of Long Beach now, and admire the perfectly restored turn-of-the century beach cottages before heading up a few winding hills to the lighthouses.

The southernmost coastal spot we visited, **Flora's Lake House B&B** in Langlois, had one of the wildest off-road rides we did all summer. The majority of the ride was on the road, partly on 101 and then heading off toward the ocean through farmland, ending with a stop at the Cape Blanco lighthouse, the most westerly lighthouse in the lower 48 states. From there we headed back to Flora's Lake House via an off-road trail that wound along the cliff edge for much of the way, and culminated in a slog through the sand along the lake. While the last mile and a half of this trail was less-than-perfect, the ocean views and utter wilderness along this trail made it one of our favorite rides.

Riding from the **Hudson House** in Cloverdale is a bit more challenging because of the hills. Fortunately, what goes up must come down, so you will have some fun downhills in addition to those uphill grinds. One of the rides in Cloverdale involves a fairly busy stretch of Highway 101, but turns off onto a 10-mile practically deserted old road that is simply breathtaking. No ocean views, but dense forests and small open meadows more than compensate for the lack of water. Taking the optional logging road cutoff (mountain bikes only) pops you out at the crest of the hill on Highway 101, where you have screaming downhill run for almost 4 miles.

Florence is one of the older towns on the Oregon coast, with a charmingly restored downtown area and a natural phenomenon unique to the northern Pacific Coast—miles and miles of sand dunes. Riding from the **Johnson House** again entails using 101 for a spell, but also offers quiet roads, many parks to stop and explore and a long, totally flat out-and-back ride along the dunes.

BOREAS BED & BREAKFAST
Sally Davis and Coleman White
607 N. Boulevard
P.O. Box 1344
Long Beach, WA 98631
Rates: $65-95

Long Beach is billed as the "World's Longest Beach," and with 28 miles of hard packed sand, they might be right. The town itself is somewhat reminiscent of Coney Island; the main drag consists primarily of bumper car arenas, colorful souvenir shops, video arcades and diners hawking everything from cotton candy to clam strips. However, just south of town is a neighborhood of impressive old Cape Cod homes, and further north on the peninsula lies the small restored Victorian town of Oysterville. A nationally acclaimed restaurant, The Ark, is also just a few miles up the road.

Boreas Bed & Breakfast is located in a quiet neighborhood one block off the busy main street, with the back of the house bordering the sand dunes. Built in the 1920s as a private beach home, the house has been extensively remodeled and turned over to guests; Coleman and Sally live in the house next door. There are four guest rooms at Boreas, each with its own personality: East, South, North and the Suite. The East and South rooms share a bath, while the North room and the Suite each have private baths.

We stayed in the East room, a cozy room with coved ceilings, a pretty semi-circle window looking back over the yard and street behind, and pale pink walls. Floral curtains in soft rose and beige tones match the spread on the queen size bed; simple artwork and antiques complete the handsome decor. In addition to finding our bedside light turned on when we returned from dinner, fresh flowers, a stuffed bunny propped up on extra pillows and fluffy robes hanging in the armoire all add a homey touch.

The shared bath across the hall is bright and airy, with a skylight and fresh white paint. Shampoo, conditioner, soap, lotion, and a hair dryer are all available for your convenience. We appreciated all the products being cruelty free!

Sharing a bath with the East room is the South room, which looks out over the dunes to the ocean. The South room is a smaller, more "modern" room, with a bright red, green and yellow bedspread, vaulted ceiling, and blue carpet.

Boreas 607 Boulevard

Bed & Breakfast
Long Beach, Washington

The North room is the largest of the second floor rooms, with the same fabulous view as the South room, a private bath, high ceilings and a romantic loft hideaway.

Downstairs, the Suite opens off the dining room. A long narrow room, more in keeping with the original house, this room has a crocheted bedspread on the daybed (which can sleep another adult), and a sitting area with a sliding glass door leading to the private oceanside deck. Done in soft mauve and gray, with floral patterns and antiques, the room is elegant and comfortable. The Suite has a private bath in gray tile with soft pink walls and a large modern bath and shower.

The living room has four huge picture windows looking out over scrubby pines and sand dunes leading down to the ocean (a fifteen-minute walk from the back deck). Classical music plays in the background throughout the day; relax in one of the two big couches or the armchair and peruse one of the many books or photo albums available. The room is simple and airy, with high raw-beamed ceilings, a giant stone fireplace and a calming view of the ocean beyond.

After all that relaxing, you'll want to take a long ride out on the peninsula, and then enjoy bubbling in the hot tub on the glass-enclosed porch!

The morning of our visit we woke early and chatted with Coleman and Sally while sipping coffee in the kitchen as they prepared breakfast. Both are knowledgeable about environmental issues surrounding development on the dunes, and had interesting tales about the changes Long Beach has seen in the past decade.

The feast they whipped up as we talked was a delight of local specialties: zucchini and coconut-banana bread, a fruit plate, and an amazing "strata" comprised of chanterelles, brie, emmanthal cheese, onions, zucchini, sweet peppers, eggs and "sea beans". We managed to sample the English muffins, juice, and coffee, too!

The name Boreas comes from the God of the North Wind, who brings crisp, clear weather. Sure enough, as we lingered over breakfast, the fog that had come in during the night burned off, and before long we were pedaling off for another sunny day in the clean salt air.

BIKING FROM THE BOREAS BED & BREAKFAST

Terrain

The Long Beach Peninsula is almost 30 miles long and very narrow, and has little in the way of hills, except near the lighthouses at the south end. The oceanside is generally windy, while the Willapa Bay side is fairly calm.

Road Conditions

The roads are in good shape, but shoulders are not overly prevalent. Some people do ride on the beach (which is 28 miles long and hardpacked; not as easy as it looks), but only if you like to clean sand out of your drivetrain for hours after a ride—fat tires work best.

Traffic

Moderate traffic on Pacific Highway 103 which runs north and south, but there are usually a few residential roads that parallel it and offer a retreat. Shoulders are not abundant on any of the roads, but most are not that heavily traveled.

Nearest Bike Shop

Bikes and Beyond
1089 Marine Dr.
Astoria, OR 97103
(503) 325-2961
(20 minutes away)

Best Time to Ride

Early spring through late fall. Winter is windy and very cool, but vacant, while midsummer fills the roads with unmaneuverable RV's and tourists, but lots of sunshine. The Washington State Kite Festival is in August.

Mountain Biking Opportunities

Nothing close by, but there are some dirt roads and such to explore near Fort Canby and the North Jetty.

LIGHTHOUSE LOOP (10.9 miles)

Northhead Lighthouse and Cape Disappointment Lighthouse are both well maintained and worth a visit for the views they command. Fort Canby is interesting, but don't miss the Lewis & Clark Interpretive Center. The displays and historical timeline is really well done; a genuine history course at your own pace. (The volunteers that staff it are very helpful.) Don't forget to check out the view over the Columbia Bar from the panorama windows.

OYSTERVILLE LOOP (30.8 miles)

Circling the Long Beach Peninsula is a great way to see the area. At the far northern end is Leadbetter Point State Park, which has some nice hiking trails and beachcombing places. Oysterville has a wonderful Historical District dating back to 1854. Stop at the Nahcotta Natural Foods for a lunch snack (or stop for dinner at the Ark Restaurant overlooking Willapa Bay off 273rd St.) On the way back, the oceanside has many places to go out and see the Pacific Ocean.

Lighthouse Loop (Road)

Pt.-Pt.	Cum	Dir.	Landmark/Street
			From Boreas B&B
0.0	0.0	**R**	**South on Boulevard Ave.**
0.0	0.0	X	5th North
0.2	0.2	**R**	**Bolstad**
0.0	0.2	**L**	**Boulevard**— immediate left
0.4	0.6	X	10th South
0.5	1.1	X	20th South
0.3	1.4	X	45 Place—Boulevard changes to **K Place**

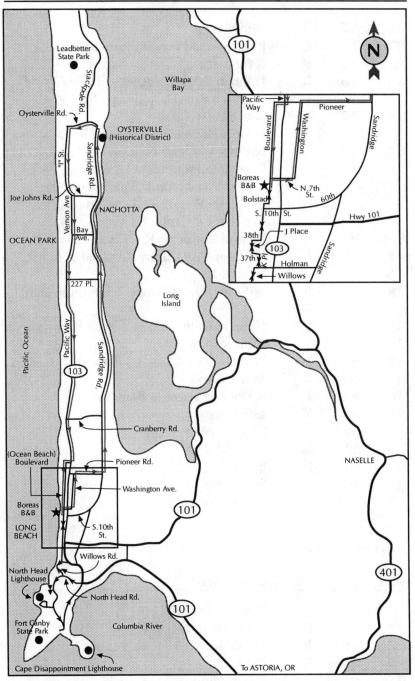

Lighthouse Loop ——————   Oysterville Loop ——————

0.3	1.7	R	**38th Place**
0.1	1.8	L	**J Place**—road curves into **37th Place**
0.1	1.9	R	**K** (unmarked)
0.4	2.3	R	**Holman (30th Street)**—road CL onto **Willow's Rd.** (1/2 mile uphill)
0.9	3.2	R	**North Head Road**
0.9	4.1	–	Beard's Hollow State Park on R
0.3	4.4	–	Northhead Lighthouse parking on R
0.8	5.2	–	Cape Disappointment Lighthouse, Fort Canby & Lewis and Clark Interpretive Center on R - go L and stay on road to Ilwaco (Fort Canby Rd./Loop 100)
0.9	6.1	–	View of Columbia River Bar to R
0.8	6.9	L	**100 Loop/Fort Canby Road** (a.k.a. North Head Rd.)
0.8	7.7	R TA	**Willows Road** (changes to **Holman/30th**)
0.9	8.6	R	**Holman (30th)**
0.1	8.7	L	**K Place**
0.4	9.1	L	**37th Place** (changes to **J Place**)
0.1	9.2	R	**38th Place**
0.0	9.2	L	**K Place** (changes to **Boulevard**)
0.3	9.5	X	45th Place
0.3	9.8	X	20th St. South
0.5	10.3	X	10th St. South
0.4	10.7	R	**Bolstad**
0.0	10.7	L	**Boulevard**
0.2	10.9	–	Boreas B&B on L

Oysterville Loop (Road)

Pt.-Pt.	Cum	Dir.	Landmark/Street
			From Boreas B&B
0.0	0.0	L	**North on Boulevard Ave.**
0.0	0.0	R	**N. 7th St.**
0.0	0.0	X	Pacific Way
0.1	0.1	L	**Washington Ave.**
0.2	0.3	X	9th North

1.0	1.3	R	**Pioneer Road**
0.3	1.6	–	Cranberry Museum on L
0.5	2.1	L	**Sandridge Rd.**
9.0	11.1	X	Bay Ave.
0.4	11.5	–	Nahcotta Natural Foods and Cafe
0.2	11.7	–	Nahcotta (Ark Restaurant to R, view of Willapa Bay)
1.0	12.7	–	Optional return point on Joe Johns Road
2.1	14.8	R	**Territory Road** to Oysterville Historical District
0.5	15.3	L	**Oysterville Road**
0.3	15.6	–	Leadbetter State Park on R
0.9	16.5	L	**I Street**
2.2	18.7	R	**295th**
0.1	18.8	L	**H Street** (CL then R and road becomes **Joe Johns Rd.**)
0.5	19.3	X	N Place
0.1	19.4	R	**Vernon** (changes into Pacific Way)
1.5	20.9	X	Bay Ave.
8.6	29.5	R	**26th North**
0.0	29.5	L	**N St.** (changes to **Boulevard Ave.**)
0.7	30.2	X	14th North
0.3	30.5	X	9th North
0.3	30.8	–	Boreas B&B on R

FLORA'S LAKE HOUSE BED & BREAKFAST
Will and Liz Brady
92870 Boice Cope Road
Langlois, OR 97450
(503) 348-2573
Rates: $90-125

The name of this B&B is derived from Flora's Lake, a narrow, 1 1/2-mile long fresh water lake separated from the ocean by just a slim sand dune. In 1910, developers convinced 400 people to move to this area (then called Lakeport) and build homes, a three-story hotel and a post office in anticipation of the canal that was to be dug between the lake and the ocean. The seaport that would result would serve as a major shipping destination between San Francisco and Seattle. Too late the developers got around to actually surveying the land, and realized the lake was 8 feet higher than the ocean; a canal would have drained the lake. The only remaining hint of this folly is a small sign in the neighboring county park, which boasts a fabulous hiking/mountain biking trail.

Today windsurfers come from miles around to take advantage of the steady breezes from the ocean and the calm waters of the lake. Will, a fanatical windsurfer himself, teaches lessons and would be happy to take you out for some cross-training if you're up to it!

Flora's Lake House is a large contemporary home on 5 acres, overlooking the lake and the ocean beyond, built by Will and Liz in 1991 to be run as a B&B. The Bradys and their two young boys, Reed and Joshua, have the run of the downstairs, while guests enjoy a spacious living room and four large guest rooms upstairs. The house is spotlessly clean, open and airy, with wonderful views from each room. The living room has 20-foot high open-beamed pine ceilings and large windows emphasizing the view. Comfortable couches and chairs covered in crisp striped and floral patterns are grouped around the woodstove and in front of the windows. While the kitchen is closed to guests, a small kitchenette with a sink, refrigerator, glasses, plates and utensils is available in the living room, and guests may feel free to use the barbecue on the deck.

Each guest room has a private bath, ceiling fans, healthy potted plants, wonderful views and access to the deck. The North Room, in the far north corner of the house, has a king-sized bed

and a day bed, a sitting area in front of a large bay window and a blue-tile fireplace. The decor is bright and sunny, with white walls and white wicker furniture, accented by a soft rose rug and a pink and green quilt on the bed.

Also in the "north wing" is the Nautical Room, done in navy and red fabrics, with a seashell-laden fish net hanging above the king-sized bed and brass headboard. An antique steamer trunk, prints of old sailing ships and window seat in red and blue striped fabric add to the nautical feel, while white wicker furniture and potted plants in the window remind you you're still on land.

Down the hall and across the living room is the Green Room, our favorite of the four. Interesting angles in the high pine ceiling lend an extra dimension to this green and white room. White duvets act as the backdrop for a multitude of green and white striped pillows on the two double beds, echoing the tiny green print on one white wall. A green directors chair, potted palm, and pine headboards and dresser round out the decor.

At the far end of this wing is the South Room, with large windows overlooking a semi-private deck to the garden and lake. A four-poster king-sized bed shares the room with wicker chairs and a table in front of the windows. The high pine ceiling makes this elegant beige room feel spacious, while the tile fireplace adds a cozy touch.

In the mornings a neighbor comes to pick up the boys while Will and Liz get breakfast ready. Coffee is put out at 6:00 a.m., and the buffet-style breakfast is ready by 8 a.m. We enjoyed having a chance to sit and chat with the Bradys over coffee before the other guests joined us for breakfast, which was served at the big dining room table by candlelight. An abundant spread of food was set out: granola, fresh fruit salad, yogurt, coffee cake, bagels and cream cheese, hard boiled eggs and a selection of juice, teas and coffee.

Will and Liz are eager, fun-loving innkeepers, anxious to hear about your ride, swap travel stories or suggest things to do in the area. At their recommendation we went to dinner at Harp's at Bandon by the Sea, a *fabulous* restaurant in nearby Bandon. Although we got there just as they were closing up, they let us in and served up one of the finest meals we've ever had: innovative, interesting dishes with a Northwest flavor in an intimate, casual atmosphere. We had great service and simply spectacular meal; it's pricey, but worth every penny. Don't miss it! The old fishing town of Bandon is fun to poke around, too.

Although located on a fairly lonely stretch of coast, Flora's Lake House B&B offers an oasis of friendly comfort, as well as one of our favorite rides of the summer. Combined with the dramatic views all around and the excellent dining just up the road, this is a getaway worth going out of your way for.

BIKING FROM FLORA'S LAKE HOUSE B&B

Terrain
The Pacific Coast in Oregon is known for its splendid scenery and great bicycling. The coastal area is flat, with hills rising to the east. Wind can be a factor at times. The Coast Trail from the airport is a wonderful adventure for its views of the ocean and the lovely groves of trees along the bluffs.

Road Conditions
All in good condition, especially Highway 101 south, as that is the direction of most cycle tourists and the Oregon D.O.T. keeps it maintained all year.

Traffic
Only Highway 101 has much traffic. Most of the other roads are very quiet.

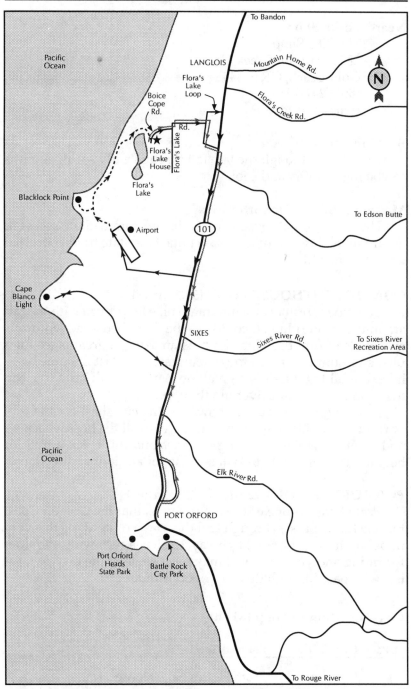

Coast/Lighthouse Loop ———   Port Orford O&B ——————

Nearest Bike Shop
>His Bike Shop
>28257 Hunter Creek Hts.
>Gold Beach, OR 97444
>(503) 247-7583
>(parts and repair)

Best Time to Ride
Year round, though the late fall through early spring months can be foggy, rainy and cool.

Mountain Biking Opportunities
The Coast/Lighthouse Loop is the most immediate access to mountain biking. For other areas contact the state trails coordinator in Salem, OR.

COAST/LIGHTHOUSE LOOP (33.5 miles)
This ride is primarily a mountain bike loop, even with the fair amount of road riding. It could best be described as adventurous and loads of fun! Blacklock Point is amazing; a great place for a picnic or simply a place to contemplate. The last 0.8 mile are a hike, but all together it's a great journey. You will need to clean the sand out of your drivetrain though.

A few words of caution, however: the cue sheet for the trail portion of the ride may be inaccurate with all the bushwhacking and sightseeing we did along the way, and this is *not* a trail for beginning riders—talk to Will and Liz for additional directions.

PORT ORFORD OUT & BACK (27.3 miles)
Port Orford is one of the many towns that the Oregon Coast Bicycle Route passes through and this was a route along this very popular stretch of road. Highway 101 has a nice wide shoulder for riding and you very well may meet some of the bicycle tourists who pass through this area every summer.

Coast Lighthouse Loop (MTB)

Pt.-Pt.	Cum	Dir.	Landmark/Street
			From Flora's Lake House
0.0	0.0	**R**	**Boice Cope Rd.**

0.2	0.2	L	**Flora's Lake Rd.**
1.5	1.7	L	**Flora's Lake Loop**
1.2	2.9	R	**Highway 101 S**
7.7	10.6	R	**Cape Blanco State Park turnoff**
3.3	13.9	–	Enter park
2.4	16.3	–	Cape Blanco Lighthouse
		TA	
5.7	22.0	L	**Highway 101**
3.0	25.0	L	**Airport Rd.**
3.0	28.0	–	County Rd. ends at Cape Blanco State Airport (trail leads off to L—go around gate—follow Blacklock Point/Flora's Lake Coast Trail)
0.7	28.7	CL	**Stay on most obvious trail** for best results! (L at sign to Blacklock Point—go past "No motor vehicle" sign)
0.5	29.2	L	**To Blacklock Point**
0.1	29.3	R	**To Blacklock Point** (follow signs)
0.3	29.6	–	Blacklock Point (leave bikes in grove of trees and explore the point on foot, lighthouse can be seen S, coastline is majestic)
		TA	
0.5	30.1	L	**Coast Trail to Flora's Lake**
0.2	30.3	CR	Viewpoint straight ahead
0.4	30.7	–	Waterfall-don't get too close to the edge, trail dissolves into windblown chaos—cross the stream and veer R
0.1	30.8	–	Hug the treeline—about midway is the difficult-to-find access to the trail. When you've found it (…you will), go L
0.3	31.1	L	**Coast Trail/Blacklock Trail** intersection
0.1	31.2	CR	**Trail** ahead is spotty—follow main trail (going north, with much portaging)
0.5	31.7	–	Down a narrow chute, beach is on the L. Take R to regain trail—you must cross the bog on the driftwood logs—then veer L
0.1	31.8	R	**Sharp R uphill away from beach**
0.4	32.2	–	At clearing, trail veers R then L

0.3	32.5	–	Follow beach north—stay off the Snowy Plover Nesting Grounds (June 15 to September 15)
0.1	32.6	**CR**	**Trail**
0.1	32.7	–	At clearing, walk north with beach on L and lake on R, trail CR around edge of Flora's Lake
0.6	33.3	–	Cross bridge—go straight uphill past park entrance on R
0.2	33.5	**R**	Flora's Lake House on R

Port Orford Out & Back (Road)

Pt.-Pt.	Cum	Dir.	Landmark/Street
			From Flora's Lake House
0.0	0.0	**R**	**Boice Cope Rd.**
0.2	0.2	**L**	**Flora's Lake Rd.**
1.5	1.7	**R**	**Flora's Lake Loop**
0.9	2.6	**R**	**Highway 101 S**
3.7	6.3	–	Pass Airport Rd. on R
1.8	8.1	–	Pass Sixes River Rd. (L goes to Sixes River Recreation Area)
1.0	9.1	–	Cape Blanco on R
3.2	12.3	–	Enter Port Orford
1.4	13.7	–	Battle Rock City Park
0.4	14.1	– **TA**	Port Orford Heads OR State Park on L
0.4	14.5	**R**	**Madrona Ave.** (Old Highway)
1.3	15.8	**CL**	**Port Orford Loop**
2.4	18.2	–	Cape Blanco on L
1.0	19.2	–	Pass Sixes River Rd.
1.9	21.1	–	Pass Airport Rd. on L
3.7	24.8	**L**	**Flora's Lake Loop**
0.8	25.6	**L**	**Flora's Lake Road**
1.5	27.1	**R**	**Boice Cope Rd.**
0.2	27.3	–	Flora's Lake House on L

THE HUDSON HOUSE
Anne and Steve Kulju
37700 Highway 101 South
Cloverdale, OR 97112
(503) 392-3533
Rates: $65-75

The Oregon coast highway winds inland a bit just below Tillamook, and although the furthest inland point is a scant few miles from the ocean, the landscape changes dramatically from the rugged coast. Rolling hills and wooded groves surround picturesque farms where cattle graze contentedly. The Hudson House is found nestled in this farmland, just three miles from the beach.

Built by the Hudson boys as a family home in 1906, this attractive Victorian farmhouse is perfectly situated to gaze out over the rolling, lush green fields and watch the cows coming in to pasture in the morning. The house is built up on a small knoll to afford the best view and avoid the road below.

Three of the four guest rooms are upstairs, reached by climbing up an elegant stairway with a window on the landing to a dark polished-wood hallway covered in a long oriental runner. Each room has hardwood floors, a private bath, country antiques and views of the fields across the road. We stayed in Louise, a warmly old-fashioned room with a queen-sized brass and white wrought iron bedstead. Blue patterned period wallpaper and an armchair by the window make this a cozy room. The bath for Louise is just across the hall.

Just down the hall is the Laura room, where a small foyer leads into a spacious room with two double beds. One is in a wood bedstead, the other in brass, and both are covered with pretty blue and white comforters. Lace curtains cover the tall window, and a light rose oriental rug covers the hardwood floors. This large room also features an antique armoire, small desk and chair and a dresser which acts as a nightstand between the two beds. Laura's private bath offers a modern shower.

At the opposite end of the hall is the Lynn room, a two-room suite with a queen-sized brass bed. This was our favorite room, the coved ceilings and deep green wallpaper making both rooms feel snug and cozy. Wicker furniture is grouped to take advantage of the view of pasture and woods from three low windows in the

THE
HUDSON HOUSE
A HISTORIC BED & BREAKFAST INN

sitting room, while a dark antique vanity and oval mirror lend a quiet air to the bedroom. The private bath in this room has a marvelous clawfoot tub and shower.

Downstairs, another larger suite opens off the dining room. This is the Emily room, two bright rooms with pine-paneled ceilings and a large bay window looking out to the fields in the sitting area. In the bedroom, a queen-sized bed in a painted wrought-iron bedstead is covered with a quilt, while in the sitting room, a brightly striped blue and white couch coordinates with the pink and white rug covering hardwood floors. A wonderful German game table made of intricately inlaid wood acts as a coffee table.

The dining room is the central shared room downstairs, seating up to eight people at two separate tables. A cookie jar collection rings the room on a high ledge, while a country hutch displays a range of goodies for sale, including a cookbook Anne has recently compiled and a selection of the regionally distributed Wholly Cow Granola, another of the Kulju's enterprises.

Just off the dining room is a small den for guests to watch television, play one of the many games on the shelf, or curl up on the couch or in the armchair and read. Be sure to check out the framed pictures of the house and surrounding area taken by Clyde Hudson in the early 1900s (Clyde Hudson continued to live in the house until 1986, and then stayed in touch with the new owners until his death at age 99).

Breakfast in the morning will more than adequately fuel you for a day of strenuous riding! We had juice and hazelnut creme coffee to start our feast, then sampled a fresh fruit plate and a bowl of Wholly Cow granola. As if on cue, the Holsteins in the pasture across the road came ambling over to the fence as we sat down to eat. Our main dish, Eggs Cristoff, was quite a creation: fluffy croissants stuffed with scrambled eggs and sautéed shallots, mushrooms and chives smothered in a white cheddar cream sauce and topped with grated cheese. British bangers accompanied the egg dish.

You likely won't need to eat again until dinner, but when you do decide to head out for sustenance, try the Riverhouse Restaurant just a few miles away in Pacific City. The restaurant is perched on the banks of the Nestucca River, and offers excellent seafood dishes in a pleasant atmosphere. Another option for a tasty lunch or more casual dinner is the Hawk's Creek Café, a tiny little spot with great sandwiches, veggie burgers and other healthy fare. Just south of Neskowin, this spot is on the Cascade Head Ride.

While it's too far from the Hudson House to include on a ride, try to arrange a stop at the Tillamook Cheese Factory some time during your visit. The factory is known throughout the world for its aged cheddars, but produces other varieties as well. The tour is fascinating, and the samples at the end of the tour make this a worthwhile detour!

This inland section of the coast highway offers a multitude of interesting spots and diverse riding—from steep climbs with ocean views to meandering spins through farmland and along quiet bays and rivers. You'll have no trouble finding places to explore from the Hudson House.

BIKING FROM THE HUDSON HOUSE

Terrain
Some hills on the east side of Highway 101, with Cascade Head having some serious climbing. The area west leads to the Pacific beaches and are slightly hilly to flat.

Road Conditions
Roads are rough in places, such as Sandlake Rd., especially before Sandlake. Highway 101 in both directions is narrower with less of a shoulder than other sections of the highway because it weaves in and out from the coast. Stay off Highway 22—beautiful scenery but it's too narrow and winding to be ridden safely.

Traffic

Lots of traffic on Highway 101 between Hebo and Hemlock, but with some shoulder. Slab Creek Rd. is almost traffic-free. Beachside roads can have many tourists but lower speeds.

Nearest Bike Shop

> Kats Bikes
> 5655 N. Highway 101
> Otis, OR 97368
> (503) 994-5242

Best Time to Ride

Almost year round riding possible, with the winters being fairly wet and cool. June through early October is best.

Mountain Biking Opportunities

Cascade Head is one area, but there is a ride over Buzzard Butte with lots of climbing. Get a good county map before you go.

SANDLAKE LOOP (29.5 miles)

The Oregon Coast is fabulous, but Highway 101 can be a bit busy. Once you have navigated that part, Sandlake Rd. is quite nice. There are a few spots along the way to access the beach and they are well worth the side trip. Another option if Highway 101 is not your cup of tea is to ride only the coast roads of the Three Capes Scenic Route as an out & back, say, up to Cape Lookout. Check the county map for options. Good view of Haystack Rock after passing Tierra Del Mar.

CASCADE HEAD RIDE (33.1 miles)

The Pacific Coast Highway leads off this route south to Cascade Head. The Scenic Drive Route is beautiful and winds through the Experimental Forest. Along the route are waterfalls and thick growth on a road that sees very little traffic. An optional route is taking a left at the crest of Cascade Head on Highway 101 on the gravel road. Follow it until you hit the Old Scenic Highway and take a left, then it's downhill until Highway 101 where you take a right to return to Cloverdale. On the way back, have lunch at the Hawk Creek Café.

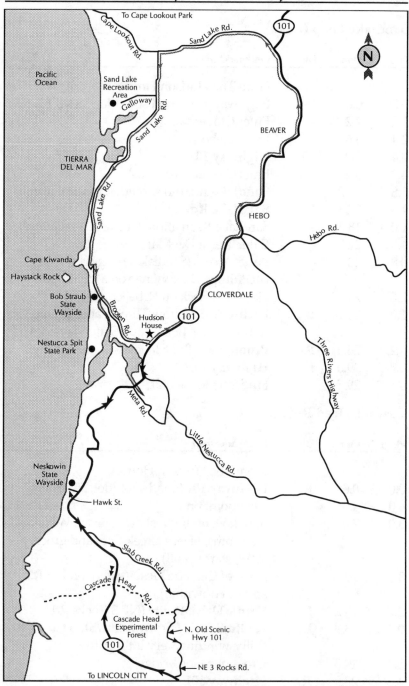

To Cape Lookout Park

Cape Lookout Rd.

Sand Lake Rd.

101

N

Pacific
Ocean

Sand Lake
Recreation
Area
Galloway

Sand Lake Rd.

BEAVER

TIERRA
DEL MAR

HEBO

Hebo Rd.

Cape Kiwanda

Haystack Rock

CLOVERDALE

Bob Straub
State
Wayside

Brooten Rd.

Hudson
House

101

Three Rivers Highway

Nestucca Spit
State Park

Meda Rd.

Little Nestucca Rd.

Neskowin
State
Wayside

Hawk St.

Slab Creek Rd.

Cascade Head Rd.

Cascade Head
Experimental
Forest

N. Old Scenic
Hwy 101

101

NE 3 Rocks Rd.

To LINCOLN CITY

Sandlake Loop ———   Cascade Head Ride ———

Sandlake Loop (Road)

Pt.-Pt.	Cum	Dir.	Landmark/Street
			From The Hudson House
0.0	0.0	L	**Highway 101** (good shoulder, 55 MPH)
2.2	2.2	–	Enter Cloverdale
2.4	4.6	–	Enter Hebo
0.4	5.0	CL	**Highway 101**
4.2	9.2	–	Enter Beaver (groceries)
3.8	13.0	L	**Sandlake Rd.** (no shoulder, healthy uphill)
4.3	17.3	L	**Sandlake Rd.**
1.0	18.3	–	Sandlake Recreation Area to R (Galloway)
4.0	22.3	–	Enter Tierra Del Mar
0.8	23.1	–	Beach access (Sandlake changes to **McPhillips Dr.**, continue on **McPhillips**)
2.0	25.1	–	Haystack Rock on R, beach access)
1.0	26.1	L	**Pacific Ave.** (follow Three Capes Scenic Route; to R is Bob Straub State Wayside)
0.2	26.3	R	**Brooten Rd.** (bike lane)
2.7	29.0	L	**Highway 101**
0.5	29.5	–	Hudson House on L

Cascade Head Ride (Road)

Pt.-Pt.	Cum	Dir.	Landmark/Street
			From The Hudson House
0.0	0.0	R	**Highway 101** (good shoulder, 55 MPH)
4.0	4.0	–	Viewpoint on R
3.0	7.0	–	Hawk St. on R (Neskowin Beach Wayside, restrooms; Hawk Creek Cafe and grocery store; start uphill)
3.5	10.5	–	Crest of Cascade Head (elevation 752 ft.; smooth downhill)
2.7	13.2	L	**Scenic Drive Route** (NE 3 Rocks Rd.)
0.7	13.9	L	**N Old Scenic Highway 101/Slab Creek Rd.** (hilly, winding, very little traffic)
5.4	19.3	–	Cross one lane bridge
4.6	23.9	R	**Highway 101**
9.2	33.1	–	Hudson House on L

THE JOHNSON HOUSE BED & BREAKFAST INN
Jayne and Ron Fraese
216 Maple Street
Florence, OR 97439
(503) 997-8000
Rates: $75-105

With its unique sand dune formations, proximity to the ocean and the Siuslaw River, and bounty of nearby parks and viewpoints, Florence offers a variety of natural attractions to explore. Old Town Florence, settled in the 1870s and now filled with shops, restaurants and restored historic buildings, provides an equally compelling reason to visit. Once a busy seaport, cannery and fishing town, Florence today is a popular tourist stop on the Oregon coast highway.

At the heart of the historic district is the Johnson House, built in 1892 for a doctor's family. Lovingly restored to reveal original woodwork and structural detail, and furnished with antiques from the late 1800s through 1935, the home has been run as a B&B for the past twelve years. The Fraeses furnished the home with antiques spanning several decades, attempting to capture the feel of a lived-in home, where pieces had been added throughout the years. The effort was successful—the inn feels much more like a beloved grandmother's house than a B&B.

Upon entering the house you find yourself in a formal foyer, with one guest room at the end of the hall and a large parlor to the left. The parlor is filled with interesting antiques, including a player piano, a chiming clock and an ancient radio which is still used in the mornings. Sling-back chairs and an afghan-covered couch are grouped comfortably in front of tall lace-covered windows. Wood floors are covered with deep red oriental rugs, complementing the period wallpaper with blue and green accents. The room is bright and sunny, opening to the equally cheerful dining room.

The dining room has several enticing heirlooms as well: a spinning wheel, large sideboard, a beautiful woodstove and a series of old photos and prints. Three tables are elegantly set with fine china and lace in the dining room, while a fourth table in the living room accommodates extra guests. An antique coffee cart is set out for early risers in the morning.

Five guest rooms are available in the main house; the adorable cottage next door acts as a sixth room. Antiques abound in all the rooms, each with a few unique pieces for character. Each room has lace curtains, mineral water set out with glasses and small vases with bouquets from the garden. Even the linens in the room are antiques: Ironed sheets with lace edges cover each gloriously soft feather bed.

The only bedroom downstairs is room 105. The room is furnished with a double feather bed in a pink wrought-iron bedstead, a striking armoire and mirror and a loveseat from the 1890s (a matching loveseat can be found on the upstairs landing). Lace curtains hang in the windows and the artwork in the room is true to the furnishings' era.

At the top of the wide stairway is a small landing with a loveseat, book-laden shelves and more wonderful photographs, prints and paintings. Sunlight streams through the tall window, making this a pleasant spot to sit and read.

Room 101 in the front corner has pretty white wallpaper with a delicate cornflower print, a double bed in a wrought-iron bedstead, and a marvelous wooden suit stand, complete with a small tray to place one's cuff links in at night. This room shares a bath with rooms 102 and 104 but has a porcelain sink in the room.

Next door is room 102, with white wallpaper in a floral print, a double bed and large armchair, and a hook rug on the hardwood floor. Dried flowers are arranged in a porcelain wash basin, while a set of button hooks and an ivory comb and brush set are laid out on the dresser.

Down the hall is room 104, a smaller room with pale pink and white wallpaper covered in tiny violets. A delicate butterfly quilt covers the feather bed, while very old stuffed bunnies are propped up in a nearby cane chair. This room also has a porcelain sink in the room, as well as a nightstand and cane dresser.

We stayed in 103, the far corner room overlooking the lovely gardens in the back of the house. This room is furnished with a large double bed with carved, dark wood foot and headboards, a velvet settee, small end tables and antique lamps, a large dresser and mirror and a wonderful hatstand. There is a porcelain sink in the room, and a private bath and shower through an adjacent door. Subdued white and tan wallpaper complements the white coverlet on the bed and lace curtains in the windows.

Walking into the cottage next door to the house is like stepping into a 1920s vacation cottage. The building itself is surrounded by climbing roses, geraniums in planter boxes and a cute front porch with green Adirondack chairs. The interior is decorated with old calendars featuring rose prints, pale pink and white walls, and hook rugs in pink, white and green. A grapevine-patterned screen hides a marvelous clawfoot tub with hand-held shower right in the room (the bathroom is just off the sitting area). A tall wardrobe, double feather bed and porcelain sink with an wrought-iron towel rack complete the furnishings.

Guests staying in both the cottage and the main house gather for breakfast in the dining room in the morning. On the morning of our visit we began our meal with coffee and fresh-squeezed orange juice, then moved onto a plate of hot cheese scones and Jayne's homemade jam. Our main course was a mouth-watering Walla Walla onion tart, accompanied by a plate of thinly sliced cantaloupe with a squeeze of lime and a sprig of mint from the garden.

Breakfast conversation is never dull at the Johnson House; both Jayne and Ron are former university professors and are knowledgeable about a mind-boggling array of topics. They are also meticulous innkeepers and clearly love their work. Ron is happy to provide guests with a multiple-page "things to do around Florence" list, complete with notes about the history, geography and wildlife of the area, which made for good reading long after our visit was complete.

The Fraeses have two other rental accommodations along the coast, both of which appeared from pictures to be spectacular retreats. Pricier than the lodging at the Johnson House, both coast houses have full kitchens and many modern amenities in addition to breathtaking views.

In addition to the many sights to see in and around Florence, eleven miles up the coast you'll find the famous Sea Lion Caves. This natural cavern is as large as a twelve-story building and in fall and winter acts as one of the largest sea lion haul-out areas on the west coast of North America. An elevator takes you down to the cave, where you can see hundreds of sea lions hauled out on the rocks inside.

Plan on spending at least a long weekend here —between the natural wonders of the region, the town of Florence and the Johnson House itself, you'll want to give yourself plenty of time to explore this diverse area.

BIKING FROM THE JOHNSON HOUSE

Terrain

The area around Florence is primarily level and spacious. The Dunes are amazing formations which shouldn't be missed. There are very few hills to speak of and generally the main concern when choosing a ride is the wind, which generally blows from north to south for most of the year.

Road Conditions

Most roads are in good condition. The Beach Access Rd. is windblown and often sand covered, but it is paved for the most part.

Traffic

In the city traffic can be rather crazy, but most of the county roads have little traffic to speak of. Shoulders are infrequent except on the main roads.

Nearest Bike Shop

Roger's Bicycle Center
2285 Highway 101
Florence, OR 97439
(503) 997-1504

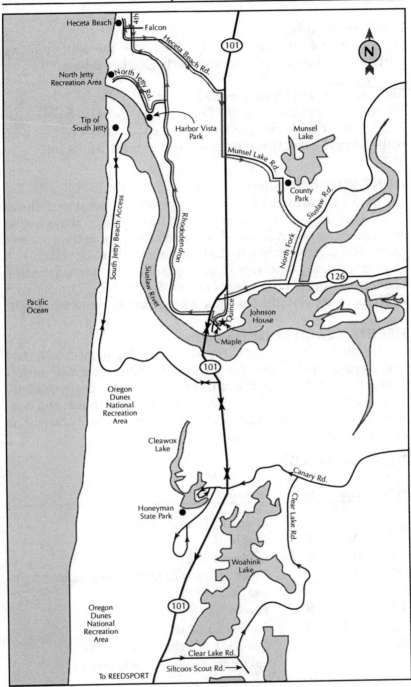

Dune Ride ———   Heceta Beach Loop ---------

Best Time to Ride

Almost year round riding possible, with the winters being fairly wet and cool. April through early October is best.

Mountain Biking Opportunities

Not much in the vicinity. "Dune riding" is not advised, one, because the dunes are fragile in some spots, and second—who really likes to clean that much sand out of their drivetrain?

DUNE RIDE (27.5 miles)

The dunes are one of the most fascinating natural formations in the Pacific Northwest. Seeing them by bicycle, you are free to stop and explore at will, and this is a great loop for getting around on the South Jetty. Riding in the beach area will make your bike a sand magnet, so take care in cleaning the drivetrain when the ride is over. The portion on Clear Lake is slightly hilly, but makes a nice loop. Highway 101 has a good shoulder and is very rideable.

HECETA BEACH LOOP (15.2 miles)

Heceta Beach is a good short ride for getting to the North Jetty and having a picnic and for exploring. There are great sunsets from here and there's a different perspective from the South Jetty area. Riding around the Munsel Lake area is an interesting contrast to the oceanside and is fairly quiet traffic-wise. Be careful on Highway 126, it can be busy.

Dune Ride (Road)

Pt.-Pt.	Cum	Dir.	Landmark/Street
			From The Johnson House
0.0	0.0	R	**Maple St.**
0.1	0.1	L	**Highway 101**
0.2	0.3	–	Cross bridge (fast traffic; metal bridge deck– use caution)
2.6	2.9	R	**Honeyman State Park**
0.1	3.0	R	**To Day Use Area**
0.3	3.3	–	Parking lot (picnic area, restrooms, groceries, espresso; trails to dunes)
		TA	
0.4	3.7	R	**Park road toward dunes**

0.2	3.9	**R**	**Toward dunes and overnight parking**
		TA	
0.2	4.1	**R**	**Toward parking lot** (lock bike and walk trails to dunes; restrooms) Follow signs to 101
0.3	4.4	**R**	**Highway 101 S**
2.5	6.9	**L**	**Clear Lake Rd.** (no shoulder, moderate traffic, rolling hills)
0.8	7.7	**L**	**Clear Lake Rd.** (don't take Siltcoos Scout Rd.)
3.4	11.1	**L**	**Canary Rd.** (nice downhill)
1.4	12.5	**R**	**Highway 101 N**
1.7	14.2	**L**	**South Jetty Rd.** (to dunes and beach)
0.6	14.8	–	Map of dunes on R
5.1	19.9	–	Pavement ends
0.3	20.2	–	Tip of South Jetty (hiking trails; mouth of river)
		TA	
6.0	26.2	**L**	**Highway 101 N**
0.7	26.9	–	Cross bridge (caution)
0.5	27.4	**R**	**Maple St.**
0.1	27.5	–	Johnson House on L

Heceta Beach Loop (Road)

Pt.-Pt.	Cum	Dir.	Landmark/Street
			From The Johnson House
0.0	0.0	**R**	**Maple St.**
0.1	0.1	**R**	**Highway 101**
0.1	0.2	**L**	**Rhododendron Dr.**
0.2	0.4	**X**	Kingwood St.
3.7	4.1	**L**	**Jetty Rd. N**
0.1	4.2	–	Harbor Vista Park to L
1.0	5.2	–	Parking lot of North Jetty Recreation Area; excellent views, picnic area, lock bikes to Coast Guard tower; hike beach)
		TA	
1.0	6.2	**L**	**Rhodendren Dr.**
1.3	7.5	**L**	**Heceta Beach Rd.**
0.1	7.6	–	Heceta Beach to R
0.3	7.9	–	Heceta Beach (lock up bikes to walk beach)

		TA	
0.1	8.0	L	**Falcon**
0.1	8.1	R	**4th**
0.2	8.3	L	**Heceta Beach Rd.**
1.9	10.2	R	**Highway 101 S**
0.5	10.7	L	**Munsel Lake Rd.** (no shoulder; light traffic)
0.8	11.5	–	County Park on L
1.3	12.8	R	**N Fork Siuslaw Rd.**
0.9	13.7	R	**Highway 126** (heavy traffic; good shoulder)
0.8	14.5	L	**Quince**
0.6	15.1	L	**Maple St.**
0.1	15.2	–	Johnson House on L

OLYMPIC PENINSULA INNS AND RIDES

Washington's Olympic Peninsula is a unique and diverse place, ranging from placid Hood Canal on the east, rugged Pacific beaches to the west, the Ho Rain Forest and towering Olympic Mountains at its interior, and dry sunny farmland on its northern edge. Rainfall on the peninsula varies from 17" in sunny Sequim to over 200" in the Ho, the only true rain forest in North America. The variety of terrain and climate allows a wide assortment of riding conditions, all within a day's drive of each other.

Looking at a map it might be tempting to ride around the peninsula, stopping at the inns in this section and creating a tour of the perimeter. Many cyclists do this in the summer months, but we've never been inclined to do so simply because of the narrow roads, limited shoulders and poor visibility along large sections of the main route. The areas we chose to ride are safe, interesting and moderately quiet, and we heartily recommend you drive to these areas and start your tours from the inns rather than linking them together.

Port Townsend is a charming Victorian seaport on the peninsula's northeastern tip; jutting out into the Strait of Juan de Fuca, Port Townsend offers views of the Olympics, the Cascade Range and water in almost every direction. On clear days it's possible to spot Victoria off in the distance. Riding from the **Annapurna Inn** you have a choice of shoreline rides, complete with a stop to explore the bunkers at historic Fort Warden, or hilly rides through the meadows and forests that extend south of town. We included a ride east of town onto Marrowstone Island, a forested island with peek-a-boo views of the water throughout the ride, and a spectacular panorama of mountains and water from Fort Flagler at the island's northern tip.

Sequim and Dungeness lie just an hour west of Port Townsend, on a flat, open plain dotted by farms. The Olympics tower above lush irrigated fields, from which stately weathered barns appear. Sea breezes whisper from the shore nearby, while eagles are often sighted soaring overhead. The riding here is magnificently flat, with open views in all directions on the north side of the highway. Loops from **Groveland Cottage** include a trip to Dungeness Spit, at six miles the longest natural jetty in the world, and a spin past the Olympic Game Farm, where over 200 animals reside in a natural habitat. South of the highway the land rises dramatically toward the mountains, providing ample opportunity for a good workout and rewarding views from the upper reaches.

Forks is on the west side of the peninsula, nestled between dense pine forest and the well-photographed rocky beaches at La Push. Rides from the **Miller Tree Inn** incorporate the best of both worlds. The first ride is a pleasant pedal to the ocean on a narrow forested road which gradually opens into marsh land and finally pops you out at a striking ocean vista. The second is a challenging off-road ride which loops through the forest on logging roads and presents stunning views of the Olympics to the east and the ocean to the west.

Further north on Highway 101 you'll come across Port Angeles, a busy industrial town at the base of Hurricane Ridge. You'll want to head south from town and ride up the road toward Hurricane Ridge for the best views, although the winding, rolling farm road through the foothills offers impressive scenes of serpentine rivers, alder groves and bucolic grasslands. If you've got a mountain bike and a lot of energy, pedal up to the Olympic Hot Springs—after a long soak in these natural pools you can coast the entire seventeen miles home! During your visit to the **Tudor Inn**, don't miss seeing the Olympic National Park Visitor Center, one of the newest and nicest of the Park's information centers.

On your way out of the peninsula, be sure to stop for a hike in the Ho Rain Forest. Interpretive signs along several short trails provide an excellent overview of this amazing ecosystem. Remember that riding is not allowed on any trails in the Olympic National Park, so you'll have to stick to the roads or stop for a hike.

THE ANNAPURNA INN
Robin Shoulberg
538 Adams Street
Port Townsend, WA 98368
(360) 385-2909 or (800) 868-ANNA
Rates: $75-105 (retreat, midweek and off-season rates available)

Port Townsend perches on the Northeast corner of the Olympic Peninsula, surrounded by the Strait of Juan de Fuca and 360° views of the Olympic and Cascade mountain ranges. Once the busiest seaport on the west coast, Port Townsend now boasts the largest collection of restored Victorian homes outside of San Francisco. Most of the homes are built on the bluff above the downtown area, taking advantage of the spectacular views. Port Townsend fairly bursts at the seams with Bed & Breakfasts, the majority taking the Victorian theme and running with it. The Annapurna Inn offers a very different type of visit; the theme here is not chintz and lace but rather health and well-being.

The inn sits in the heart of the Historic District on the corner of Clay and Adams, among an ambitious new landscaping of edible herbs and flowers. Built in 1881, the house originally was a sea captain's home; three years ago Robin Shoulberg completely renovated the home to create The Annapurna Inn. Robin wanted to invent a surrounding that would cater to a visitor's total well-being, and by combining her years of experience as a licensed massage therapist with this tranquil setting, she has done just that.

The front porch is enclosed with round portal-like openings, reflecting the home's nautical past. Several seats offer a pleasant place to sit and view the neighborhood, though you may vie with resident felines Ralphina or Newman for the comfiest chair.

Entering the house you pass through a fairly narrow hallway to the living room and dining room. The light-walled living room is commodious, with two comfortable white couches, several tables with interesting reading material on a variety of diet, health, and spiritual matters piled high, and old oriental rugs down over light oak floors. The living room opens onto the dining room, with a long table that acts as an office throughout the day. Plants abound in this casual mix of antique and comfort. The Annapurna Inn feels like a friend's house; you feel entirely comfortable going barefoot, putting your feet up on the couch, or leaving your door open.

The four rooms are all fairly large. Two open off the front hall-way, looking out over the garden, one opens from the dining room, and the fourth room is a separate cottage behind the house.

Our room, off the dining room, had pale peach walls and a white ceiling, a very pretty floral bedspread on a firm futon (the other rooms have mattresses), the same blond oak floors with a patterned oriental rug, and three windows, two tall and narrow, and one smaller one in the center. Fabric matching the bedspread hung imaginatively and mixed with lace served as curtains. A large dark armoire with full-length mirror stood between two doors, one of which leads to a tiny hallway heading out to a small deck, and the other opens into the private bath.

All the rooms have an open, peaceful feel. Dried wreaths and bouquets of wildflowers add an extra touch. One of the rooms in front has a wonderful madrona tree mural painted in an alcove with an extra bed—perfect for a family traveling with children.

In this tranquil atmosphere, Robin and her partner Tim offer several different types of massage, including cranio/sacral therapy and foot reflexology, as well as more traditional Swedish massage and injury treatment. We forgot we'd ridden 40 miles after we were treated to a sample massage before bed! Robin will work with you to explain the benefits of each type of treatment, and help select a technique for you.

Annapurna Inn provides a retreat package for 3 days and 2 nights that includes healthy, vegetarian meals, lodging, several full massage treatments, and two early-morning yoga classes. This is heaven for a cyclist; good meals, a restful, casual atmosphere, a sauna and steam room, and licensed massage practitioners in the living room! Robin encourages people to take advantage of the retreat package, to more fully experience The Annapurna Inn and what it has to offer.

Robin is an energetic and charming hostess, whose heartfelt convictions about health, diet and healing are reflected in her devotion to providing personal attention to each of her guests. In keeping with her philosophy about diet (influenced by John Robbins, Dr. John McDougall and Dr. Dean Ornish), the delicious breakfasts served in the morning are entirely vegan—Robin and Tim will be happy to accommodate any special dietary needs guests may have. We started our morning feast with a fruit frappé, fresh fruit salad and organic coffee. A delicious homemade granola was available on the table. We moved on to wheatless waffles served with real maple syrup and blueberry-apple compote, and finished with a tofu sauté of shitake mushrooms, green pepper and nasturtium blooms.

Although it is a short 50-mile drive and a ferry ride from Seattle, Port Townsend seems to exist in a different era. The Annapurna Inn provides an exceptionally relaxing base from which to explore the unique Victorian atmosphere and overwhelming natural beauty of this little town.

BIKING FROM ANNAPURNA INN

Terrain
Port Townsend sits at the northeast end of the Quimper Peninsula and commands views of both the Strait of Juan de Fuca and Puget sound. It can be quite hilly in places and has both forested and farm land. Marrowstone Island is flat and quite pleasant for riding, a beautiful rural and wooded area with no road shoulders, but minimal traffic.

Road Conditions
Cape George Road is rough and narrow in some spots. East 116 is narrow and winding, as is Irondale Road. Discovery Rd. has no shoulder and some blind curves.

Traffic

The main spots for heavy traffic are: Airport Cutoff Road, Irondale Road, and Four Corners Road. The intersection at Four Corners is hairy, so pay particular attention. Highway 20 can be busy but generally has a good shoulder.

Nearest Bike Shop

> Port Townsend Cyclery
> 215 Taylor St.
> Port Townsend, WA 98368
> (360) 385-6470

Best Time to Ride

Almost anytime is good riding in Port Townsend. The town sits in the rain shadow of the Olympics and sees quite a few days of sunshine. April through October are the better though, avoiding the potential cool days and slick roads of winter.

Mountain Biking Opportunities

There are some short rides possible at Fort Worden, but the better off-road riding is in the Olympic National Forest. Contact the local bikeshop for trails and destinations.

FORT FLAGLER LOOP (42.8 miles)

Fort Flagler is at the north end of Marrowstone Island, a very quiet island to the northeast of the main Olympic Peninsula. The park has swimming, beachcombing and hiking. The fort was one of three installations built to defend Admiralty Inlet in the 1890s

FORT WORDEN LOOP (16.0 miles)

The Annapurna Inn sits at the heart of the hilltop area of Port Townsend, and therefore gives you a nice jumping off point for any portions of the Quimper Peninsula you wish to explore. The short loop we chose leaves from the Annapurna Inn and traverses counterclockwise on a loop connecting Fort Worden State Park and the Cape George area with views of Admiralty Inlet.

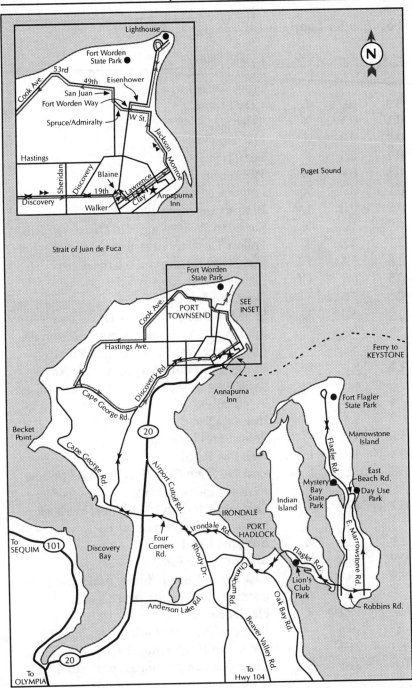

Fort Flagler Loop ———   Fort Worden Loop ‒ ‒ ‒ ‒ ‒

Fort Flagler Loop (Road)

Pt.-Pt.	Cum.	Dir.	Landmark/Street
			From Annapurna Inn
0.0	0.0	L	**Clay Street**
0.1	0.1	X	Tyler St.
0.2	0.3	X	Harrison St.
0.2	0.5	X	Benton St.
0.1	0.6	R	**Walker St.**
0.1	0.7	X	Lawrence St.
0.1	0.8	L	**Blaine** (turns into **19th**)
0.9	1.7	X	Sheridan (19th changes to **Discovery Rd.**)
2.1	3.8	X	Follow Discovery Rd. through intersection
2.6	6.4	CL	Discovery Rd. curves to left
0.5	6.9	CL	Stay left on Discovery Rd.
0.7	7.6	–	Slow, gradual climb
0.4	8.0	X	State Road 20 (Be careful, this is a very busy intersection; once past the intersection the road changes to **Four Corners Road**)
1.3	9.3	R	**Merge right onto Airport Cutoff Road** (watch for traffic merging from the left; get in left lane)
0.3	9.6	L	**Irondale Road**
1.8	11.4	–	Enter Port Hadlock
0.1	11.5	L	**Oak Bay Road**
0.8	12.3	L	**East 116 State Road/Flagler Road** (follow signs for Indian Island)
0.7	13.0	–	Cross onto Indian Island (Port Hadlock Lions Club Park on right)
2.1	15.1	R	**Robbins Road**
0.9	16.0	L	**Marrowstone Road**
2.9	18.9	L	**East Beach Road** (County park with public restrooms and pretty beach to R)
0.2	19.1	R	**Flagler Road**
0.3	19.4	–	Mystery Bay State Park to L
1.9	21.3	–	Enter Fort Flagler State Park
0.6	21.9	S	**Continue straight ahead**, past turns for fishing pier and campgrounds.

0.1	22.0	**TA**	Enjoy views! Pay phone, soda machine, interpretive display and park office available. Turn around and head back down hill.
0.2	22.2	**S**	**Continue straight ahead toward gate.**
0.6	22.8	**S**	**Flagler Road.**
2.5	25.3	–	Pass through Nordland; small moorage on R, small grocery on left
2.4	27.7	**CR**	**Flagler Road** (back to Indian Island)
2.8	30.5	**R**	**Oak Bay Road**
0.9	31.4	**R**	**Irondale Road**
1.9	33.3	**R**	**Rhody Drive**
0.3	33.6	**L**	**Quick left back onto Four Corners Rd.** Dangerous intersection!
1.2	34.8	X	Highway 20; continue straight.
0.4	35.2	–	Descent
0.6	35.8	–	View of Discovery Bay to the left
0.1	35.9	**CR**	**Discovery Road**
0.5	36.4	–	Pass Chevy Chase Golf Course
4.7	41.1	X	Sheridan (Discovery changes to **19th**, then into **Blaine**)
0.9	42.0	**R**	**Walker St.**
0.1	42.1	X	Lawrence St.
0.2	42.3	**L**	**Clay St.**
0.1	42.4	X	Benton St.
0.1	42.5	X	Harrison St.
0.2	42.7	X	Tyler St.
0.1	42.8	–	Annapurna Inn on R

Fort Worden Loop (Road)

Pt.-Pt.	Cum.	Dir.	Landmark/Street
			From Annapurna Inn
0.0	0.0	**R**	**Clay St.**
0.1	0.1	**L**	**Monroe St.**
0.3	0.4	**R**	**Roosevelt St.**
0.1	0.5	**L**	**Jackson St.** (short, steep climb)
0.7	1.2	**L**	**W Street**
0.3	1.5	**R**	**Fort Worden Way**

0.1	1.6	R	**Eisenhower** (toward lighthouse)
0.3	1.9	L	**Follow loop** to batteries
0.1	2.0	–	Marine science center and beach to R, view of Admiralty Inlet and Indian Island
0.6	2.6	TA	Lighthouse (loop back to main road)
0.2	2.8	–	View batteries; park bikes and hike in. Follow loop to the right.
0.5	3.3	R	**Eisenhower** (barracks and museum and Park Office to R)
0.1	3.4	L	**Fort Warden Way**
0.3	3.7	R	**W Street**
0.2	3.9	CR	W St. changes to **Spruce** (Around Ft. Worden military cemetery)
0.1	4.0	–	Spruce turns into **Admiralty**
0.2	4.2	R	**San Juan**
0.1	4.3	L	**49th St.**
0.9	5.2	L	**53rd St.**
0.3	5.5	L	**Cook Ave.** (views of Admiralty Inlet on right)
1.6	7.1	R	**Hastings**
2.4	9.5	CL	**Hastings** (turn right to do additional Cape George Loop—10.6 miles)
0.6	10.1	L	**Cape George Road**
2.1	12.3	L	**Discovery Road**
2.0	14.3	X	Sheridan (Discovery Road changes to **19th**, then into **Blaine**–long downhill)
0.9	15.2	R	**Walker St.**
0.1	15.3	X	Lawrence St.
0.2	15.5	L	**Clay St.**
0.1	15.6	X	Benton St.
0.1	15.7	X	Harrison St.
0.2	15.9	X	Tyler St.
0.1	16.0	–	Annapurna Inn on R

GROVELAND COTTAGE
Simone Nichols
4861 Sequim-Dungeness Way
Dungeness, WA 98382
(360) 683-3565 or (800) 879-8859
Rates: $55-90

Sequim and Dungeness lie on flat, open fields which slope gently to the Straight of Juan de Fuca to the north, and rise dramatically to the Olympic Mountains to the south. The proximity of the mountains and the water have created a "rain shadow" in this area; Sequim receives just 19" of rain a year, compared to 40" and up just a few miles in either direction. The spectacular views, temperate climate and miles of flat terrain offer a perfect year-round cycling destination.

Groveland Cottage is located in Dungeness, a few square miles on the water just north of Sequim. Built at the turn-of-the-century for Charles Seal, a local merchant and trader, the house still retains much of its original charm and decor. The inn is surrounded by gardens and a small creek, with views of the Olympics and Mount Baker in the Cascades. Innkeeper Simone Nichols is an ardent gardener, cook and hostess, never too busy too stop and chat or answer questions.

We entered the inn through a rose-covered arbor and across a wide porch with comfortably-worn furniture positioned to take advantage of the panoramic views. The front foyer has a built-in bookcase groaning with books and puzzles, a wide staircase leading to the rooms upstairs, and a doorway to the old Great Room on the right. This large room has been converted into a small neighborhood store, offering gifts, groceries, fine wines and video rentals (you are welcome to select a complimentary video to watch in your room). The massive river rock fireplace on one wall recalls the room's days as a magnificent ballroom.

Four of the five rooms at Groveland Cottage are upstairs, while the fifth is in the detached cottage behind the inn. Each room has a distinct personality, all comfortable and homey, with an eclectic blend of antiques and artwork, as well as modern extras such as a television and VCR.

Oriental rugs cover blue-painted floors in the Happy Room, while an antique rocking chair offers a place to sit and contemplate the mountain view out over the gardens. This smaller room

features a queen-sized bed and shares the bath down the hall with Mr. Seal's Room. The bathroom is sunny and bright, with an enormous skylight above the fabulous whirlpool tub and shower.

We stayed in Mr. Seal's Room at the end of the hall. One of the largest rooms, it has a king-sized bed and a separate sitting area, including a couch which doubles as a single bed. Floor-to-ceiling windows at the alcove end of the room offer views of Mount Baker and the lush fields surrounding the inn.

The two other rooms in the house have private baths. The Waterfall Room is a large room with hardwood floors, a plush white rug, king-sized bed, and in-room shower. Elegant fabrics and turn-of-the-century paintings decorate this east-facing room. The cozy French Room, also facing east with views of Mount Baker, features country antiques, a dormer nook with an antique sink and washstand, and hardwood floors painted a cheerful blue.

The Secret Room, in the cottage outside, has a private bath, queen-sized bed and small kitchen area. It looks out through the gardens and fruit orchard.

The living room and dining room are shared areas downstairs in the main house. The sunny, museum-like living room is filled with interesting antiques, a piano, comfortable couches and chairs, a cozy woodstove and a wonderful Prohibition-era liquor cabinet and hutch. Opening off the living room, the long narrow dining room offers spectacular views of the Olympics and features an elegant table that comfortably seats 10-12 people.

The breakfast served in the morning is truly an event. You'll have coffee or tea delivered to your door with the morning paper before wandering down to the dining room with the other guests. We began our feast with more coffee and fresh-squeezed orange juice, accompanied by a dish of apples, grapefruit and sprigs of mint from the garden. Simone then brought out hot scones and bowls of steaming "Groveland Hot Cereal", a delicious cross between oatmeal and granola, topped with peaches, blueberries, brown sugar and cream. Just when we thought we'd completed our meal, out she came again, with individual servings of poached eggs over salmon and a plate of buttered toast. Beware Simone's cheerful urgings to have a second helping or you may not be able to rise from the table!

The relaxed atmosphere at Groveland Cottage is reminiscent of a favorite relative's summer cottage. You feel free to ask for seeds or a recipe, put your feet up on the couch, or share a sunny chair with the cat. Time slows down as you wander about the gardens and orchard, sit on the porch with a book and take in the mountain views and gentle sea breeze, or enjoy leisurely rides through the surrounding countryside.

BIKING FROM GROVELAND COTTAGE

Terrain

The Dungeness valley on the north side of the Olympic Peninsula is flat, with good views of both the Strait of Juan de Fuca and the Olympic Mountains. Any hills are mainly on the south side of Sequim.

Road Conditions

Most of the roads around Dungeness are in good condition; the Old Olympic Highway was being repaved in the summer of 1994. South of Highway 101 the roads are not marked very consistently.

Traffic

Highway 101 through Sequim can be a nightmare of gridlocked RV's because it is the main peninsula route. Cross it with care. Other roads have no shoulders, but much less traffic.

Nearest Bike Shop
      D & G Cyclery
      551 W. Washington
      Sequim, WA 98382
      (360) 681-3868

Best Time to Ride
    Almost year-round riding is possible, due to the area being in the rain shadow of the Olympics. Early spring through late fall are perfect.

Mountain Biking Opportunities
    There are an infinite number of routes in the foothills of the Olympics. Contact D & G Cycles for where to go and what map to bring.

HAPPY VALLEY LOOP (27.2 miles)
    The terrain on the south side of Sequim/Dungeness is much more wooded and hilly then the northern water side and is less populated. This ride gives you a taste of both. The Dungeness River is not crossable on the south side except for Highway 101, but there are some logging roads which go up into the Olympic Mountains if you care to explore them. Get a good county map before you head out on any logging roads or trails.

SPIT SPIN (16.4 miles)
    Here's a nice route out to the Dungeness Spit for an afternoon of hiking; pack a lunch and make a day of it. The hike is about 7 miles one way and there is a lighthouse at the end and a vast array of birds to watch too. The Strait of Juan de Fuca stretches out in front of you and on a clear day you can see Canada to the north and the Olympic Mountains to the south—it really is quite incredible.

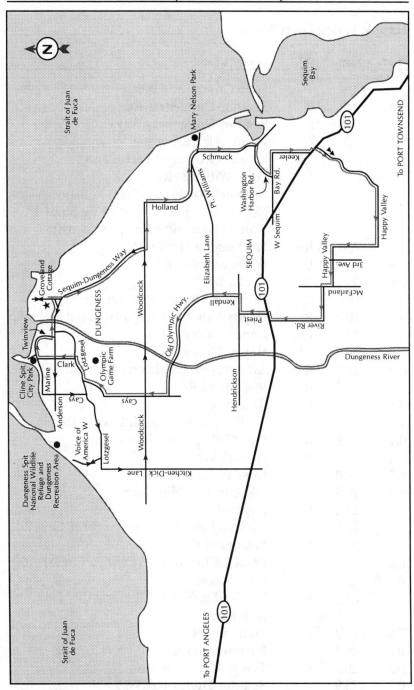

Spit Spin ——————   Happy Valley Loop ~~~~~~~~

Happy Valley Loop (Road)

Pt.-Pt.	Cum.	Dir.	Landmark/Street
			From Groveland Cottage
0.0	0.0	R	**Sequim-Dungeness Rd.**
0.2	0.2	L	**Sequim-Dungeness Way**
2.1	2.3	L	**Woodcock Rd.** (narrow, no shoulder)
1.1	3.4	CR	Woodcock changes to **Holland**
1.6	5.0	L	**Point Williams Rd.**
1.5	6.5	R	**Schmuck Rd.** (to L is Point Williams/Mary Nelson Park. Great views of the Strait of Juan de Fuca and hiking, restrooms)
1.4	7.9	R	**Washington Harbor Rd.**
0.8	8.7	L	**W Sequim Bay Rd.**
0.5	9.2	R	**Keeler Rd.**
0.8	10.0	L	**Highway 101** (heavy traffic, be careful)
0.2	10.2	R	**Happy Valley Rd.** (gradual uphill first mile)
3.0	13.2	CR	**Happy Valley Rd.**
1.0	14.2	CL	**Happy Valley Rd.**
0.3	14.5	X	3rd Ave. (go straight on Happy Valley Rd.)
1.0	15.5	R	**McFarland Rd.**
0.5	16.0	R	**River Rd.**
1.7	17.7	R	**Highway 101** (be careful, heavy traffic)
0.1	17.8	L	**Priest Rd.** (no shoulder, narrow)
0.8	18.6	R	**Hendrickson**
0.4	19.0	L	**Kendall Rd.**
0.5	19.5	L	**Old Olympic Highway**
2.5	22.0	R	**Cays Rd.**
0.5	22.5	X	Woodcock Rd. (continue straight on Cays Rd.)
1.5	24.0	R	**Lotzgesell Rd.**
0.5	24.5	L	**Clark Rd.** (across from Olympic Game Farm)
0.5	25.0	X	E Anderson Rd.
0.3	25.3	R	**Marine Dr.** (to L is Cline Spit City Park, restrooms)
0.6	25.9	L	**Twinview Rd.**
0.6	26.5	L	**E Anderson Rd.**
0.3	26.8	L	**Towne Rd. Extension**
0.1	26.9	L	**Sequim-Dungeness Way**
0.3	27.2	–	Groveland Cottage on L

Spit Spin (Road with MTB option)

Pt.-Pt.	Cum.	Dir.	Landmark/Street
			From Groveland Cottage
0.0	0.0	R	**Sequim-Dungeness Way**
0.2	0.2	R	**East Anderson Rd./Sequim-Dungeness Way**
0.9	1.1	R	**Marine Drive** (great views of Dungeness Bay and lighthouse)
1.6	2.7	L	**Cays Road**
1.0	3.7	R	**Lotzgesell Road**
1.6	5.3	R	**Voice of America Road** into Dungeness Spit National Wildlife Refuge and Dungeness Recreation Area.
1.0	6.3	TA	On the right there is an area to lock up bikes for hiking out on the spit or to visit the wildlife area.
0.2	6.5	–	Mountain Bike option: take left hand trail and follow trails down to lower parking near entrance. Road bikes turn around, reverse route through campgrounds.
0.8	7.3	–	Trail rejoins road
0.3	7.6	R	**Lotzgesell Road**
0.2	7.8	L	**Kitchen Dick Road**
1.0	8.8	L	**Woodcock Road**
1.5	10.3	X	Continue straight on Woodcock Road, crossing Dungeness River
3.1	13.4	L	**Sequim-Dungeness Way**
2.2	15.6	R	**Sequim-Dungeness Way** (follow signs for 3 Crabs Restaurant)
0.4	16.0	TA	Near restaurant- great view of Dungeness Bay, turn around and return to inn.
0.4	16.4	–	Groveland Cottage on R

MILLER TREE INN
Ted and Prue Miller
654 East Division Street
P.O. Box 953
Forks, WA 98331
(360) 374-6806
Rates: $35-60

The past decade's troubles in the timber industry have taken their toll on Forks. Once a booming logging town, Forks is now struggling to carve out a new economic niche. Its proximity to the Olympic mountains and the Pacific Ocean, combined with the lack of amenities north and south of town and the friendly residents themselves make tourism a natural choice. The demise of the timber industry has had a benefit to cyclists: miles and miles of abandoned logging roads wind up through the forests behind town, offering fabulous mountain biking opportunities and incredible vistas of the Olympics to the east and the ocean to the west.

The Miller Tree Inn has weathered the changes in Forks over eleven years as a B&B. Ted and Prue Miller bought the former Winifred Ford Peterson home in 1984 from a descendant of the first owner. The home was built by one of the first three homesteading families in Forks in 1917, and retains its original farmhouse feeling.

The atmosphere at the inn encourages guests to make themselves comfortable, and since frequent visitors are biologists or forestry workers working nearby, the inn is home-away-from-home for many guests. The roomy downstairs is divided into two living rooms and a dining area. The pine-paneled front room, opening from a full front porch outside with big wicker furniture to lounge in, has a comfortable couch and several easy chairs, a piano and a wide table for spreading out puzzles or the scrapbooks the Millers have compiled about the area and the house's history.

The smaller second room has hardwood floors covered in shag rugs, overstuffed couches and chairs cozily arranged around a gas-log wood stove and television/VCR, a large bay window, and built-in bookshelves with a wide offering of reading material. This second sitting area opens into the dining room, with big picture

windows overlooking the yard and pasture outside. A small sunporch area has a table for two, while other guests share the big country-tile table and blue-cushioned benches.

The guest rooms are all on the second floor. In summer you have six rooms to choose from; in winter one of the second-floor rooms is not used. In busy seasons, or when a large group comes to stay, two additional rooms on the third floor are occasionally rented out. The main rooms on the second floor are the Sunset, Elk View, Country Clover, Cedar Creek, Blue Jay and Minnie Rooms.

Sunset has a private bath and looks out on the neighboring pasture. The two twin beds are covered in pale peach spreads which complement lace curtains in the window. Elk View is a corner room with lots of windows, a rocking chair, television, and queen-sized bed. It shares a bath with the Minnie room. Minnie is a small room with a double bed, pine headboard, walk-in closet and lace curtains. It looks out through the large trees on the side of the house.

The Country Clover room, with a private half-bath, is a bright room with light pink carpet, matching floral curtains and bedspread on the queen bed, white walls and two large windows. A small desk provides a nice spot to read. The Blue Jay room has a queen-sized bed, large dresser, and antique loveseat in a small floral print. Soft blue-gray carpet matches cheerful blue curtains hanging in the big bay window. A desk and chair in front of the window affords a spot to sit and gaze out over the pasture. This room shares a full bath with the Cedar Creek room just down the hall.

The Cedar Creek room was our favorite: stretching the length of the front porch, this big room has a treehouse feel, with views of the pasture and big trees just outside the large windows on the south side. Two twin beds and a queen-sized bed easily share the space with a separate sitting area, a television, an armoire and large vanity.

We visited the Miller Tree Inn the weekend daylight savings time ended in the fall, and had forgotten to reset our clocks the night before. Hoping to get an early start in the morning, we rose early and crept downstairs for breakfast at the earliest possible time—6:30 a.m. The fact that it was actually *5:30 a.m.* and the Millers cheerfully started coffee and made us breakfast before letting us in on the time change is a testament to their easy-going natures and willingness to oblige! Breakfast is generally early, in order for fisherman, workers and cyclists to get a jump on the day. Prue puts juice, coffee, cereal and fruit out on the sideboard for guests to start, and then creates toast, eggs, sausage, French toast or whatever else guests ask for.

With the myriad of nearby activities, from mountain biking in the forest to riding out to the beach, or taking a day trip 30 miles away to the Ho Rain Forest, you'll have no trouble filling your days in Forks. After a long day exploring you'll want to slip into the hot tub on the side of the house and marvel at the stars while you plan your next day's adventure.

BIKING FROM THE MILLER TREE INN

Terrain
As the timber capitol of the Olympic Peninsula, Forks and the surrounding area is lush with trees and water. To the west is the Pacific Coast with flat, open areas leading to the saltwater. The eastern portion rises up into the Olympic Mountains and paved roads are less frequent.

Road Conditions
Highway 101 is the main artery through town and has a good shoulder for most of its length. Forest Service Rd. 29 is paved, but narrow. Roads to the ocean beaches are winding and narrow.

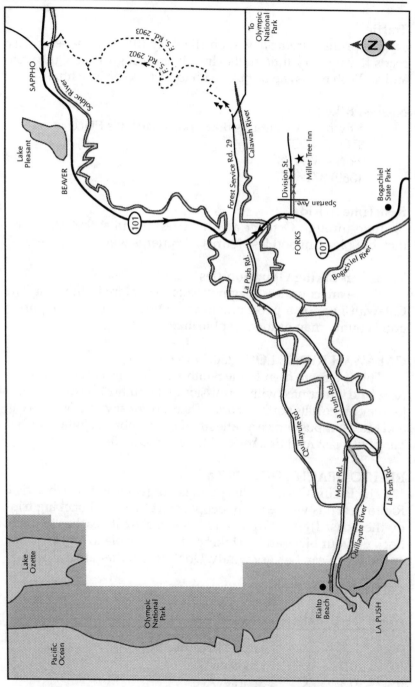

Calawah Ridge Loop ———   Rialto Beach Loop ········

Traffic

The primary traffic flow is on Highway 101, with the secondary roads having very little traffic. In July and August the Quillayute and La Push roads can be busy with tourists, so be watchful.

Nearest Bike Shop

>Olympic Mountains Bike Shop/Shirley's Place
>P.O. Box 2377
>Forks, WA 98331
>(360) 374-9777

Best Time to Ride

June through October are the driest months; the fall is predictably pleasant and less touristy. Winter is wet around here.

Mountain Biking Opportunities

There are countless logging roads to explore in the area. The Calawah Loop is a good one to try, while any others require a good county map or topographic map.

CALAWAH RIDGE LOOP (30.3 miles)

This is a route from Kathe Smith's book, *Olympic Peninsula Off-Road* (and is reprinted with permission of the author). It is an excellent journey in the hills north of Forks. There are great views of the ocean and Mt. Olympus and very little strenuous climbing. Highway 101 is busy but a fast road ride back with a good shoulder.

RIALTO BEACH LOOP (29.7 miles)

The Pacific Ocean at this point is gorgeous and worth a visit. Rialto Beach is where many people start their backpacking trips up the Coast Trail to Ozette and has some great beaches to roam. Lock up your bikes and go hiking. It is advisable to bring a jacket as the beach can be very windy. Don't forget the camera.

Calawah Ridge Loop (MTB)

Pt.-Pt.	Cum.	Dir.	Landmark/Street
			From Miller Tree Inn
0.0	0.0	L	**Division St.**
0.3	0.3	X	Spartan Ave.
0.1	0.4	**R**	**Highway 101**

0.3	0.7	–	Tillicum Park on R
1.5	2.2	**R**	**Forest Service Road 29**
3.6	5.8	**L**	**Forest Service Road 2902** (before bridge)
		–	Washout in 1/2 mile - follow trail along edge
3.8	9.6	–	Views of Olympus and Pacific Ocean
1.1	10.7	**CR**	**Forest Service Road 2902** (FS Rd 2924 on L)
1.2	11.9	–	Alternate route on FS Rd 2903 to R
2.2	14.1	**CR**	**Forest Service Road 2902** (FS Rd 300 on R)
1.2	15.3	–	End of alternate route FS Rd 2903
1.3	16.6	**L**	**Unmarked paved road (FS Rd 2902)**
1.0	17.6	**L**	**Highway 101 south** (Sappho Cafe is R; Rayonier park straight ahead)
10.5	28.1	–	FS Rd 29 on L
1.8	29.9	**L**	**Division St.**
0.1	30.0	X	Spartan Ave.
0.3	30.3	–	Miller Tree Inn on R

Rialto Beach Loop (Road)

Pt.-Pt.	Cum.	Dir.	Landmark/Street
			From Miller Tree Inn
0.0	0.0	**L**	**Division St.**
0.3	0.3	X	Spartan Ave.
0.1	0.4	**R**	**Highway 101**
1.5	1.9	**L**	**La Push Road**
3.1	5.0	**R**	**Quillayute Rd.**
6.8	11.8	**R**	**Mora Rd.**
0.5	12.3	–	Enter Olympic National Park
2.3	14.6	–	Rialto Beach parking area (trails, restrooms, picnic spots, windy)
0.0	14.6	**TA**	**Turn around**
3.0	17.6	X	Quillayute Rd./Richwine
2.0	19.6	–	Narrow one lane bridge
0.4	20.0	**L**	**La Push Road**
4.6	24.6	**CR**	**La Push Road**
3.1	27.7	**R**	**Highway 101 south**
1.6	29.3	**L**	**Division St.**
0.1	29.4	X	Spartan Ave.
0.3	29.7	–	Miller Tree Inn on R

THE TUDOR INN
Jane and Jerry Glass
1108 South Oak
Port Angeles, WA 98362
(360) 452-3138
Rates: $85-110

Port Angeles is the largest community on the peninsula, with an active lumber mill and a busy downtown area, but is best known for being the jumping off point to both Victoria, British Columbia and the beautiful Hurricane Ridge area. The Tudor Inn is in a quiet residential neighborhood within walking distance of town and just a short ride from the Olympic National Park Visitor Center, which is the newest of the Park's visitor centers and well worth a visit. Mountains tower behind the house, while just past town, down the hill, the Strait of Juan de Fuca sparkles in the distance.

Jane and Jerry Glass worked in Europe for ten years before becoming innkeepers, all the while collecting antiques with hopes of starting an antique store when they retired. Upon their return to the States in 1981, Jerry was transferred to Seattle, and they began making weekend trips to the peninsula. They found the Tudor Inn for sale on one of their trips, and impulsively decided to abandon the antique store and open a B&B instead. Guests are lucky they did—they're natural hosts with a beautiful home and naturally, exquisite antiques throughout the house.

Since our visit, the house has undergone an extensive remodel, adding private baths and enlarging several rooms. We have not had the opportunity to revisit the Tudor Inn since the changes were made, but have altered our original description of the rooms based on Jerry's portrayal of the remodel. We trust the ambiance and general decor will remain the same, so the only deviations from our description should be pleasant surprises!

As one might guess from the name, the house was built in the classic English Tudor style, and the furnishings and atmosphere throughout the house perpetuate the English feel, right down to the fine teas offered in the afternoon. The shared areas downstairs are at once elegant and comfortable. Polished hardwood floors glisten beneath a large green oriental rug in the living room, coordinating with an overstuffed green-and-white striped loveseat and armchair set. An antique red velvet couch and glass-topped cof-

fee table face the multi-paned windows which look out on the street, while a woodstove inset in a large white brick hearth wards off the evening chill. Guests are welcome to try a tune at the grand piano or peruse the guest book, scrapbooks and guide books on the coffee table. The living room opens to the dark-paneled formal dining room to the left, dominated by a long antique dinner table surrounded by high-back chairs. A gorgeous hutch sits at one end of the room, while a large mirror reflects the view out the multi-paned window at the other end.

The five guest rooms are reached by climbing a regal hardwood staircase covered with dark red carpet held in place by polished brass rods. All the accommodations have crisp linens, private baths, and select European antiques accenting the unique nature of each room. Steam radiators throughout the house sigh quietly on chilly evenings, adding an authentic old-fashioned flair.

The Wedgwood Room features a queen-sized bed with brass headboard and fluffy down comforter, stained glass in the window looking back toward the mountains, and delicate blue walls.

True to its name, the Oriental Room has a decidedly Asian feel, with a queen-sized bed in a black lacquered bedstead, ornate dresser, and deep salmon-colored walls accented by a plum tree branch stencil. This corner room enjoys views of the water.

The Country Room has been transformed in the recent remodel to a luxurious suite, with a private balcony to take in spectacular mountain views, a gas-log fireplace and a full-size clawfoot tub in the private bath. The country charm is still evident in turn-of-the-century artwork and pastel floral bouquet stencils dotting the white walls.

Another corner room, the Bayleaf Room, has also been recently enlarged. Deep green walls with an ivy stencil create a peaceful environment to sit and marvel at the mountain view out the window, while a marvelously ornate carved oak headboard cradles a king-sized bed topped with a white coverlet.

Our favorite of the room choices was the Tudor Room, in the northeast corner. This room enjoys both mountain and water views from a striking four-poster canopy bed. Light peach walls and soft carpeting set off an elaborate antique dresser with a built-in vanity and mirrors, while the big corner windows make the room bright and cheery.

Breakfast is served in the mornings between 8:30 and 9 a.m., unless you're catching the ferry to Victoria, in which case breakfast can be as early as 7 a.m. (the Glasses will also encourage you to leave your car in line at the dock the night before and will drive you down after breakfast). The morning of our visit we met a fun bunch of travelers from all over the country while enjoying fine coffee and orange juice, a lavish fruit plate, and heart-shaped waffles served with bacon. We all enjoyed chatting over coffee with Jane and Jerry about their European adventures, and didn't get going on our ride until almost noon!

Even if you linger over the breakfast table as long as we did, you'll still have time to choose from a number of good rides. Whether you head toward the mountains for a long rewarding climb, up to the hot springs for a refreshing dip, or choose to stick closer to town and enjoy the water views, you're sure to relish the beauty of this area and the serenity that surrounds you at the Tudor Inn.

BIKING FROM THE TUDOR INN

Terrain
Port Angeles is on the north Olympic Peninsula, between the Strait of Juan de Fuca and Hurricane Ridge. The land rises up from the waters edge to the foothills of the Olympics, so it's flat to rolling near the water and progressively hillier as you go south.

Road Conditions
Narrow two-lane roads cross Highway 101, with Little River Rd. being partially gravel. Highway 101 has a wide shoulder for most of its length.

Traffic
Highway 101 is busy, but most other roads have moderate traffic except for Hurricane Ridge Road which can be filled with tourists during July and August.

Nearest Bike Shop
Pedal 'n Paddle
120 E. Front st.
Port Angeles, WA 98362
(360) 457-1240

Best Time to Ride
June through late September are the driest months, but the temperatures throughout the year are moderate near the water, with winter bringing snow to the foothills and Hurricane Ridge areas.

Mountain Biking Opportunities
Foothills Trail System off Little River Road offers some nearby singletrack, but there are also a large number of logging roads available for exploration. Pick up maps and Kathe Smith's *Olympic Peninsula Off-Road* book at Pedal 'n Paddle (or call Kathe at 360-457-1640 to order a copy—it's a great little resource).

LAKE DAWN LOOP (16.3 miles)
This ride is just plain fun and offers great access to the Foothills Trail system. One of the advantages to this area is the proximity to trails right from town. You could combine this ride

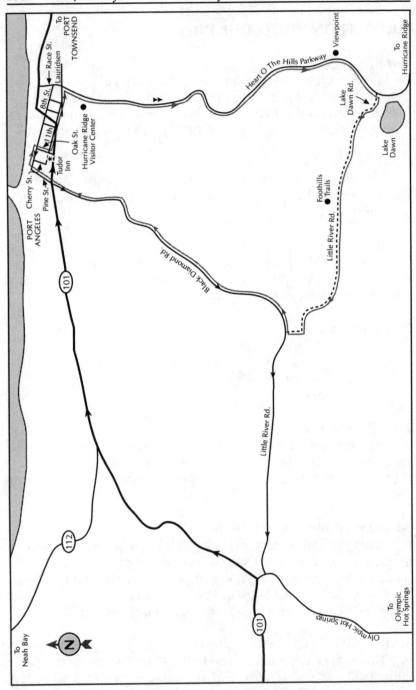

Little River Loop ———   Lake Dawn Ride ———

with the Little River Ride for a longer trek. The Hurricane Ridge Visitor's Center is worth a visit and the views are glorious from the viewpoint before Lake Dawn Road. For the full day climb you can ride all the way up to Hurricane Ridge itself.

LITTLE RIVER RIDE (17.0 miles)

This makes a nice paved loop with the option of taking a left at Little River Road and riding up the Elwah River. The climb to get to Olympic Hotsprings is arduous and long, so if you decide to do it be prepared for a long day. Otherwise this is a pleasant tour through the west side of Port Angeles. Highway 101 is busy but has a wide shoulder.

Lake Dawn Loop (Road)

Pt.-Pt.	Cum.	Dir.	Landmark/Street
			From the Tudor Inn
0.0	0.0	L	**Oak St.** (north)
0.0	0.0	R	**11th St.**
0.2	0.2	X	Lincoln St.
0.2	0.4	X	Peabody St.
0.3	0.7	X	S. Eunice St.
0.1	0.8	R	**Francis**
0.0	0.8	L	**Lauridsen**
0.0	0.8	CL	**Race St./Mt. Angeles Rd.** (winding stretch)
0.4	1.2	–	Hurricane Ridge Visitor's Center on R (worth a look inside)
0.1	1.3	CR	**Heart O' The Hills Rd.** (to Hurricane Ridge)
4.6	5.9	–	Viewpoint
0.5	6.4	R	**Lake Dawn Rd.** (chipseal)
0.3	6.7	CR	**Little River Rd.** (gravel)
3.0	9.7	–	Foothills Trails to R (mountain biking area)
0.9	10.6	R	**Black Diamond Rd.**
4.6	15.2	–	Black Diamond changes to **Pine St.**
0.6	15.8	R	**W. 8th St.** (cross bridge on sidewalk—yield to pedestrians)
0.2	16.0	R	**S. Cherry St.**
0.2	16.2	L	**11th St.**
0.1	16.3	–	Tudor Inn on R

Little River Ride (Road)

Pt.-Pt.	Cum.	Dir.	Landmark/Street
			From Tudor Inn
0.0	0.0	L	**Oak St.** (north)
0.2	0.2	L	**W. 8th St.**
0.2	0.4	X	Cherry St.
0.2	0.6	L	**Pine St.** (winds through residential area)
1.3	1.9	–	Pine changes to **Old Black Diamond Rd.** (winding & rolling climbs; farms and forests)
3.7	5.6	–	Black Diamond changes to **Little River Rd.**
3.4	9.0	R	**Olympic Hot Springs Rd.** (Olympic Hot Springs is to the L on Olympic Hot Springs Rd.—8 miles uphill on part gravel, then a 2-mile hike; lock up bikes at trailhead and go for a soak)
0.3	9.3	R	**Highway 101** (wide shoulder)
7.4	16.7	L	**Oak St.**
0.3	17.0	–	Tudor Inn on L

SAN JUAN AND PUGET SOUND ISLANDS INNS AND RIDES

Islands have a special magic. Nowhere else is the beauty of the Northwest so abundant and the concerns of daily life so removed. Whether your destination is one of the closer islands such as Bainbridge or Whidbey, or one of the more remote San Juan Islands, the sense of adventure upon boarding the ferry is the same; you truly feel as though you're getting *away*. An island may not provide the unlimited riding opportunities that the mainland does, but the quiet pace and spectacular scenery at every turn more than compensate for the number of miles you've put in.

Bainbridge Island is a sleepy residential island just minutes by ferry from downtown Seattle. With winding roads and hilly climbs, it offers a number of challenging rides. The rides we selected from the **Bombay House** include a visit to a winery, a section of the annual Chilly Hilly bicycle ride route, a detour past the shops and art galleries in downtown Winslow and a trip through the bicycles-only Fort Ward State Park. Mountain bike and hiking trails abound on the island as well; stop by the excellent Chamber of Commerce visitors center to pick up more information about things to do on Bainbridge Island.

Whidbey Island, a long, thin island, is the largest we visited. Several charming towns dot the island's perimeter, among them Clinton, Langley, Freeland, Greenbank and Coupeville. Oak Harbor, the largest town on the island, is host to a large naval base. The **Inn at Penn Cove** is centrally located in Coupeville, the second-oldest town in the state. Rides in this area pass museums and historic sites well worth a visit. An excellent little brochure entitled "Ebey's Landing: A Driving and Bicycling Tour" discusses many of the points of interest on our Fort Casey Loop.

The San Juan Islands are a tremendously popular vacation spot among Northwesterners and visitors alike—with very good reason. A nearly-perfect climate, abundant wildlife, any number of enchanting small towns and unparalleled scenery make these islands a favorite destination year-round. Due to their overwhelming popularity, we really can't recommend that you visit during the peak summer months unless you have a penchant for long lines and lots of traffic. Traveling before Memorial Day or after Labor Day assures a much more enjoyable visit, with safer roads, shorter ferry lines and happier inhabitants!

While we chose rides from each inn that remained on the island we were visiting, many cyclists "island hop" during their visit. You can ride to the ferry dock, wheel your bike on the ferry and spend the day pedaling around one of the neighboring islands before heading back to your B&B for the night. Shaw Island has no overnight accommodations, but offers some great cycling opportunities.

Lopez Island, one of the smaller islands in the San Juan chain, has long been a favorite among cyclists because of its relatively flat terrain and smaller population. While the area closest to the **Inn at Swift's Bay** is a bit hilly, the south part of the island is fairly level and affords excellent views from any one of the small inlets and bays which punctuate the south end.

San Juan Island is the second largest and the most populated of the islands. Forest and farmland slope gently to the water's edge in this rolling terrain. At the windswept southern end of the island one finds **Olympic Lights**, removed from the bustle of Friday Harbor on the north end both geographically and philosophically. After one of our favorite rides of the summer, the Outer Island Loop, this was a spectacular place to finish the day—sunsets and mountain views are dramatic from the inn.

Having been married there, we have a special place in our hearts for Orcas Island. Offering by far the most strenuous cycling in the San Juans (riding 30 miles on this island will feel like 60 on any other), this densely forested, hilly island also offers the greatest rewards. The ride to Doe Bay from **Turtleback Farm Inn** culminates with a luxurious soak in the natural hotsprings, and if you can bear the seven-mile grind up Mount Constitution, the sight of the entire island chain stretching out below you will take your breath away (once you've regained it, that is).

When your daily routine gets to feeling too frantic, consider taking a trip to one of these islands. As the ferry pulls away from the dock and that tiny speck in the distance begins to loom on the horizon, you sense time slowing down. By the time you arrive at one of these inns, you'll feel worlds away from home and ready to pedal off on a new adventure.

BOMBAY HOUSE BED & BREAKFAST
Bunny Cameron and Roger Kanchuk
8490 Beck Road
Bainbridge Island, WA 98110
(206) 842-3926
Rates: $55-125 per night

Bainbridge Island is home to the Pacific Northwest's first official cycling event of the season, the February Chilly Hilly. While you may visit at less chilly times of the year, you won't find it any less hilly in July than in February!

Despite its close proximity to Seattle, Bainbridge Island is a quiet island with lovely homes, narrow winding roads, and diverse scenery ranging from farms to forests. It isn't possible to do much more than a 30-mile loop on the island, but with the addition of a few dozen serious hills, you won't miss the extra mileage.

The Bombay House is located in the southern half of the island, on a steep hill overlooking Rich Passage. Built in 1907 by Frank Beck, a Master Shipbuilder, the house retains its original charm while providing modern comforts.

There are five rooms to select from, each with its own personality. The Red Room opens off the living room on the first floor and has a private bath with tub and shower across the hall. The room has a Victorian ambiance, with a queen-sized brass bed, deep red walls, and a velvet couch. The Red Room overlooks the gardens, which explode with color almost year-round.

The other room on the first floor is the King Room, which also looks out over the gardens and the rustic rough-cedar gazebo on the lawn outside. The room features a private bathroom and an antique blue tin soaking tub in the room. The decor is antique country, with a light pine armoire, dresser, desk and chair, and a king sized bed.

Upstairs is the Morning Room, a sunny room with both double and single beds in white wrought-iron bedsteads, pale yellow walls, and a view of the grounds. The room shares a bath with the Crow's Nest down the hall.

The Crow's Nest is the smallest room in the house, but one of our favorites. From the double bed in the morning we could look out to the water and see the ferries heading for Seattle. The room is bright and cozy, with a small desk, pine furniture, and a won-

derful old steamer trunk turned on its side and converted into a dresser. Both the Crow's Nest and Morning Rooms have fluffy robes in the closet for your use.

The most luxurious room in the house is the Captain's Suite, a deep green room which occupies the entire east half of the second floor. Views of the gardens, gazebo, woods and water are all possible from one of the many windows. More like a small apartment than a room for the night, in addition to the queen-sized bed and antique wood-inlay furniture the Captain's Suite has a television and VCR, a small refrigerator, an unfolding futon couch and a woodstove. The private bath includes a heated towel rack and a tub behind wooden doors, which can be opened to the room. A sherry decanter and wine glasses, several plants and a ceiling fan all add an extra touch of home.

The living room downstairs extends almost the length of the house, but is filled at one end by an enormous loom and therefore appears much cozier. Old stained glass hangs in the windows on either side of the brick-hearth fireplace, while books and magazines slide over antique steamer trunks used as end tables on either side of the couch. The blonde wood floors and plants in the bay window create a cheerful, bright setting.

Breakfast is served in the kitchen in front of bay windows overlooking the deck and water beyond; an immense table is laden with food. Bunny is the author of a wonderful cookbook, and she's always eager to have you taste as many recipes as you can possibly consume. As just an example of the spread we sampled, the morning we visited there was zucchini jam bread, zucchini marmalade, peach yogurt, fresh-picked grapes from the arbor outside, fruit salad, mixed-fruit bran muffins with orange butter, homemade granola, "fall blend" juice, Australian pa-pa/banana jam, cranberry bars, berry muffins, an apple tart, pear bread, toasted beer bread, raspberry-boysenberry jam, and a pear and apple plate. We enjoyed chatting with the other guests about Rex, the Red Classic Tabby Cornish Rex cat who rules the kitchen at breakfast, and admiring the trompe d'oeil on the kitchen cabinets while we tried to digest enough to stand up!

If you can bear to think about eating again, make reservations at either Ruby's or the Pleasant Beach Grill before you head out for the day. We enjoyed the selection of local wines, attentive service and creative menu at Ruby's, but Pleasant Beach Grill came highly recommended, too. Both are just a mile from the inn.

BIKING FROM THE BOMBAY HOUSE

Terrain
Rolling hills abound on Bainbridge Island, and a few really steep ones as well, but there are always the corresponding downhills too. The really steep ones are Toe Jam Hill (worth riding just so you can say you rode up a steep hill with a name like that), Baker Hill Rd. and Bucklin Hill Rd. Most of the island is very treed, and very populated.

Road Conditions
Roads are good for the most part, with quite a few deadends near the shoreline of the island (like between South Beach Rd. and Bean's Bight).

Traffic
Highway 305 coming from Poulsbo and going to Winslow is heavily traveled and high speed. Most other streets and roads are not as busy except for in the town of Winslow. There are few shoulders on any road, and any traffic can feel too close, so stay aware.

Nearest Bike Shop
Reliable Cycle
10255 N. E. Valley Dr.
Bainbridge Island, WA 98110
(206) 842-0654

Best Time to Ride

Early spring or late fall. The first organized ride of the year, called the Chilly Hilly, happens here in February. As with most areas at this latitude and with saltwater so near, the temperatures are moderate year-round.

Mountain Biking Opportunities

The closest mountain biking is in the DNR lands off Mandus Olson Road from Koura Road or from New Brooklyn. At present, only a portion of the area's 280 acres have marked trails.

FAY BAINBRIDGE LOOP (19.5 miles)

This route follows the center of the island up to the north end where Fay Bainbridge State Park is located. There are some splendid views of Seattle from the Skiff Point and Sunrise Rd. area. For a side trip you can hike in the Grand Forest off of Miller Rd.

WINSLOW LOOP (24.4 miles)

This loop weaves around the south end of Bainbridge Island, through Fort Ward State Park (Battery Vinton was built in 1900) and into the town of Winslow. There are some serious hills on this island, but conversely there are the downhills as well. Visit the Bainbridge Island Winery and see the vista from Strawberry Hill Park.

Fay Bainbridge Loop (Road)

Pt.-Pt.	Cum.	Dir.	Street/Landmark
			From the Bombay House (corner of Beck & Blakely Ave)
0.0	0.0	L	**W Blakely Ave. NE**
0.1	0.1	L	**Blakely Ave. NE**
1.5	1.6	S	Blakely changes to **Bucklin Hill Rd.**
0.3	1.9	–	Bucklin changes to **Eagle Harbor Dr.**
0.2	2.1	CR	Eagle Harbor changes to **Wyatt St.**
0.1	2.2	L	**Finch Rd.**
0.2	2.4	CR	**Sportsman Club Rd.**
0.3	2.7	X	High School Rd.
0.6	3.3	X	New Brooklyn Rd.

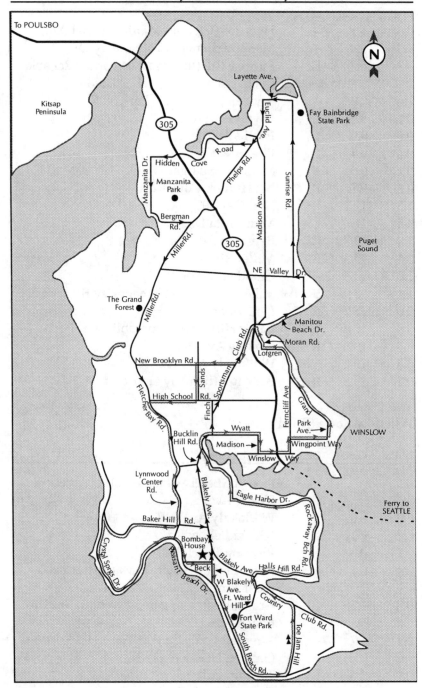

To POULSBO

Kitsap
Peninsula

Layette Ave.

305

Euclid Ave.

Fay Bainbridge
State Park

Road

Manzanita Dr.

Hidden Cove

Phelps Rd.

Sunrise Rd.

Manzanita
Park

Bergman
Rd.

Madison Ave.

305

Puget
Sound

Miller Rd.

NE Valley Dr.

The Grand
Forest

Miller Rd.

Manitou
Beach Dr.

Club Rd.

Moran Rd.

New Brooklyn Rd.

Sands Rd.

Finch

Sportsman

Lofgren

Ferncliff Ave

Grand

Fletcher Bay Rd.

High School

Wyatt

Park
Ave.

WINSLOW

Bucklin
Hill Rd.

Madison

Winslow Way

Wingpoint Way

Lynnwood
Center
Rd.

Blakely Ave.

Eagle Harbor Dr.

Ferry to
SEATTLE

Baker Hill Rd.

Rockaway Bch Rd.

Crystal Springs Dr.

Bombay
House ★

Beck

Pleasant Beach Dr.

Blakely Ave.

Halls Hill Rd.

W Blakely
Ave.
Ft. Ward
Hill

Country

Fort Ward
State Park

Club Rd.

Toe Jam Hill

South Beach Rd.

Fay Bainbridge Loop ——————   Winslow Loop ——————

0.8	4.1	X	Hwy 305 (CR onto **Manitou Beach Dr.**)
1.3	5.4	–	Manitou changes to **NE Valley Dr**.
0.3	5.7	R	**Sunrise Rd.** (Jiffy Mart on corner. Reliable Cycle 1/4 mi up on Valley Dr. on L)
2.6	8.3	–	Fay Bainbridge State Park on R
0.1	8.4	L	**Layfayette Ave.**
0.6	9.0	L	**Euclid Ave.**
0.4	9.4	L	**Phelps Rd. NE**
0.1	9.5	X	Madison/Spargar
0.2	9.7	R	**NE Hidden Cove Rd.**
1.5	11.2	X	Highway 305
0.5	11.7	L	**Manzanita Dr.**
1.0	12.7	CL	**Bergman Rd.**
0.6	13.3	R	**Miller Rd.**
1.0	14.3	–	Grand Forest on R
1.4	15.7	S	Miller changes to **Fletcher Bay Rd.**
2.0	17.7	R	**Lynnwood Center Rd.**
0.9	18.6	L	**Baker Hill Rd.** (steep uphill, but short)
0.4	19.0	R	**Blakely Ave. NE**
0.4	19.4	CR	**W Blakely Ave. NE**
0.1	19.5	R	**Beck Rd.** (Bombay House on R)

Winslow Loop (Road)

Pt.-Pt.	Cum.	Dir.	Street/Landmark
			From the Bombay House (corner of Beck & Blakely Ave)
0.0	0.0	R	**W Blakely Ave. NE**
0.1	0.1	X	NE Oddfellow Rd.
0.2	0.3	L	**Pleasant Beach Rd.**
0.4	0.7	–	Enter Ft. Ward State Park (restrooms, picnicking)
0.8	1.5	R	Gravel stretch to gate, then onto **South Beach Rd.**
0.2	1.7	–	Alternate route up Fort Ward Hill Rd. on L (Salmon Hatchery on R)
0.9	2.6	L	**Toe Jam Hill**
1.2	3.8	L	**Country Club Rd.**

0.6	4.4	–	End of alternate route on Ft. Ward Hill Rd.
0.2	4.6	R	**Blakely Rd.**
0.3	4.9	CL	**Halls Hill Rd.**
0.7	5.6	–	Halls Hill Rd. changes to **Rockaway Beach Rd.**
1.2	6.8	CL	**Eagle Harbor Drive**
2.4	9.2	R	**Eagle Harbor Drive**
0.1	9.3	CR	**Wyatt** (more traffic)
0.9	10.2	R	**Madison**
0.3	10.5	L	**Winslow Way**
0.3	10.8	X	Olympic Drive/Highway 305 (for Bainbridge Island Vineyards & Winery, take Hwy. 305 to L 0.3 mi)
0.2	11.0	L	**Ferncliff Ave.**
0.2	11.2	R	**Wingpoint Way**
0.7	11.9	L	**Park Ave NE**
0.3	12.2	CL	**Grand Ave.**
0.9	13.1	R	**Ferncliff Ave.**
0.4	13.5	CL	**Lofgren Rd.**
0.4	13.9	CR	**Moran Rd.**
0.3	14.2	L	**Sportsman Club Rd.** (X Highway 305)
0.9	15.1	R	**New Brooklyn Rd.**
0.6	15.7	L	**Sands Ave. NE**
0.5	16.2	R	**High School Rd.**
0.2	16.4	–	Strawberry Hill Park and Bainbridge Island Historical Museum
0.5	16.9	L	**Fletcher Bay Rd.** (to Lynnwood)
1.4	18.3	R	**Lynnwood Center Rd.**
0.9	19.2	R	**Baker Hill Rd.** (long uphill and steep downhill)
1.6	20.8	L	**Crystal Springs Drive**
2.9	23.7	R	**Pleasant Beach Drive**
0.3	24.0	L	**Beck Rd.**
0.2	24.2	X	Lytle Rd.
0.2	24.4	–	Bombay House on L

THE INN AT PENN COVE
Gladys and Mitchell Howard
702 N. Main Street
Coupeville, WA 98239
(360) 678-8000 or (800) 688-COVE
Rates: $60-125

This inn is actually two completely separate homes, moved next to one another several years ago. The Italianate Kineth House was built in 1887 by one of the first settlers in the area. The second house, the Coupe-Gillespie House, was built in 1891 as a wedding present for town-founder Captain Coupe's daughter. The Coupe-Gillespie house was moved twice before coming to settle in its present location.

Today the homes serve as the Inn at Penn Cove, with three guest rooms in each house. Each of the guest rooms is named for one of the previous owner's daughters or granddaughters. The Kineth House is the posher of the two, with a formal parlor and dining room where guests staying in either house meet for breakfast in the morning. The rooms in this house are slightly larger and more elaborately furnished than those next door.

The Coupe-Gillespie House is a little more laid-back, with a comfortable library and game room downstairs and three cozy guest rooms upstairs. Larger groups or families with kids may prefer the Coupe-Gillespie House's less formal atmosphere. The library in this house is impressive. We spent hours poring over the shelves crammed with every genre of literature imaginable. Wide pine floors covered with oriental rugs, high ceilings and a large bay window make the room feel big, while casual groupings of cushioned wicker furniture and high-back armchairs divide the room into smaller reading nooks. A carom board provides more lively entertainment for those so-inclined.

Across the hall from the library is a very relaxed game room, with puzzles, books and games stacked on low shelves about the room. A large table and plenty of chairs provide space to spread out and listen to the stereo or have a complimentary soda from the refrigerator.

The three guest rooms in the Coupe-Gillespie House are up a wide staircase. We stayed in Audrey's Room, a pretty white room with wisteria stenciled about the border. This room has wonder-

ful views of Penn Cove and Mount Baker, a queen-sized bed with a delicious down comforter and lots of pillows and a beautiful antique armoire. The huge closet has fluffy robes for trips across the hall to the shared bath.

The other two rooms were occupied during our visit, but we know that Miriam's room, which shares the bath with Audrey's Room, offers the best views of Mount Baker and Penn Cove in the house. This room also has a queen-sized bed, down comforter and is furnished with antiques.

Carol's Room is furnished much the same, with a queen-sized bed and antiques, has great views of the Cove and Mount Baker, and has a private bath with a shower.

Next door at the Kineth House, all guests are invited to tea on the sun-porch in the late afternoon The glassed-in, light peach porch is cozy almost year-round, with spectacular views out to the water. Cushioned wicker and cane furniture is grouped around a glass-topped table, upon which a bountiful spread of treats is offered. The table seats six for tea, and four for breakfast.

The sun-porch opens into the dining room, a large room with two tables seating four apiece. Wide pine floors, an antique sideboard, lace curtains in the tall windows and a fireplace at one end make the room warmly elegant.

The formal parlor at the Kineth House opens from the dining room and has a second fireplace and the same tall lace-curtained windows. Unique heirlooms abound, including an organ, antique china hutch, and working symphonium, which Mitch is happy to show guests how to use. Large armchairs are arranged about the room around a cream oriental rug atop the pine floors.

The guest rooms upstairs are larger than those next door, with fireplaces and private baths in each. Desiree's Room is the grandest of the three, with a king-sized bed and a sitting room adjoining the spacious bedroom. Victorian-era antiques furnish the suite, which offers a lovely view of the Puget Sound and the mountains. The private bath boasts a Jacuzzi tub for two in addition to the shower.

Elizabeth's Room has a pretty sitting area in front of a large bay window, with views of Mount Baker and the water. A queen-sized bed sits next to an antique armoire with built-in mirrors in the bedroom, while the bathroom has a unique double-pedestal sink (rescued from a turn-of-the-century hotel in Seattle) and a large clawfoot tub and shower.

Amanda's Room also has a sitting area, this one furnished with embroidered armchairs in front of the fireplace. The queen-sized bed has a handsome headboard and down comforter; other antiques grace the room. In the bathroom one can soak in the antique soaking tub.

Guests from both houses gather in the dining room at the Kineth House for breakfast. Mitch and Gladys both bustle about seating guests and bringing out juice and coffee. We had a fabulous Nantucket cranberry pie and plate of sliced cantaloupe to start our meal the morning we visited. Our main dish consisted of low-fat turkey sausage served with a tasty apple French toast concoction. Mitch cranked up the symphonium during our meal, the sound of which added a nostalgic authenticity to the surroundings.

The Inn at Penn Cove offers a variety of accommodations to suit a casual weekend trip or a more luxurious excursion. We liked the easygoing feel of the Coupe-Gillespie House, but also enjoyed the regal air of the Kineth House. Whichever you choose, you're sure to enjoy the Howards' enthusiastic hospitality and the wonderful riding opportunities that await you on Whidbey Island.

BIKING FROM THE INN AT PENN COVE

Terrain

Central Whidbey Island has a wide variety of hills, wooded areas, wetlands and farms. Penn Cove is bordered by manzanitas, while Ebey's Landing looks out over Admiralty Inlet.

Road Conditions
Most roads are in good condition and well maintained.

Traffic
With the exception of Highways 20 and 525, which have good shoulders, most of the area's roads have little traffic. The Keystone ferry landing at the end of Fort Casey Rd. can be busy when the boats come in or leave.

Nearest Bike Shop
All Island Bicycles
302 N. Main
Coupeville, WA 98239
(360) 678-3351

Best Time to Ride
Almost year round riding possible, with the winters being fairly wet and cool. Early spring through late fall is best.

Mountain Biking Opportunities
There are no real designated off-road areas.

FORT CASEY LOOP (19.7 miles)
Ebey's Landing National Historic Reserve is a place of interest as a rural community with a long history. Central Whidbey Island has been inhabited for many hundreds of years, first by the Salish tribes and now preserved as it evolved into prairies, farms and wooded hillsides. Fort Casey was part of the same defense triangle as Fort Worden and Fort Flagler, all built in the late 1890s. Pick up the brochure, "Ebey's Landing: A Driving and Bicycling Tour" for more highlights of the area.

PENN COVE RIDE (22.3 miles)
Fort Ebey was built in 1942 near Lake Pondilla (the lake is a remnant of the Vashon Glacier) and is a nice spot for a picnic and views of Admiralty Inlet. To explore the bunkers you need a flashlight. An optional ride is to continue on Sherman before taking a left on Cook to the trailhead leading out to Perego's Lake for a short hike.

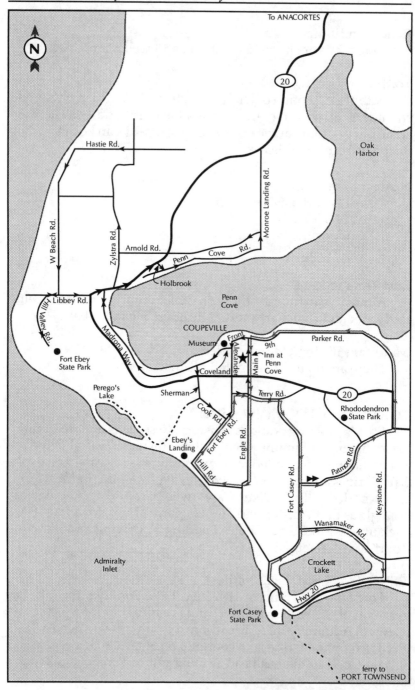

Fort Casey Loop ———   Penn Cove Ride ———

Fort Casey Loop (Road)

Pt.-Pt.	Cum.	Dir.	Street/Landmark
			From Inn at Penn Cove
0.0	0.0	R	**Main Ave.** (south)
0.4	0.4	X	Highway 20
0.4	0.8	X	SW Terry St. (Main changes to **Engle Rd.**)
1.4	2.2	R	**Hill Rd.**
1.2	3.4	CR	**Fort Ebey Rd.** (Ebey's Landing)
1.3	4.7	R	**Terry Rd.**
0.3	5.0	X	Main St.
0.5	5.5	R	**Fort Casey Rd.**
2.2	7.7	L	**Wanamaker Rd.**
1.7	9.4	R	**Keystone Rd.**
0.3	9.7	R	**Highway 20** (wide shoulder)
2.1	11.8	–	Fort Casey State Park straight ahead
0.5	12.3	R	**Fort Casey Rd.**
1.5	13.8	R	**Patmore Rd.** (uphill)
1.4	15.2	–	Rhododendron Park to L
0.5	15.7	L-R	**Patmore Rd.**
0.1	15.8	L	**Highway 20**
0.6	16.4	R	**Parker Rd.** (rolling hills; turns into 9th)
3.2	19.6	L	**Main St.**
0.1	19.7	–	Inn at Penn Cove on R

Penn Cove Ride (Road)

Pt.-Pt.	Cum.	Dir.	Street/Landmark
			From Inn at Penn Cove
0.0	0.0	L	**Main Ave.** (north)
0.2	0.2	L	**Front St.**
0.1	0.3	L	**Alexander St.** (museum on R)
0.0	0.3	R	**Coveland**
0.1	0.4	CL	**Madrona Way** (town park on R)
0.1	0.5	X	NW Broadway St. (follows edge of Penn Cove; madrona trees)
3.1	3.6	R	**Highway 20**
0.9	4.5	R	**Holbrook Rd.**

0.1	4.6	L	**Penn Cove Rd.**
1.9	6.5	L	**Monroe Landing Rd.**
0.4	6.9	L	**Arnold Rd.**
1.6	8.5	X	Highway 20
0.7	9.2	R	**Zylstra Rd.**
2.0	11.2	L	**Hastie Lake Rd.**
1.0	12.2	L	**West Beach Rd.** (beach access and wayside on R)
2.3	14.5	R	**Libbey Rd.**
0.3	14.8	L	**Hill Valley Rd.**
0.6	15.4	–	Entrance Fort Ebey State Park (great views, picnic area, gun emplacements)
		TA	
0.9	16.3	R	**Libbey Rd.**
0.8	17.1	L	**Highway 20**
0.2	17.3	R	**Madrona Way**
2.5	19.8	R	**Sherman Rd.**
0.3	20.1	X	Highway 20
0.3	20.4	L	**Cook Rd.**
0.5	20.9	L	**Fort Ebey Rd.**
0.4	21.3	R	**Terry Rd.**
0.3	21.6	L	**Main St.**
0.3	21.9	X	Highway 20
0.4	22.3	–	Inn at Penn Cove on L

THE INN AT SWIFT'S BAY
Christopher Brandmeir and Robert Hermann
Route 2 #3402
Lopez Island, WA 98261
(360) 468-3636
Rates: $75-155

Throughout our travels this summer we kept hearing about the Inn at Swift's Bay. Guests and innkeepers alike continually suggested this inn as the epitome of a fine B&B experience. We took their word for it and have to concur: this is truly a remarkable spot, and these innkeepers have thought of absolutely everything.

The inn is tucked away on the northeast corner of the island, in a woodsy area just off Swift's Bay. Tall trees and natural landscaping surround the contemporary wood and brick home. Upon entering you are ushered through the front hall into the sunken living room to the right, where comfortable couches and a glass-topped coffee table are grouped in front of the long hearth with an inset woodstove. Exposed beam ceilings, light carpet and a large bay window reflect the open feel of the room. Shelves and tables about the room hold plenty of interesting reading material, while a large hutch offers tasteful souvenirs and gift items. This room is relaxed and commodious, a perfect spot to sip a glass of sherry in the evenings, or add to the ongoing mystery written by guests.

The dining room is part of the living room, up two steps at the far end of the room. Several small tables are arranged in front of the window to take advantage of the peek-a-boo water view through the trees. Delicate stenciled vines wind around the edge of the ceiling.

At the other end of the house are the three downstairs guest rooms. Each room is quietly decorated, with light gray wall-to-wall carpeting and refined watercolors or etchings on the walls. All the rooms at the inn have sumptuous down or lambswool comforters, fine linen sheets, fluffy robes for the trip to the hot tub, fresh flowers, walking sticks and scented potpourri in bowls throughout the rooms.

Room 1, a snug room with a view of the woods outside, has cream walls, a pretty floral rose and cream coverlet to match the curtains and a queen-sized bed. Two straight-back armchairs and

INN
AT
SWIFTS
B A Y

a dresser complete the furnishings. This room shares a bath across the hall.

Room 2 is a slightly larger room, with lithographs depicting English hunting scenes hung on forest-green walls and a view out over the lawn. Furnishings consist of a queen-sized bed covered in a green-and-cream comforter, beautiful dresser and mirror, a small desk and two chairs. This room shares the bath across the hall with Room 1.

The largest of the downstairs accommodations is Room 3. This room is an open two-level suite, with a sunny sitting area in the upper level furnished with a natural wicker couch and chairs. The lower level features a queen-sized bed with a brightly-colored spread and pillows in front of a cozy gas-log fireplace. Light streams in from a large picture window and French doors which open to the back patio. This airy room has a private bath with two sinks and a shower.

Back down the hall and to the left one enters the intimate den and library. An impressive video library offers over 100 films, which can be viewed in front of the fire while curled up on the couch or in one of the spacious armchairs. A CD player and selection of music is available, or you can try your hand at the piano. French doors lead out to the landscaped patio and trail to the secluded hot tub—guests are encouraged to use the sign-up sheet to schedule private tub time.

The French doors are also the way to the two upstairs accommodations, Rooms 4 and 5, each with a private staircase entrance and a small deck looking back over the woods and patio below. Room 4 is to the left, a long narrow suite with a sloping ceiling and lots of skylights. Cream walls are accented with a blue floral wallpaper border throughout the suite. In the front half of the suite a couch sits in front of the gas-log fireplace, across from a tall mirrored wardrobe. The other half of the room is devoted to a skylit queen-sized sleigh bed, two handsome antique chairs and a rocker. The private bath has a shower and another skylight.

We stayed in Room 5, the most deluxe of the available accommodations. Like Room 4, the room is long and narrow, with skylights. This suite is also divided into two rooms, a sitting area with gas-log fireplace and television/VCR, and the bedroom. The sitting area has light walls and carpet, two skylights, a maroon-and-green print couch in front of a low coffee table, and Victorian floral prints on the walls. A small writing desk and chair are located beneath one of the skylights.

The bedroom has deep raspberry-colored walls, with a paisley wallpaper border around the top edge. A huge skylight above the queen-sized bed affords a view of the tall cedars and pine outside. A big armchair and reading light are situated below a narrow lattice window at the far end of the room, adding to the cozy attic-room feeling. A matching dresser and huge mirrored armoire round out the tranquil decor. Black and white photos depicting island scenes decorate the walls in the bedroom and private bath, which has a double head shower and skylight.

Breakfast at the inn is famous for miles around. Specialties include Hazelnut waffles with local berries topped with créme fraiche and fresh crab cakes, which we were privileged enough to sample during our visit. We began our meal with dark roasted coffee and a delicious fruit blend concoction, served with homemade pear muffins. The delicate crab cakes were served with a poached egg and tangy lemon tarragon sauce lightly drizzled on top. An exotic assortment of artfully arranged sliced kiwi, pears and pomegranate seeds accompanied the crab cakes. In addition to Christopher and Robert's superb culinary skills, the occasional substitute innkeepers happen to be gourmet chefs, so you'll never be left hungry here! (There's no need to suffer with blasé fare at dinner, either: the nearby Bay Cafe is well-known throughout the islands for their exceptionally innovative cuisine.)

While the atmosphere at the Inn at Swift's Bay doesn't encourage one to do anything but lounge about and be thoroughly pampered, you won't want to miss some of the excellent riding opportunities on the island. You'll need to work off some of those fine meals, and besides, you need to *earn* that late-night hot tub under the stars!

BIKING FROM THE INN AT SWIFT'S BAY

Terrain
Most of the island is made up of gradual hills and open vistas, with periodic forests along the road.

Road Conditions
Most roads are in fair to good condition, with little to no shoulders.

Traffic
Pretty quiet on most roads with slightly more traffic on Center Rd. from the ferry landing to Mud Bay Rd.

Nearest Bike Shop
> Lopez Bicycle Works
> Fisherman Bay Rd.
> Route 2, Box 2700
> Lopez Island, WA 98261
> (360) 468-2847

Or   Cycle San Juans
> Rt. 1, Box 1744
> Lopez Island, WA 98261
> (360) 468-3251

Best Time to Ride
Winters are quiet on the island, cool, but not too cold. Late fall and early spring are wonderful.

Mountain Biking Opportunities
There are no designated areas.

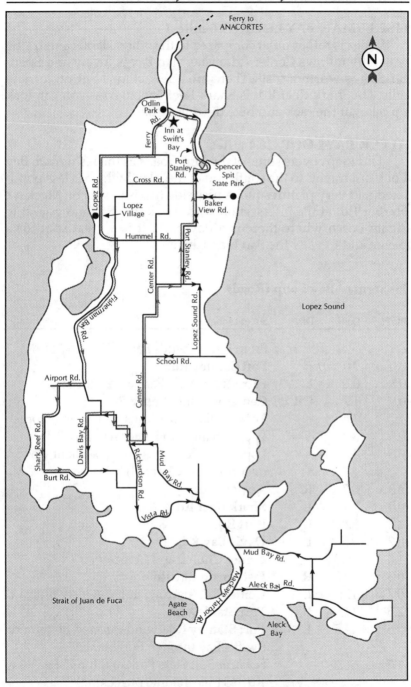

Fisherman Bay Loop ———   Aleck Bay Loop ———

FISHERMAN BAY LOOP (17.8 miles)

Lopez is rather quiet compared to the other islands and traffic generally follows Center Rd. Fisherman Bay is lovely and Spencer Spit is worth a visit. There are a few climbs but no terrible hills. On Shark Reef Rd. is Shark Reef Sanctuary—you can lock up bikes at the rack and hike the quiet trails.

ALECK BAY LOOP (28.4 miles)

This loop covers some of the same roads as the Fisherman Bay Loop but travels to the south end of the island which is less populated and very picturesque. A nice side trip is to stay on Mackaye Harbor Rd. at the intersection with Aleck Bay Rd. and go out to Agate Beach where there is a day park. It is a great spot for a picnic and to view the San Juan Channel.

Fisherman Bay Loop (Road)

Pt.-Pt.	Cum.	Dir.	Street/Landmark
			From Inn at Swift's Bay
0.0	0.0	L	**Port Stanley Rd.**
0.8	0.8	L	**Ferry Rd.** (Odlin Park across the street)
0.9	1.7	CR	**Center Rd.** onto **Lopez Rd.**
1.7	3.4	–	Lopez Village to R (museum, shops, store)
0.5	3.9	–	Lopez changes to **Fisherman Bay Rd.**
0.5	4.4	–	Lopez Bicycle Works on L (excellent views over San Juan Channel)
2.3	6.7	R	**Airport Rd.**
0.4	7.1	L	**Shark Reef Rd.**
1.7	8.8	L	**Burt Rd.**
0.7	9.5	L	**Davis Bay Rd.**
1.0	10.5	–	Center Church and Cemetery
0.3	10.8	R	**Fisherman Bay Rd.**
0.7	11.5	L	**Center Rd.** (narrow; traffic at ferry times)
2.5	14.0	R	**Port Stanley Rd.**
0.5	14.5	L	**Port Stanley Rd.** (winds around fields and Swift's Bay through Port Stanley)
1.7	16.2	–	Spencer Spit State Park to R (on Baker View Rd. 0.5 mile, hiking, picnicking)
1.6	17.8	–	Inn at Swift's Bay on L

Aleck Bay Loop (Road)

Pt.-Pt.	Cum.	Dir.	Street/Landmark
			From Inn at Swift's Bay
0.0	0.0	R	**Port Stanley Rd.**
1.6	1.6	L	**Baker View Rd.**
0.5	2.1	–	Spencer Spit State Park (hiking, picnicking)
		TA	
0.6	2.7	L	**Port Stanley Rd.**
1.7	4.4	L	**Lopez Sound Rd.**
1.4	5.8	CR	**School Rd.**
1.1	6.9	L	**Center Rd.**
1.0	7.9	R	**Fisherman Bay Rd.**
0.8	8.7	L	**Davis Bay Rd.**
1.2	9.9	CL	**Davis Bay Rd.**
1.1	11.0	R	**Richardson**
0.6	11.6	CL	**Vista Rd.**
1.3	12.9	R	**Mud Bay Rd.**
1.1	14.0	R	**Mackaye Harbor Rd.** (Bike Rest Stop behind fire station)
0.9	14.9	L	**Aleck Bay Rd.**
1.6	16.5	L	**Aleck Bay Rd.**
0.5	17.0	L	**Mud Bay Rd.** (unmarked; turn at yield sign)
1.2	18.2	–	Store on L
2.9	21.1	CR	**Center Rd.**
1.5	22.6	R	**School Rd.**
1.1	23.7	L	**Lopez Sound Rd.**
1.4	25.1	R	**Port Stanley Rd.**
3.3	28.4	–	Inn at Swift's Bay on R

OLYMPIC LIGHTS
Christian and Lea Andrade
4531-A Cattle Point Road
Friday Harbor, WA 98250
(360) 378-3186
Rates: $70-105

The sense of goodwill that resonates from this house and land has a long history. In 1900 the old Johnson Farm, today Olympic Lights, was the site of largest working farm in the chain of San Juan Islands. Wealthy farmer Johnson acted as a banker for other farmers throughout the islands, collecting I.O.U.s in exchange for cash. Shortly before his death, Johnson took all the notes he'd collected and ripped them up, canceling all debts and leaving his neighbors free and clear.

Maybe it's Johnson's kind spirit hanging around, or maybe it's the breathtaking view of the Olympics rising across the water, or maybe it's just the wildflowers in the windswept fields all around, but whatever it is, this inn has a wonderful light, peaceful feeling.

Almost 6 miles from Friday Harbor on San Juan Island, Olympic Lights is on the south end of the island, near the American Camp National Historic Park. The American Camp and the British Camp, its corresponding National Historic Park on the north end of the island, are holdovers from a fascinating piece of island history.

In the mid 1800s, when American territory borders were being negotiated between the British and the Americans, a dispute arose over the where the line had been drawn in the 49th parallel. British and American citizens set up residence on opposite ends of San Juan Island, waiting for a decision. In 1859 a pig from the British Camp wandered down to the American Camp and was promptly shot. The long-standing tension between the two camps erupted, leading to troops and warships being called in on both sides. Both sides held their ground for thirteen years, although neither side was anxious to go to war over a pig, and they actually invited each other to holiday events. In 1872 the islands were given to the Americans, thus ending the so-called Pig War. Today interpretive signs at both camps provide an interesting glimpse at this rather amusing bit of history.

Olympic Lights
a place of comfort and joy.

Olympic Lights is within walking distance of American Camp, surrounded by pretty gardens and wild meadows. A beautiful herb, vegetable and flower garden has paths through it and a couple of Adirondack chairs from which to sit and admire the panoramic mountain and water vista. Cats Pia, Perry, Pedra, Pepper and Pippin may join you for a stroll on the grounds. The 1895 farmhouse has been renovated to create a relaxing retreat; the chickens clucking in their coop outside and simple furnishings inside retain a hint of its farmhouse days.

Christian and Lea live next door, so guests have the run of the main house. An ample sitting room has two couches and a couple of chairs in front of the woodstove, shelves with books and puzzles to peruse, an antique china cabinet and lots of plants in the big bay window. You're welcome to help yourself to a glass of sherry beside the fire in the evening.

We stayed in the only downstairs room, the Garden Room, which looks out at the meadows behind the house. This is a large room with private bath, a king-sized bed covered in a goose down comforter, and an antique armoire. Pretty pastel colors and watercolors on the wall add to the tranquil feeling.

The four rooms upstairs each have queen-sized beds with goose down comforters and share two full sunny bathrooms. The North Star Room, up a couple of stairs, is a cozy room, the white walls, curtains and comforter adding a bright touch. An antique armoire and small floral prints complete the decor. Guests fall asleep at night listening to the large Oakselberry tree whispering outside.

The Heart Room is the largest of the upstairs rooms, with a single bed in addition to the queen-sized bed. Both beds are covered in pale rose comforters. The simple furnishings include a separate sitting area and table in front of the window.

In the southeast corner, the Ra Room enjoys brilliant morning sun from the large bay windows which look south over the wildflower meadows and east to the water. Two low chairs and a table sit in front of one window. White fabrics and simple artwork complement the natural light this room receives.

Our favorite room was the Olympic Room, with its stunning views down to the ocean and the Olympics beyond. A white spread on the bed further brightens the room, while comfortable chairs and a table in front of the window provide a place to contemplate the scenery.

Christian and Lea, as with most innkeepers on the islands, are flexible about breakfast times because of the ferry schedule. The morning we visited our fellow guests were trying to catch the first ferry, and since we were anxious to start on our ride, we joined them for an early breakfast. We began with juice, coffee, hot scones and bananas in yogurt. Our main dish was a delightfully light chili puff, made with fresh eggs from the inn's hens. Meals at Olympic Lights are always vegetarian, and the Andrades are happy to accommodate special dietary needs. Lea wrapped up the leftover scones for us, which we enjoyed for lunch later in the day.

The Outer Island Loop ride we did from here was our favorite ride of the summer. Give yourself the whole day, since you'll come across numerous places to stop and enjoy the view, check out a historic monument, or have a bite to eat. We were lucky enough to see a pod of Orcas breaching off shore; keep your eyes peeled around Lime Kiln Lighthouse! Whales or no whales, you're sure to fall in love with the riding and relaxation offered at Olympic Lights.

BIKING FROM OLYMPIC LIGHTS

Terrain

San Juan Island is rather open and dry, with sweeping vistas of the surrounding waters and the Olympic Mountains. Hills are rolling and easy. There's a large contrast in surroundings between the American Camp and the British Camp and you'll enjoy visits to both areas.

Road Conditions

Most roads on San Juan are paved and well maintained. The main thoroughfare is Roche Harbor Rd. and it's wide enough for riding with good visibility. False Bay Rd. is gravel, as is the driveway to Olympic Lights.

Traffic

Friday Harbor is typically busy in the summer months and one should use caution when riding through. Other roads have traffic but are wide enough for a fairly comfortable passing zone.

Nearest Bike Shop

Island Bicycles
P. O. Box 1609
360 Argyle
Friday Harbor, WA 98250
(360) 378-4941

Best Time to Ride

Year around riding here, with winters having the least traffic, but also the least amount of festivals and events. Weather is very moderate, with temperatures not ever too hot or cold.

Mountain Biking Opportunities

No designated areas but there are many gravel roads (like Cady Mountain Rd. or the road to Trout Lake) that are explorable.

INNER ISLAND LOOP (18.3 miles)

Riding the loop will give you a good perspective on the tranquil nature of this islands' farming community. When in season, the blackberries are delicious. The roads have generally less traffic in the center of the island and offer splendid views from its higher vantage point.

OUTER ISLAND LOOP (32.1 miles)

This is one of the finest rides in the book. Maybe it was the pod of Orcas we saw, or the ginger soda, or the brilliant sunshine, but frankly, this is an outstanding ride. There are many sidetrips to take and we'd suggest taking the whole day to make your way around. There is a lot to see. The American and British Camps alone take a few hours to explore. Enjoy.

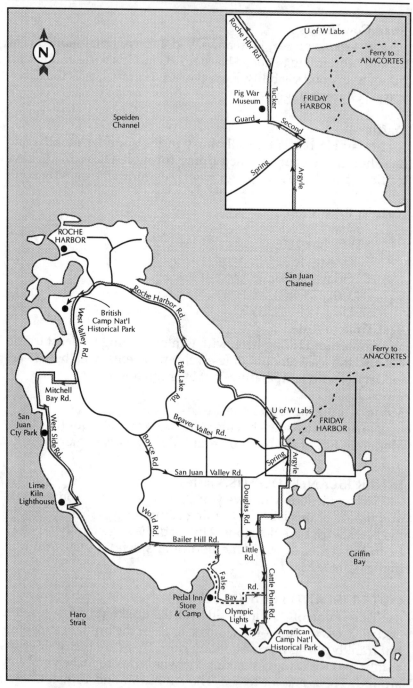

Inner Island Loop ——————   Outer Island Loop ——————

Inner Island Loop (Road)

Pt.-Pt.	Cum.	Dir.	Street/Landmark
			From Olympic Lights
0.0	0.0	–	Olympic Lights gate
0.3	0.3	L	**Cattle Point Rd.** (changes to **Argyle**)
4.9	5.2	R	**Spring St.**
0.1	5.3	X	Haines St./Blair Ave.
0.1	5.4	X	Intersection of Spring and Argyle
0.1	5.5	L	**Second St.**
0.2	5.7	–	Second changes to **Guard St.**
0.5	6.2	CR	**Beaverton Valley Rd.**
4.0	10.2	L	**Boyce Rd. N**
1.0	11.2	CL	**San Juan Valley Rd.**
1.3	12.5	–	Great views and blackberries on R
1.3	13.8	R	**Douglas Rd.**
1.5	15.3	L	**Little Rd.**
0.4	15.7	R	**Cattle Point Rd.**
2.3	18.0	R	**Olympic Lights driveway**
0.3	18.3	–	Olympic Lights

Outer Island Loop (Road)

Pt.-Pt.	Cum.	Dir.	Street/Landmark
			From Olympic Lights
0.0	0.0	–	Olympic Lights gate
0.3	0.3	L	**Cattle Point Rd.** (changes to **Argyle**)
4.9	5.2	R	**Spring St.**
0.1	5.3	X	Haines St./Blair Ave.
0.1	5.4	X	Argyle
0.1	5.5	L	**Second St.**
0.2	5.7	–	Second changes to **Guard St.**
0.1	5.8	R	**Tucker Ave.** (Pig War Museum on L)
0.4	6.2	CL	**Roche Harbor Rd.**
7.8	14.0	L	**West Valley Rd.** (to R is Roche Harbor—2.0 miles)
1.3	15.3	–	British Camp National Historic Park on R
1.6	16.9	R	**Mitchell Bay Rd.**

1.3	18.2	**CL**	**Mitchell Bay Rd.**
1.8	20.0	–	San Juan County Park on R (uphill)
2.4	22.4	–	Lime Kiln Lighthouse (Whale Watch Park over Deadman Bay)
2.6	25.0	**CL**	Mitchell changes to **Bailer Hill Rd.**
2.6	27.6	**R**	**False Bay Rd.** (gravel)
1.8	29.4	–	False Bay Rd. changes to **False Bay Drive**
0.8	30.2	–	Pedal Inn on R (bicycle campground, go in and talk to the owner, buy a ginger soda and see Loki the magic sheep-herding dog)
0.9	31.1	**R**	**Cattle Point Rd.**
0.7	31.8	**R**	**Olympic Lights driveway**
0.3	32.1	–	Olympic Lights

TURTLEBACK FARM INN
William and Susan Fletcher
Route 1 Box 650
Eastsound, WA 98245
(360) 376-4914
Rates: $70-150

We had no idea that some of the other San Juan Islands were actually almost flat, since we'd previously done all our bike touring on hilly Orcas. Having ridden the other islands now, we still find Orcas offers some of the greatest riding in the island chain. With its arduous climbs and rapid descents offering views of mountain lakes and madrona-lined bluffs, this island is not for the casual cyclist, but presents spectacularly rewarding vistas from every vantage point.

Turtleback Farm, once an 80-acre dairy farm, is located on the less-hilly western half of the horseshoe-shaped island. Here the terrain slopes more gradually, encompassing rolling meadows and bucolic farms in the shadow of Turtleback Mountain and Mount Constitution in the distance. The green and white clapboard inn sits on a small ridge overlooking a picturesque duck pond and meadows where sheep still graze. The Fletchers completed an impeccable renovation of the 100-year-old farmhouse and opened the inn in 1985; Turtleback Farm has since become known as one of the finest B&Bs in the Northwest.

Interesting heirlooms, including a turn-of-the-century rocking horse, an antique highchair, crystal doorknobs and light fixtures rescued from the remodeling of the Savoy Hotel in Seattle and pedestal sinks and beveled glass from the Empress Hotel in Victoria, grace the simple interior. Wide pine floors shine throughout the house, while ivory linen curtains on wooden dowels rustle in the breeze in each wide window. The living room centers around a large pine-mantled brick fireplace, in front of which sits a long couch and antique sea chest. Armchairs and a chess table (with a carved wooden seafarer chess set) provide other spots to gather for a game or a glass of sherry in the evening.

The dining room is part of the big country kitchen in the next room. Tables for two dot the cheerful room, which opens onto a wide deck where breakfast is served on sunny summer mornings. Indoors or out, tables are set with silver, bone china and nice linens, accompanied by small bouquets of flowers from the garden.

There are seven rooms to choose from at the inn, each with a private bath. Two of the four rooms on the first floor are located in the north wing of the house. The Nook is the smallest room, with a view of the gardens in front of the inn. The double bed is covered with a white spread, complementing creamy pink walls and a small throw rug. The private bath has a tub and hand-held shower.

Next door is the tranquil Valley View room, a spacious corner room nestled beneath an ancient elm outside and overlooking the farm below. Furnishings include a queen-sized bed with a white down comforter, a small writing desk and chair, a marble-topped nightstand, a rocking chair and white cushioned loveseat. Botanical flower prints accent the taupe walls, while dappled sunlight plays through French doors opening to a private deck. The private bath has a pull-chain toilet and clawfoot tub and shower.

Meadow View is in the south wing, an equally spacious corner room with a view of the rolling meadow outside. This sunny cream and tan room features a king-sized bed with a floral spread, a sofa bed, an antique armoire and an attractive straight-back armchair. Sun streams in French doors leading to a sunny private deck. The private bath has a wonderful clawfoot tub and shower.

Down the hall in the south wing is the Garden View room, with a delightful view of the English garden just outside the window. Ivory walls and a white floral print bedspread on the queen-sized bed coordinate with a nubby cotton throw rug and the small botanical print artwork. A cushioned rattan chair rests beside an antique dresser topped with fresh flowers.

There are three more guest rooms upstairs. We stayed in the Orchard View room, a corner room in the front of the house which looks out through floor-to-ceiling windows over the orchard and sheep pasture down below. Good reading lamps stand on either side of the queen-sized bed, while a dresser and armchair in the sunny corner round out the furnishings. Etched floral prints hang on the light tan walls.

Across the hall is the Maple View room, a sunny corner room on the meadow side of the house. Two large maples and a towering elm rustle outside the tall windows. A dainty floral border accents pale green walls, while a white coverlet covers the queen-sized bed. The room is furnished with a glass-topped nightstand, a comfortable armchair, a small desk and a pedestal sink. The private bath has a clawfoot tub and overhead shower.

The last room in the house, Elm View, is reached through the upstairs foyer, where an antique desk and chair sit amid old photos, woodcuts and prints. The Elm View's tall windows feature a view of the gigantic elm outside. The queen-sized bed is topped with a white comforter and pale blue pillows which complement the peaceful sea-foam walls. A small pastel-patterned loveseat, antique nightstand and dresser comprise the remaining furnishings.

Breakfast at Turtleback Farm is always a treat. Amid the pastoral surroundings out on the sunny deck we were first brought apple juice made from apples in the orchard and a pot of coffee. Soon fruit cups and a bowl of the inn's award-winning granola arrived, topped with yogurt and raisins. We completed our feast with a stack of banana pancakes drizzled with honey-butter. Resident canines Vicar and Spud, a French Briard and a Jack Russell Terrier, waited patiently for us to finish dining so they could join us for a walk down to the duck pond.

Turtleback Farm Inn provides a touch of luxury in a relaxed country setting. The Fletchers are helpful hosts with a wealth of knowledge about the island, including good ride suggestions and the latest information about the ever-changing road conditions. Toward the end of the summer, when you've had a chance to put some miles in, come enjoy the invigorating rides and indulgent accommodations at Turtleback Farm.

BIKING FROM TURTLEBACK FARM

Terrain

Orcas has the lions share of hills for the San Juan islands, but don't let that dissuade you from exploring its beauty. The woods are very much a part of this island, and most views of the water are caught in glimpses. The best view is from Mt. Constitution; it's a long climb but you can always take a dip in Cascade Lake when you get down!

Road Conditions

Roads are paved but can be rough in spots. All roads are narrow and winding, so keep aware of automobiles needing to pass. Dolphin Bay Rd. is gravel and was in the process of being partially paved in the summer of 1994.

Traffic

Traffic is generally low, with the exception of the ferry landing at Orcas and the town of Eastsound. Dolphin Bay and Doe Bay Roads have little traffic.

Nearest Bike Shop

Dolphin Bay Bicycle
(To the right of the ferry dock)
P. O. Box 1346
Eastsound, Orcas Island, WA 98245
(360) 376-4157

Best Time to Ride

Almost year round riding possible, with the winters being cooler. June through early October is best. Well into the summer is better for swimming in Cascade Lake, the cool water is invigorating! A note for your well being; near the ferry, let all the traffic that is loading or unloading do so. There's no hurry to try and ride in the flurry of cars, bikes and people. Let them pass by.

Mountain Biking Opportunities

There is no designated off-road riding. Most trails in Moran State Park are hiking only and are better suited for it anyway.

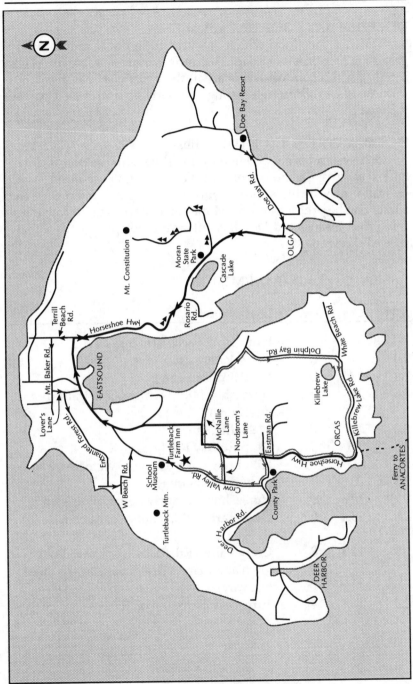

Doe Bay O & B ——————   Dolphin Bay Loop ~~~~~~~~

DOLPHIN BAY LOOP (16.7 miles)

This is a nice loop which has very little traffic and is partly gravel on Dolphin Bay Road. The route is more suitable for MTBs if only for the comfort. They are in the process of paving it, but for now it's a rolling trek through a relatively untraveled part of the island.

DOE BAY OUT & BACK (31.8 miles)

Orcas Island is shaped like a horseshoe with the points down and so all cross-island travel leads you through Eastsound. It can be quite busy in the summer and weekends but the rest of the island can be pretty tranquil. Moran State Park is good for swimming and hiking and Doe Bay offers the hotsprings for a truly splendid reward.

Dolphin Bay Loop (Road/MTB)

Pt.-Pt.	Cum.	Dir.	Street/Landmark
			From Turtleback Farm Inn
0.0	0.0	L	**Crow Valley Rd.**
1.4	1.4	L	**Nordstrom's Lane**
0.6	2.0	CL	**Horseshoe Highway** (caution–traffic both directions)
0.8	2.8	R	**McNallie Lane**
0.5	3.3	CR	**Dolphin Bay Rd.** (gravel)
5.0	8.3	CR	**Killebrew Lake Rd.** (not White Beach Rd.)
2.3	10.6	–	Dolphin Bikes on R
0.2	10.8	S	**Horseshoe Highway** (ferry landing on L)
2.6	13.4	L	**Deer Harbor Rd.** (county park on L down steps)
0.9	14.3	R	**Crow Valley Rd.** (deli on L; Deer Harbor town and marina straight ahead, 4.1 miles one way)
2.4	16.7	–	Turtleback Farm Inn on R

Doe Bay Out & Back (Road)

Pt.-Pt.	Cum.	Dir.	Street/Landmark
			From Turtleback Farm
0.0	0.0	R	**Crow Valley Rd.**
0.3	0.3	–	Crow Valley School Museum on L
0.9	1.2	X	West Beach Rd.
0.6	1.8	L	**Horseshoe Highway** (toward Eastsound)
1.2	3.0	R	**Horseshoe Highway** (into Eastsound)
1.2	4.2	R	**Horseshoe Highway** (long uphill ahead)
3.2	7.4	–	Enter Moran State Park
0.4	7.8	–	Moran State Park (restrooms on L; shores of Cascade Lake)
0.9	8.7	–	Road to top of Mt. Constitution on L (5 miles uphill; worth the climb on a clear day)
3.0	11.7	L	**Pt. Lawrence Rd./Doe Bay Rd.** (Café Olga on L)
3.3	15.0	R	**Doe Bay Resort** (views, hikes, café, hotspring tubs, kayaking)
		TA	
3.3	18.3	R	**Horseshoe Highway**
6.5	24.8	S	**Terrill Beach Rd.**
0.5	25.3	L	**Mt. Baker Rd.**
1.2	26.5	L	**Lover's Lane**
0.2	26.7	R	**Enchanted Forest Rd.**
2.6	29.3	L	**West Beach Rd.**
1.3	30.6	R	**Crow Valley Rd.**
1.2	31.8	–	Turtleback Farm on R

WESTERN WASHINGTON INNS AND RIDES

The inns we covered in this section span the largest geographical area in the book. Western Washington, technically everything west of the Cascades, is a fairly broad term; we used it mainly as a catchall for these last few areas we wanted to be sure you have a chance to experience! With the exception of Spokane, the largest cities in the state are concentrated along the north-south Interstate 5 corridor. Bellingham, La Conner and Olympia are all along this route, while Poulsbo sits to the west on the Kitsap Peninsula. Despite the growth adjacent to the corridor, each of the areas covered here afford excellent cycling opportunities.

Our first stop in Western Washington is the capital city of Olympia. One of the larger cities included in our guide, Olympia is a well laid out, manageable city with an abundance of good road riding within minutes of the **Harbinger Inn**. From the inn one can spin along the marina on East Bay Drive, enjoying sights of the snow-capped Olympics off in the distance, out to the rolling hills and water views of the Boston Harbor area, and then back past small family farms and peaceful neighborhoods. For a change of pace, some of the most ideal mountain biking territory on the West Coast is just a twenty minute drive away in the Capital Forest. Boasting over 100 miles of single track, with hundreds more miles of logging roads, the forest is rapidly becoming a destination spot for mountain bikers from all over the West. Although the summer is the best time to ride as far as weather goes, the trails are shared by motorcyclists and equestrians from April to November. A winter ride may be a bit muddy, but you'll have the trails to yourself!

Jumping over to the Kitsap Peninsula you'll find rolling hills and farms. Poulsbo was settled in the 1880s by Scandinavian fisherman, and its heritage remains very much alive today. On one ride from the **Manor Farm Inn** you'll cycle through downtown and have a chance to check out authentic Norwegian bakeries, a busy waterfront park and the Poulsbohemian Cafe. Another ride will take you out of town into the rolling hills at the heart of the peninsula, and along the water to the historic town of Port Gamble, a true company town from the 1800s with several original Victorians in excellent repair.

La Conner is about as flat as it gets in the Northwest, allowing effortless rides of 40 miles and more. With exceptionally fertile soil, moderate rainfall and a temperate climate, orderly farms growing everything from broccoli to rutabagas stretch as far as the eye can see. The region is probably best known for the few weeks in spring when the tulip and daffodil farms draw visitors from all over the Northwest to see acre after acre of the sunny red and yellow blooms. If you come to see the spring display, you'll definitely want to be on a bicycle, since the traffic backs up for miles along the country lanes. Our rides from the **Rainbow Inn** will take you through the fields and out along the Padilla Bay Nature Trail to Samish Island, or into Mt. Vernon along the dry slough road.

Bellingham, an outdoorsy college town, is the last major stop before the Canadian border. Bellingham is just north of La Conner along Chuckanut Drive, an extremely narrow winding road which is popular with cyclists for the views, although the traffic makes it a hair-raising ride at best. **Schnauzer Crossing** is located in a tranquil suburban neighborhood, just a few pedal stokes away from the start of a long ride which winds along Lake Whatcom and out into the country. The area surrounding Bellingham is largely agrarian, with views of the North Cascades looming above the picturesque farmland which characterizes so much of Western Washington.

HARBINGER INN
Terrell and Marisa Williams
1136 East Bay Drive
Olympia, WA 98506
(360) 754-0389
Rates: $55-90

We've lived in Olympia for eight years, and even after traveling all over the Northwest, we think it offers some of the best cycling around. Low traffic roads, bucolic countryside, and views of both water and mountains make biking a pleasure here. The Harbinger Inn, located on a hill across the road from the water, is perfectly situated to take advantage of several great rides, as well as easy access to downtown Olympia and the beautiful capitol grounds.

Despite our resident status, we learned a little something new about Olympia's history during our stay at the Harbinger Inn. In the early 1900s, a stately Victorian home was built on the west side of the water. The builder's estranged brother, in a fit of one-up-man-ship, bought the property directly across the narrow tip of Puget Sound. In 1910 he proceeded to build the handsome asher block residence that is now the Harbinger Inn, complete with a large mirror at the end of the front hall, which perfectly reflected the front door of his brother's home! The Victorian across the water still stands, now home to the Seven Gables Inn, one of the fancier restaurants in Olympia.

The jealous brother certainly had good taste. Enormous white pillars and wide balconies grace the front of the house, while blond hardwood floors, high ceilings and tall narrow lace-covered windows inside convey distinguished grace. Despite numerous remodelings, innkeepers have kept the original wall stencils and used turn-of-the-century furnishings throughout the house, preserving the feel of the home's early days. Arts and Crafts-period stained glass, a remarkable mirror/hatstand/bench combination piece in the hall, and original light fixtures throughout the house contribute to the authentic feel.

Entering the house we crossed a wide porch with wicker furniture set out to take advantage of sunsets over the water. Once inside we were drawn to the magnificent library through oak pocket doors on the right. Deep green walls with tulip stencils at the ceiling, built in bookshelves filled with magazines and old

first edition classics, a Craftsman-era Morris couch, and wonderful black-and-white photos of Olympia in the 1900s invite one in to browse. Guests are welcome to sample one of the Washington wines Terry often sets out in the evening, watch a movie or listen to a CD.

Across the hall, the living room is brighter, with the same tall windows and high ceilings. Antique chairs and a velvet-covered loveseat border an oriental rug on the floor. The living room opens to the large dining room, dominated by the elegantly-set table for eight. Coffee and tea are set out on an antique sideboard, while a gas-log fireplace warms the room on chilly mornings.

Your choice of four rooms are all on the second floor. Seltzer and ice are set out on the large hall hutch, where binoculars, a hair dryer, and an iron and ironing board can also be found. Guests are encouraged to enjoy the spectacular views of the Sound and Olympic Mountains from the shared second floor verandah which opens from the hall. All but the Blue Heron Suite share baths, one upstairs and one down, both with white tile floors, a tub/shower combination and a pull-chain toilet. Each room features towels and robes for the trip down the hall.

The Coral Room is in the front corner, with excellent views, a king-size bed (which can be converted to two twins) and several lovely antiques. Dark wood headboards complement a handsome armoire which contains fluffy robes. Pale coral walls add a soft light to the large room.

The Blue Heron Suite, in the other front corner, has the best views in the house. With a small separate sitting room and private bath, it is also the largest. The double bed with a wrought iron bedstead is covered with a pretty lace coverlet, matching the delicate curtains in the windows. Sky blue walls soften dark wood floors, creating a cozy getaway.

Down the hall is the Victoria room, a small, quiet room in the back of the house with a bit of a bay view, within earshot of the artesian waterfall in the back of the house. White wicker furniture and a wrought iron bedstead on the queen bed brighten the small room, while white floral print wallpaper complements a lace coverlet and curtains. Guests staying in the Cloisonné room can also hear the waterfall, and they have the same side view of the Sound. This cream and yellow room is also smaller, but manages to fit a double bed with a dark wood bedstead, a rattan chair and footstool, and a wonderful antique vanity with three-quarter mirror into the room quite nicely.

Breakfast in the morning is generally a simple affair, although far more generous than the "continental breakfast" we had been led to expect. We enjoyed raspberries and slivered almonds in a delicious sauce, hot oatmeal, granola, scones and juice and coffee. Innkeeper Marisa entertained us with stories of the house's past while we ate, and then took us on a tour of the basement afterwards. It seems the basement doubled as a sheep barn in the early days, and the artesian spring which cascades behind the house still bubbles into a cement trough along one wall. A wood door on the other wall opens to a narrow tunnel which travels under the house and out to the road below; in 1910 the road was a pasture and the sheep could be let out to graze at the water's edge without leaving the house. Today the tunnel just serves as a fine passageway for wheeling your bikes out for a ride!

BIKING FROM HARBINGER INN

Terrain

Gradual hills and wide open flats characterize most of the riding around Olympia. South of Olympia are flat farmlands, while the finger peninsulas to the north are treed and hilly, offering some beautiful glimpses of the Olympics and Cascades.

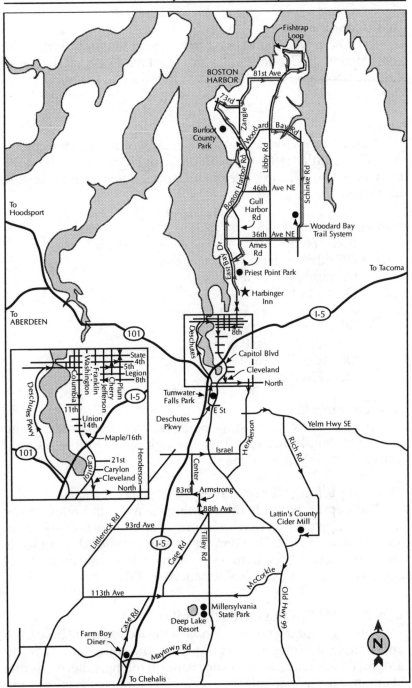

Fishtrap Loop

BOSTON HARBOR

81st Ave

73rd

Burfoot County Park

Zangle

Woodard Bay Rd

Libby Rd

Schinke Rd

Boston Harbor Rd

46th Ave NE

Gull Harbor Rd

Woodard Bay Trail System

36th Ave NE

Ames Rd

East Bay Dr

Priest Point Park

To Tacoma

★ Harbinger Inn

To Hoodsport

To ABERDEEN

101

Deschutes

8th

Capitol Blvd

Cleveland

North

I-5

Tumwater Falls Park

E St

Deschutes Pkwy

Yelm Hwy SE

Israel

Henderson

Rich Rd

Inset map:

Deschutes Pkwy

101

Columbia

Washington
Franklin
Jefferson
Cherry
Plum

State
4th
5th
Legion
8th

I-5

11th

Union
14th

Maple/16th

21st
Carylon
Cleveland
North

Capitol

Henderson

Center

Armstrong

83rd

88th Ave

Lattin's County Cider Mill

Littlerock Rd

93rd Ave

I-5

Case Rd

Tilley Rd

McCorkle

Old Hwy 99

113th Ave

Case Rd

Millersylvania State Park

Deep Lake Resort

Farm Boy Diner

Maytown Rd

To Chehalis

N

Boston Harbor Loop ‒‒‒‒‒‒ **South County Loop** ‒‒‒‒‒‒

Road Conditions

Roads are well maintained throughout the area, with some construction on Capitol Boulevard. Most roadways on the South County Loop are narrow, two-lane affairs, with little or no shoulders, but quiet.

Traffic

Traffic in the city can be rather crazy, but most of the county roads have little traffic to speak of. Yelm Highway can be quite busy at times, as is any stretch of Capitol Boulevard the further north you go.

Nearest Bike Shop

    Bike Stand
    407 4th Ave. East
    Olympia, WA 98506
    (360) 943-1997

Or   Bike Tech
    1931 4th Ave. East
    Olympia, WA 98501
    (360) 754-2453

Best Time to Ride

Almost year round riding possible, with the winters being fairly wet, cloudy and cool. June through early October is best if you enjoy riding in sunshine.

Mountain Biking Opportunities

The Capitol Forest is fifteen minutes away and offers many miles of singletrack-get a map from the local shops before you go. Most trails are marked but don't overestimate your abilities—this area is demanding and hard on equipment. If you are on the trails and have questions, the D.N.R. Mountain Bike Patrol can help.

BOSTON HARBOR LOOP (22.4 miles)

This is one of the favorite loops of the local Capital Bike Club and a great morning or evening ride. The route takes you up around Dickerson Point on some beautiful rolling, quiet roads that alternate between canopies of trees and wide open views of mountains. Woodard Bay Rd. crosses the bay of the same name and displays one of the fascinating natural marine environments of the South Sound.

SOUTH COUNTY LOOP (33.1 miles)

This route shows off the diversity of the South Sound region. Starting at the end of Budd Inlet the ride goes south through the farms and woodlands that make up this area. Make sure to explore Millersylvania State Park, grab a snack at Deep Lake Resort, or lunch at the Farm Boy and see Tumwater Falls on the way back into town. There's a little bit of everything on this route.

Boston Harbor Loop (Road)

Pt.-Pt.	Cum.	Dir.	Street/Landmark
			From Harbinger Inn
0.0	0.0	R	**East Bay Dr.** (Bike lane)
1.0	1.0	–	South entrance to Priest Point Park
0.6	1.6	CL	**East Bay changes to Boston Harbor Rd.**
1.9	3.5	–	Gull Harbor Store to R
1.0	4.5	–	Views of Olympics at Woodard Bay Rd.
0.3	4.8	–	Climb to Zangle
1.1	5.9	–	Burfoot County Park on L
0.3	6.2	CR	**Boston Harbor Rd.**
0.2	6.4	R	**73rd Ave NE** (steep climb-L at 73rd goes to marina/store)
0.8	7.2	L	**Zangle** (at N. Olympia Fire Station 2)
0.3	7.5	CR	**Zangle** (no shoulder)
0.2	7.7	CL	**Zangle**
0.5	8.2	R	**81st Ave NE** (rolling up and down)
1.1	9.3	L	**Libby Rd.**
0.3	9.6	CR	**Libby Rd.** (narrow, winding, no shoulder)
1.2	10.8	L	**Fishtrap Loop NE**
0.9	11.7	L	**Fishtrap Loop NE**
0.8	12.5	R	**Libby Rd.**
1.9	14.4	L	**Woodard Bay Rd.**
0.8	15.2	CL	**Woodard Bay Rd.** (over bridge)
0.3	15.5	CR	**Schinke Rd.**
2.5	18.0	–	Woodard Bay Trail system on R

0.2	18.2	R	**36th Ave NE**
2.0	20.2	L	**Gull Harbor Rd.**
0.6	20.8	R	**Ames**
0.3	21.1	L	**East Bay Dr.**
0.2	21.3	–	North entrance to Priest Point Park (picnics, trails, views)
1.1	22.4	–	Harbinger Inn on L

South County Loop (Road)

Pt.-Pt.	Cum.	Dir.	Street/Landmark
			From Harbinger Inn
0.0	0.0	L	**East Bay Dr.**
0.6	0.6	X	State Ave.
0.1	0.7	X	4th Ave.
0.1	0.8	X	Legion Way
0.1	0.9	R	**8th**
0.1	1.0	X	Jefferson
0.2	1.2	X	Franklin
0.1	1.3	L	**Capitol Blvd.**
0.1	1.4	X	Union
0.1	1.5	X	11th (Washington State Capitol on R)
0.2	1.7	X	14th Ave.
0.1	1.8	S	Pass Maple/16th
0.3	2.1	X	21st
0.7	2.8	S	Pass Carlyon
0.2	3.0	L	**Cleveland** (from far L lane of Capitol Blvd.)
0.1	3.1	L	**North** (narrow, busy)
0.9	4.0	R	**Henderson** (good shoulder)
1.0	5.0	L	**Yelm Hwy. SE** (bike lane)
0.7	5.7	X	Boulevard Rd.
0.5	6.2	R	**Rich Rd.**
0.8	7.0	CL	**Rich Rd.** (no shoulder)
3.5	10.5	–	Lattin's County Cider Mill on L (juice up!)
0.7	11.2	L	**Old Hwy 99**
0.9	12.1	R	**McCorkle** (narrow, hilly)
1.4	13.5	CR	**113th Ave.**
1.2	14.7	L	**Tilley Rd.**

1.0	15.7	–	Millersylvania State Park on R
0.1	15.8	–	Deep Lake Resort on R (store, cafe)
0.7	16.5	R	**Maytown Rd.** (after railroad tracks)
2.6	19.1	R	**At stop sign (Maytown Rd.)**
0.1	19.2	–	Farm Boy Restaurant on R (local hangout)
0.1	19.3	R	**Case Rd.** (views of Black Hills & Olympics)
2.0	21.3	R	**113th Ave.** (over I-5)
0.2	21.5	L	**Case Rd.** (Scott Lake Grocery on R)
2.4	23.9	X	93rd Ave SW
0.6	24.5	L	88th (irregular intersection with Tilley Rd.)
0.3	24.8	R	**Armstrong Rd. SW**
0.5	25.3	CL	**83rd Ave. SW**
0.2	25.5	R	**Center St.**
0.9	26.4	X	Linderson/Airdustrial Way
0.4	26.8	R	**W. Israel Rd.**
0.5	27.3	L	**Capitol Blvd.**
0.2	27.5	X	E. Dennis St.
0.6	28.1	X	Lee St.
0.2	28.3	X	Trosper Rd.
0.5	28.8	S	Pass Linwood Ave.
0.3	29.1	L	**E Street**
0.1	29.2	CR	**Deschutes Pkwy.** (follow to 5th St.)
0.1	29.3	–	Tumwater Falls Park on R
0.1	29.4	X	Boston (Olympia Brewery to R)
2.2	31.6	CR	**5th St.**
0.2	31.8	X	Simmons St SE
0.1	31.9	X	Water St.
0.0	31.9	X	Columbia
0.1	32.0	X	Capitol Blvd.
0.0	32.0	X	Washington
0.1	32.1	X	Franklin
0.2	32.3	L	**Cherry**
0.1	32.4	R	**4th Ave.** (get in far L lane for next turn)
0.1	32.5	L	**Plum St.**
0.1	32.6	X	State St.
0.5	33.1	–	Harbinger Inn on R

THE MANOR FARM INN
Jill Hughes
26069 Big Valley Road NE
Poulsbo, WA 98370
360-779-4628
Rates: $95-190 per night, double occupancy

You'd never know you're just an hour from Seattle at The Manor Farm Inn. The tidy farm sits on a sprawling 25 acres in a wide valley bordered by trees, and the pace is anything but hurried. It isn't much of a stretch of imagination to picture the farm the way it was in 1890; Coopworth sheep graze in the pasture, cows, pigs and horses look up with interest as you stroll the grounds, and chickens cluck from the coop. Feel free to wander through the large herb garden, or grab a fishing rod from the porch and try to catch a trout in the pond out back.

The inn consists of an old farmhouse with two wings added to form a courtyard, where flowers bloom all summer. You'll enter through a wall covered in ancient climbing roses, and follow the covered walkway to the entrance.

The inn is run by a large, friendly and exceedingly capable staff, who will be happy to show you around the place, offer you a sample of whatever is baking in the enormous kitchen and help you to your room.

There are seven rooms, all with private baths, to choose from at Manor Farm: the Cow, Stable, Tack, Carriage, Pig and Sheep rooms are on the lower level in the two new wings, each with a private entrance. The Loft Room is upstairs in the main house, reached by a staircase near the kitchen. All the rooms are decorated simply, with pine antiques and king-sized beds covered with eiderdown comforters.

The Cow, Pig and Sheep rooms all look out over the pasture to one side, and through the courtyard to the barn on the other. The Cow Room has a lofted ceiling with exposed beams. The Pig and Sheep rooms were our favorites, with big wing chairs in front of wood burning fireplaces. The Pig Room is light and bright with a private deck, while the Sheep Room is spacious yet cozy.

The larger Stable and Tack rooms are located in the west wing. Both have private garden areas overlooking the barn, king-sized beds, and lofted ceilings with exposed beams. Each room also has a sitting area with table and chairs.

The Carriage Room is one of the largest rooms, open and airy with a slight Japanese feel. One wall is formed by huge wooden carriage doors, original to the house. Big overstuffed armchairs look out the picture window to the pasture.

We stayed in the Loft Room, a roomy suite with a view down to the courtyard or out to the sheep meadow and barn. Sliding French doors separate the bedroom from a cheerful sitting area with couch and highback armchair.

In the afternoons, enjoy a cup of tea and an assortment of cookies in the west wing drawing room. High ceilings and French doors, groupings of mauve chairs and couches, framed photos of life at the farm, views out to the barn and pastures, and music playing softly in the background create a peaceful ambiance.

For an additional charge, the Inn serves a spectacular 4-course dinner in the evenings. You'll begin in the drawing room, sipping a glass of sherry in front of the fire and listening to the wine steward describe the meal and help you select your wine. You'll then amble through the courtyard to be seated in the dining room.

The dining room is simple and elegant, with country pine furniture, white cloths on the tables, French doors leading out to the patio, and quiet classical music playing. You have a choice of three seasonal entrées with your meal; during our visit we had the Sturgeon in Champagne Sauce and Farm-Raised Roast Venison with Juniper, Red Wine, Thyme and Roasted Garlic. Save room for one of the mouth-watering desserts!

In the morning, sip fresh-squeezed juice and munch hot scones before wandering to the dining room for a three-course breakfast at 9 a.m.. During our visit we had a grapefruit with blueberries, hot porridge in cream, a farm egg with bacon and sausage, and an apple crepe. You'll have some riding to do after this meal. . .

BIKING FROM THE MANOR FARM INN

Terrain
The Kitsap Peninsula, which separates Hood Canal from the Puget Sound, is a relatively flat piece of land with an occasional hill or two sprouting. Fields and farms are interspersed with stands of fir on the interior, while the populated areas border the water.

Road Conditions
Most roads are in good condition, though narrow. Some construction was taking place on Bond Rd. as it approaches Poulsbo as of fall 1994.

Traffic
Bond Rd. is the most intense of the thoroughfares, use it with caution. Port Gamble Rd. is very pleasant, especially around the town of Port Gamble. Within the city limits of Poulsbo traffic can be heavy. Shoulders are infrequent except on the main roads.

Nearest Bike Shop
Silverdale Cyclery
9242 Silverdale Way
Silverdale, WA 98383
(360) 692-5508
(20 minutes away)

Best Time to Ride
Almost year-round riding is possible, due to the maritime environment. June through late October will probably afford the warmest weather.

Mountain Biking Opportunities
Green Mountain on the central Kitsap Peninsula is the closest, just west of Bremerton, past Wildcat Lake.

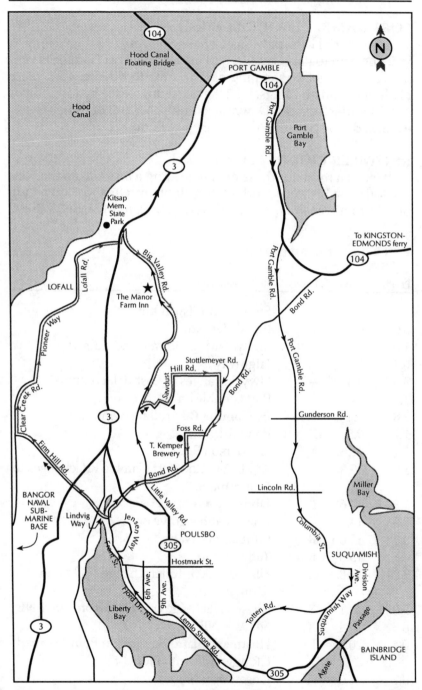

Rootbeer Ride ———— Port Gamble Loop ————

PORT GAMBLE LOOP (26.1 miles)

The central Kitsap Peninsula has some very pleasant riding as you go north to Port Gamble, and the town of Port Gamble is very interesting. It's like stepping back in time to ride between these old homes and buildings. Visit the museum, see the historic homes and Victorian seaport. Downtown Poulsbo is full of things to see, eat and do. Be careful on any stretch of Bond Rd.

ROOTBEER RIDE (16.4 miles)

Here's a route for those of you needing a break from the winery tours—a brewery tour! A good climb or two and then a mug of cold rootbeer should make your day. Be careful on Bond Road.

Port Gamble Loop (Road)

PtPt.	Cum.	Dir.	Street/Landmark
			From Manor Farm Inn
0.0	0.0	L	**Big Valley Rd.**
1.0	1.0	–	Molly Yard (good cafe and nursery)
0.4	1.4	R	**Highway 3**
3.0	4.4	–	Hwy 3 changes to East 104 (continue)
1.2	5.6	–	Port Gamble on L
2.8	8.4	R	**Pt. Gamble Rd.** (rolling, winding)
1.1	9.5	X	Bond Rd.
2.1	11.6	X	Gunderson Rd.
1.2	12.8	–	At Lincoln Rd., Port Gamble Rd. changes to **Columbia St.**
1.8	14.6	R	**Division Ave.**
0.3	14.9	–	Chief Sealth's grave on L
0.1	15.0	R	**Suquamish Way**
0.6	15.6	R	**Totten Road**
2.2	17.8	X	Highway 305–Totten changes to Lemlo Shore Rd.
2.3	20.1	X	9th Ave. NE–Lemlo changes to **Fjord Drive NE**
0.3	20.4	X	6th Ave. NE
0.4	20.8	L	**Hostmark St.** (to downtown Poulsbo–road CR downhill into Front St.)
0.2	21.0	X	Jensen Way NE
0.1	21.1	–	Poulsbohemian Coffee House on L

0.8	21.9	R	**Bond Rd.** (busy intersection, poor shoulder)
0.4	22.3	X	Highway 305
0.4	22.7	L	**Big Valley Road**
3.4	26.1	–	Manor Farm Inn on L

Rootbeer Ride (Road)

Pt.-Pt.	Cum.	Dir.	Street/Landmark
			From Manor Farm Inn
0.0	0.0	R	**Big Valley Rd.**
2.3	2.3	L	**Sawdust Hill Road** (steep uphill)
2.1	4.4	R	**Stottlemeyer Rd.**
0.6	5.0	R	**Bond Road** (good shoulder, moderate traffic)
0.5	5.5	R	**Foss Road**
0.3	5.8	–	Kemper Brewery on R (tours, tasting)
0.2	6.0	R	**Bond Road** (narrow shoulder, moderate to heavy traffic)
1.6	7.6	X	Highway 305
0.4	8.0	R	**Lindvig Way**
0.2	8.2	X	Viking Ave. NW (Lindvig changes to **Finn Hill Road**, gradual uphill)
0.5	8.7	–	Cross Highway 3 overpass
1.5	10.2	R	**Clear Creek Road** (no shoulder)
0.6	10.8	CR	**Pioneer Way**
2.4	13.2	L	**Lofall Road**
1.0	14.2	–	Manor Farm's Beach Cottage on L
0.5	14.7	L	**Highway 3**
0.2	14.9	–	Kitsap Memorial Park on L
0.1	15.0	R	**Big Valley Road**
1.4	16.4	–	Manor Farm Inn on R

RAINBOW INN
Ron Johnson and Sharon Briggs
1075 Chilberg Road
P.O. Box 15
La Conner, WA 98257
(360) 466-4578
Rates: $75-95

L a Conner is a perfect place to spend a spring bicycling weekend—besides the acres and acres of tulips in bloom, the flat country terrain is forgiving to even the most inactive winter cyclist. Miles go by effortlessly as you try to guess what is growing in each farmer's field: mustard, rutabaga, turnips, potatoes, wheat, peas, barley, carrots, broccoli and cucumbers are among the many crops grown in the fertile Skagit Valley. Just a few miles from the jump-off point for the San Juan Islands and in the shadow of snow-covered Mount Baker, La Conner offers cyclists quiet roads and wonderful views in every direction.

The Rainbow Inn is ideally located to explore both the quaint downtown area and the adjacent miles of farmland. Built for a prosperous dairy farmer at the turn of the century, the large three-story house was easily converted to a spacious, comfortable inn. The house has a somewhat "masculine" feel, with dark wood trim and solid lines throughout the house, but flowers and cheery curtains and fabrics add a softer touch. The large open living room downstairs features an enormous Swedish fireplace, which radiates heat for the first floor, and several overstuffed chairs and couches grouped comfortably about the sitting area. The formal dining room, just off the living room, has oak floors and a woodstove with a large brick hearth to warm chilly mornings. Rich red floral print wallpaper and china cabinets filled with colorful china further warm the room, where you can have a cup of tea and peruse the next morning's breakfast menu.

The only guest room downstairs is the Rose Room, so named for the early 1900s rose chandelier. The real treat in this room is the sunken Jacuzzi tub in the private bath, surrounded by wood and burgundy tiles.

The second floor hosts four more rooms: the Violet, Tulip, Daisy and Heather Rooms. Each has a private bath, though the Heather Room's bath (a huge room with an enormous clawfoot tub and a view of the Cascade foothills) is down the hall. The Heather Room

is done in soft rose-colored floral patterns, with a door to the shared second floor balcony and views of the fields and mountains in the distance. The Tulip Room also has a private bath and a door to the balcony, and looks out through a 100-year-old chestnut tree to the fields below. A pretty antique chest and mirror was converted to an in-room sink, tiled with pretty tulip tiles.

In the Daisy Room one can soak in the big blue tub while viewing the Cascades through the window. Cool blue carpet and trim throughout the good-sized room; a queen-sized bed and single daybed could accommodate an extra person.

We stayed in the Violet Room, a large front-corner room with an ornamental antique wood burning stove and door to the balcony. The spread on the queen-sized bed was white and covered in tiny green and purple violets, complementing a pale blue carpet and ceiling. We appreciated use of the desk and chair, placed in front of a window looking out through the chestnut tree.

Down the hall, past the bookcase overflowing with every possible book imaginable and lots of board games, is the staircase downstairs to the hot tub or up to the third floor. Upstairs you'll find three more rooms, which share the large bathroom—complete with clawfoot tub, skylights and clouds painted on the ceiling—in the hall. Done in deep blue tones, the Belle Room is quite large, with both a queen-size and a double bed, and looks east to Mount Baker and the Cascades.

The peaceful Sadie Room has peaked ceilings, a queen-sized bed and rocking chair, and stays cool in summer in the shade of the chestnut tree. The Ginger Room also has a rocking chair, and the added feature of a cozy window seat tucked in the south window, perfect for reading or contemplating tulips as far as the eye can see!

Before dropping off to sleep at night, don't overlook the hot tub in the back yard. The tub is elevated in a gazebo which feels very private, but offers great views in almost every direction while you are bubbling away.

In summer guests dine on the glassed-in porch, taking advantage of the sunny mornings at small French cafe tables, where you are served by Ron and Sharon. These enthusiastic hosts are also excellent cooks: our cantaloupe and kiwi plate was accompanied by zucchini bread with a unique jalepeño pepper jelly. Our main course was a delicious green chili fritata, smothered in peppers fresh avocado. We sipped coffee and juice and chatted with other cycling guests as we finished up our meal.

Innkeepers Sharon and Ron are knowledgeable about the area and particularly good at scouting out good bike routes—they were armed with several photocopied bike maps which they handed out to guests. Ron also has his captain's license and a small sailboat, and is organizing sails in the Anacortes area during the summer. They clearly enjoy innkeeping, are filled with ideas for expanding and improving their business, and convey their love of the area to their guests. If the surroundings and the cycling aren't enough to ensure a wonderful weekend, Sharon and Ron's enthusiasm will clinch the deal!

BIKING FROM THE RAINBOW INN

Terrain

Flat. Not many other words could describe the majority of the land here. Small roads meander around tulip and dahlia farms, while the Skagit River and its forks wind their way to Puget Sound which frames the western edge of the Skagit Valley.

Road Conditions

Most roads are two-lanes and very narrow, some concrete, like Calhoun Rd., others asphalt. Occasionally some of the farm roads will be gravel for a short distance.

Traffic

Very little except during the spring tulip blossoming season when it is bumper to bumper cars around La Conner. Highway 20 is busy due to being the link from I-5 to the San Juan ferries in Anacortes. Be careful when crossing the Division St. bridge out of Mt. Vernon. Watch for tractors and dogs.

Nearest Bike Shop

> Cascade Sports
> 509 S. 1st St.
> Mount Vernon, WA 58257
> (360) 336-6641

Best Time to Ride

Mid-March through May shows the color of the valley during tulip season, but also more traffic. Midsummer there are different flowers in bloom in the fields; while fall has ideal temperatures and less people.

Mountain Biking Opportunities

Not much, as it is mainly an agricultural area. The Padilla Bay Trail is smooth enough for both road and mountain bikes. Closest off-road area is the Walker Valley-Cavenaugh Trail out of Mt. Vernon.

PADILLA BAY RIDE (36.1 miles)

This is a very pleasant ride along Padilla Bay and is a distinct change from the farmland that surrounds it. The Padilla Bay Shore Trail is also used by pedestrians, so ride with them in mind. Highway 237 is narrow but flat and fast.

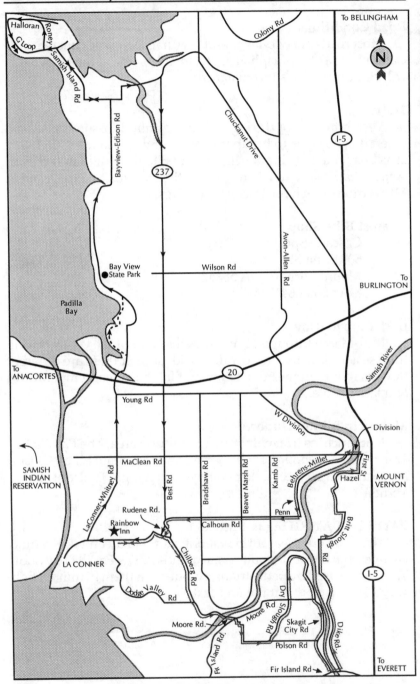

Skagit Loop ——— Padilla Bay Ride ———

SKAGIT LOOP (28.7 miles)

This ride is a good taste of the Skagit Valley and all the flower fields which have made it popular. Needless to say, when the tulips are in bloom it is gorgeous, but also clogged with cars full of people wanting to get that awesome photo. The bike is your only way through.

Padilla Bay Ride (Road)

Pt.-Pt.	Cum.	Dir.	Street/Landmark
			From Rainbow Inn
0.0	0.0	R	**Chilberg Road**
0.7	0.7	R	**La Conner-Whitney Road**
4.1	4.8	X	Highway 20 (La Conner-Whitney changes to **Bayview-Edison Rd.**)
0.9	5.7	L	**Onto Padilla Bay Shore Trail** (packed gravel, no cars! Watch for pedestrians)
2.3	8.0	L	**Bayview-Edison Road** (end of trail)
0.6	8.6	–	Bayview State Park entrance
0.5	9.1	–	Breazeale-Padilla Bay Interpretive Center on R
4.1	13.2	L	**Samish Island Road**
2.3	15.5	CL	**Samish Island Rd.**
0.4	15.9	R	**Roney Road**
0.5	16.4	L	**Halloran Road**
0.2	16.6	–	County park on L (restrooms)
0.8	17.4	L	**G Loop** (becomes **Samish Island Rd.**)
4.0	21.4	X	Bayview-Edison Road (continue on Samish Island Road)
1.3	22.7	X	Samish River
0.3	23.0	R	**Highway 237** (no shoulder, watch for traffic)
7.9	30.9	X	Highway 20 (cross traffic does not stop!)
1.8	32.7	X	McClean Road (cross traffic does not stop!)
1.8	34.5	R	**Rudene Road**
0.1	34.6	R	**Chilberg Road**
1.5	36.1	–	Rainbow Inn on R

Skagit Loop (Road)

PtPt.	Cum.	Dir.	Street/Landmark	Rainbow Inn
			From Rainbow Inn	
0.0	0.0	L	**Chilberg Road**	
4.3	4.3	L	**Moore** (watch curve for oncoming traffic)	
0.9	5.2	L	**Polson Road**	
1.4	6.6	L	**Dry Slough Road**	
1.3	7.9	X	Unmarked road–watch for dogs!	
3.8	11.7	–	Dry Slough changes to **Skagit City Road**	
1.2	12.9	L	**Fir Island Road**	
0.4	13.3	L	**Dike Road**	
3.9	17.2	R	**Britt Road**	
2.1	19.3	R	**Hazel W**	
0.1	19.4	R	**Hazel Street**	
0.3	19.7	L	**Cleveland**	
0.4	20.1	X	Kincaid (Cleveland changes to 1st)	
0.1	20.2	X	Gates	
0.2	20.4	L	**Division** (WARNING: horrible bridge crossing; walk bike across on pedestrian sidewalk)	
0.3	20.7	L	**South Baker**	
0.1	20.8	R	**Ball Street** (also known as Behren Millet Road)	
1.1	21.9	L	**Penn** (gravel road)	
2.0	23.9	X	Kamb Road (Penn changes to **Calhoun**; concrete surface)	
0.8	24.7	X	Beaver Marsh Road	
1.0	25.7	X	Bradshaw Road	
1.0	26.7	L	**Best Road**	
0.4	27.1	R	**Rudene Road**	
0.1	27.2	R	**Chilberg Road**	
1.5	28.7	–	Rainbow Inn on R	

SCHNAUZER CROSSING
Vermont and Donna McAllister
4421 Lakeway Drive
Bellingham, WA 98226
(360) 733-005 or (800) 562-2808
Rates: $110-180

Yes, there really are schnauzers here—in fact, Chuck and Bärbel are likely to greet you as you pull in the driveway of this luxurious B&B. Schnauzer Crossing is regarded by other innkeepers and guests alike as the epitome of the Bed & Breakfast experience in a tasteful and relaxing environment. The grounds are lovely, with winding paths and Japanese wood screens throughout the property. A hot tub, centrally located, is surrounded by tall cedars and looks through trees down to the lake. Monty and Donna McAllister have lived in this house for 22 years, and have been remodeling pretty much ever since, creating three special choices of accommodations.

The Master Suite and Queen Room are located in the McAllister's home, a contemporary, open house oriented to take advantage of spectacular views of Lake Whatcom just down the hill. The Queen Room is light, quiet and elegant, with a partial lake view. White carpet and walls with deep pink and blue accents complement a white goose down comforter and crisp deep blue sheets on the queen size bed. A large heron print adorns one wall. A beautiful glass-front bookcase is filled with good books, while the large walk-in closet holds more books, slippers and fluffy robes. A well-appointed private bath is just outside the door in the hall.

The Master Suite features a larger version of the same elegance. Pale orange carpet warms the airy rooms, which include a large fireplace with a pale wood mantle and brick hearth, a huge armoire, large armchairs in front of the fire, and a king-size bed with an iris floral pattern bedspread. Through a set of French doors one finds a sun porch sitting room, with a brightly-patterned futon couch, lots of plants and a door to the private garden outside, lush with ferns, azaleas and rhododendrons. The rooms have extra touches throughout, such as an ice bucket and glasses, a stereo, television, VCR, a desk and chair and small refrigerator. The luxurious private bathroom has skylights and a wood-framed Jacuzzi tub and double shower.

   While the Master Suite and Queen Room are certainly deluxe accommodations, we were royally spoiled in The Cottage. The Cottage sits tucked among tall cedars at the far end of the property, a short walk from the main house and hot tub, but very secluded feeling. Entering through a glass door to a hardwood entry with a sloped ceiling and enormous skylight, you see a spectacular view of the lake through the door to the deck. To the right, the room is divided by a low built-in shelf which contains a cozy gas log fireplace. On this side of the cottage there is a large couch with deep cushions, complete with matching footstools, under a huge window that looks down to the lake. The king-sized bed is opposite the sitting area, covered in a delightful rich blue, green and purple fish print bedspread with matching bolsters. A bamboo headboard echoes the glass-top table and cushioned bamboo chairs against the wall, adding to the Oriental feeling of the room. Western touches are plentiful but unobtrusive: a television, VCR and CD player with a wide variety of CDs are available should you tire of the view. To the left of the entry a small, well-appointed kitchenette offers a microwave, refrigerator, sink (with instant boiling water for tea), and the all-important bean grinder and coffee maker. Naturally, the Schnauzer's Crossing blend is plentiful. The bathroom is white and spotlessly clean; the Japanese feeling continues here, with wooden shelves to hold extra towels, and a sunken Jacuzzi tub.

Back in the main house, guests are invited to share the huge living room and dining room, which looks out over the meticulously landscaped yard down to Lake Whatcom. The main wall is almost entirely glass, allowing stunning views of water and sky. Skylights and glass doors on the other two sides complete the feeling of being outside, while the pretty couches and light rug bring a coziness to the room. Tables of games, baskets of brochures and beautiful flower arrangements dot the room.

The breakfast served in the morning will fuel even the longest ride. We enjoyed the company of two other cycling couples as we began with orange juice and coffee, accompanied by yogurt, granola and fresh blueberries served in tall parfait glasses. We sampled homemade muffins and a coffee cake before rounding out our meal with a delicious hearty spinach and artichoke heart fritata. We all felt so at home (and pleasantly full!) after breakfast we ended up sitting and chatting for almost two hours after breakfast, setting us all back in our riding schedules!

Donna and Monty are gracious hosts who cater to their guests. Donna made a trip to the Visitors Center in advance of our visit in order to provide us with maps, menus from local restaurants and bicycle-specific information for the area. Monty spent time with us in the afternoon showing us his favorite bike rides on a map, adding advice about road conditions, wind direction and mountain biking options. They've anticipated guests every possible need, and added some surprises besides (we had to promise we wouldn't give away all the details, but just a hint: check in the closet)!

BIKING FROM SCHNAUZER CROSSING

Terrain
The area around Bellingham is moderately hilly, with a large number of greenway corridors throughout the city.

Road Conditions
Main roads in Bellingham are in good condition, with secondary roads more narrow and winding. Some bike paths exist, connecting main roads with a no-traffic alternative.

Traffic

Bellingham is fairly bicycle-friendly, with some roads having marked bicycle routes. Downtown Bellingham can be somewhat busy, but Highway 9 and the Mount Baker Highway have good shoulders to follow.

Nearest Bike Shop

Kulshan Cycles
100 East Chestnut
Bellingham, WA 98225
(360) 733-6440

Best Time to Ride

Early spring through late fall have the best temperatures and parks (of which there are many) have their best showing.

Mountain Biking Opportunities

Galbraith Mountain area has a number of trails, but there are also a few greenways to follow including the popular Interurban Trail, the Lost Lake Trail and short trails in Whatcom Falls Park.

LAKE SAMISH LOOP (32.9 miles)

Just south of Bellingham, this loop has both town and country riding and access to the lake, so bring your swim suit. The roads around the lake are narrow, but the area is very scenic.

STEWART MTN. LOOP (43.5 miles)

This route circles Stewart Mountain to the northeast of Bellingham. It is amazing how remote this area feels, yet you are never too far from the city. Lake Whatcom Blvd. is narrow and winding, so be careful. Midway is Everybody's Store and Exotic Grocery—worth a look inside and a great rest stop.

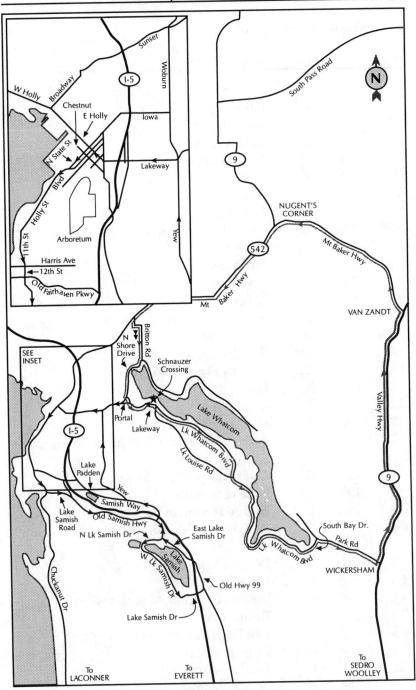

Lake Samish Loop ——— Stewart Mtn. Loop ———

Lake Samish Loop (Road)

Pt.-Pt.	Cum.	Dir.	Street/Landmark
			From Schnauzer Crossing
0.0	0.0	R	**Lakeway Dr.**
0.1	0.1	R	**Lakeway Dr.**
0.4	0.5	R	**Lakeway Dr.**
1.7	2.2	X	Yew (heavy traffic)
0.8	3.0	X	Lincoln
0.1	3.1	X	King
0.1	3.2	X	I-5 entrance
0.3	3.5	X	5 way intersection (Lakeway changes to **E. Holly**)
0.1	3.6	X	Indian St.
0.1	3.7	X	N Garden
0.1	3.8	X	N Forest St.
0.1	3.9	L	**N State** (one way)
0.0	3.9	X	E Chestnut
0.4	4.3	CR	**E Holly**
1.4	5.7	CL	**E Holly changes to 11th**
0.5	6.2	X	Harris Ave.
0.2	6.4	X	Donovan
0.2	6.6	CL	**Chuckanut Dr./11th**
1.1	7.7	CL	**Samish Lake Rd.** (yield to oncoming traffic; winding, hilly)
4.6	12.3	R	**Old Samish Highway**
0.8	13.1	CR	**N Lake Samish**
0.9	14.0	L	**Bridge at Samish Park**
0.1	14.1	L	**W Lake Samish Rd.** (view of lake; narrow shoulder)
0.9	15.0	CL	**W Lake Samish Rd.**
1.6	16.6	S	**Lake Samish Rd.**
1.4	18.0	–	View of Galbraith Mountain area
0.5	18.5	S	**Bridge over I-5**
0.9	19.4	L	**Old Highway 99** (rough shoulder)
2.4	21.8	–	Cross under I-5
0.1	21.9	R	**E Lake Samish Dr.**
2.5	24.4	R	**N Lake Samish**

0.9	25.3	**CR**	**Samish Way** (cross bridge over I-5; past Texaco on L)
2.6	27.9	**R**	**Yew St. Rd.** (no shoulder; great downhill)
2.8	30.7	**R**	**Lakeway Dr.**
1.7	32.4	**CL**	**Lakeway Dr.**
0.4	32.8	**L**	**Lakeway Dr.**
0.1	32.9	**L**	**Driveway to Schnauzer Crossing**
0.1	33.0	–	Schnauzer Crossing on L

Stewart Mtn. Loop (Road)

Pt.-Pt.	Cum.	Dir.	Street/Landmark
			From Schnauzer Crossing
0.0	0.0	**R**	**Driveway to Lakeway Dr.**
0.1	0.1	**L**	**Lakeway Dr.**
0.5	0.6	**L**	**Lake Whatcom Blvd.** (very narrow, winding along lakeshore, rolling hills)
4.5	5.1	**CL**	**Lake Whatcom Blvd.**
2.8	7.9	**CL**	**South Bay Drive**
3.7	11.6	**R**	**Park Road** (immediately after railroad tracks)
2.8	14.4	**L**	**Highway 9** (good shoulder, fast traffic; along wide valley bottom)
9.1	23.5	–	Enter town of Van Zandt (Everybody's Store on L at 23.7 miles)
2.3	25.8	**L**	**W 542/N 9/Mt. Baker Highway**
3.1	28.9	–	Mt. Baker Vineyards on R (tours and tasting)
1.5	30.4	–	Stay on Mt. Baker Highway/542 through Nugent's Corner (N 9 veers R. Cross Nooksack River on sidewalk, it's safer)
7.1	37.5	**L**	**Britton Road** (uphill)
1.9	39.4	**R**	**North Shore Drive**
0.7	40.1	**L**	**North Shore Drive** (North Shore Drive changes to Electric Ave.)
1.0	41.1	**L**	**Portal Drive**
0.1	41.2	**L**	**Lakeway Dr.**
0.9	42.1	**L**	**Lakeway Dr.**
1.3	43.4	**L**	**Driveway to Schnauzer Crossing**
0.1	43.5	–	Schnauzer Crossing on L

RECIPES

Surely one of the great joys of cycling is the ability to eat without counting calories. The recipes in this final chapter reflect the diversity of the inns we visited: some are hearty and comforting, while others are more complex and sophisticated. We hope these recipes will inspire you to visit more of the inns we've described, or perhaps remember a pleasant weekend by recreating the delicious breakfast!

The recipes that follow are in alphabetical order by the inn from which they originate.

Alexander's Country Inn
Applesauce Raisin Strudel

Yield: Four 9" by 9" pans

4 cups applesauce	4 cups granulated sugar
1 tsp. cinnamon	4 eggs
1/2 lb. melted butter or margarine	3/4 cup raisins
3/4 cup granola	6 cups flour
4 tsp. salt	4 tsp. baking soda

Topping

1 cup finely chopped pecans	1 cup brown sugar
1 tsp. cinnamon	

1. Preheat oven to 375°.
2. In a large bowl, combine applesauce, sugar and cinnamon. Mix well.
3. Add eggs and mix thoroughly, then add melted butter and mix again.
4. Add raisins and granola, mix well and let stand for 15 minutes to moisten.
5. Sift together flour, salt and baking soda, then add to the mixture above.
6. Combine topping ingredients and set aside.
7. Grease four 9" by 9" pans. Pour batter into first 1/3 of pans, then sprinkle with topping. Add another 1/3 of batter and sprinkle with topping.

8. Bake for 1 hour or until toothpick inserted in the center comes out clean.
9. Let cool for 10 minutes on a wire rack before serving.

❦ ❦ ❦

Annapurna Inn
Fabulous French Toast

Yield: 4 servings

4 slices whole wheat bread	1/4 lb. tofu
pinch of turmeric for color	salt and pepper to taste
1/4 cup soy, rice, cashew or millet milk	

1. Blend tofu, milk, salt, pepper and turmeric. Pour into shallow dish.
2. Dip bread into tofu/milk mixture.
3. Fry lightly in a skillet coated lightly with a half oil and half lecithin mixture until golden brown.
4. Serve with a warm fruit compote and real maple syrup.

Comments: This French toast is a toast to people who wish to eat a plant-based diet!

❦ ❦ ❦

Bombay House
Paradise Punch

Yield: 2 gallons of punch

46 oz. can pineapple juice, unsweetened
46 oz. can apricot nectar
12 oz. can lemonade concentrate, frozen
12 oz. can orange juice concentrate, frozen
12 oz. can cranberry concentrate, frozen
4 liters ginger ale

1. Mix the first five ingredients together in a gallon container. Refrigerate at least five hours.

2. When you are ready to serve, pour the punch base into a large 2-gallon punch bowl.
3. Add the ginger ale. Serve over ice.

Comments: If you want to serve this fruit punch as a breakfast drink, mix in club soda instead of ginger ale and omit the ice. For a wine punch substitute a white zinfandel, Johannesburg Riesling or a chenin blanc for the ginger ale. To avoid diluting, prepare ice cubes with some of the punch ingredients.

꿩 꿩 꿩

Boreas B&B
Mexican Quiche

Yield: 6 servings

3-4 small flour tortillas
1/2 medium onion, chopped
1/2 cup Monterey jack cheese
1 cup plain yogurt or sour cream
1/2 tsp. cumin
salt and pepper to taste

1/4 lb turkey sausage
1 can diced chilies, small
1/2 cup cheddar cheese
4 eggs
1/2 tsp. oregano

1. Sauté turkey sausage and onion in olive oil. When cooked, stir in green chilies.
2. In an 8" greased pie pan, layer tortillas to cover the bottom and leave scalloped edges around the sides of pan.
3. Mix together the 2 cheeses and spread half the mixture in on top of the tortillas.
4. Pour the turkey sausage mixture on top of the cheese.
5. In separate bowl, beat together the eggs, yogurt or sour cream, cumin, oregano, salt and pepper.
6. Pour the egg mixture over the turkey sausage and onion. Top with remaining cheese.
7. Bake at 350° for 35-45 minutes. Serve with salsa.

Campus Cottage
Southwest Baked Eggs

Yield: 1 baked egg (allow one egg per serving)

2 Tbs. canned black beans	1 tsp. butter
1 tsp. canned mild green chilies	1 egg
2-4 Tbs. grated cheddar cheese	1 Tbs. cream
Freshly ground pepper to taste	

1. Preheat oven to 400°.
2. Spray ramekins with non-stick cooking spray.
3. Put butter in the bottom of ramekin. Layer black beans and chilies on top.
4. Gently break the egg into the ramekin, being careful not to break the yolk.
5. Sprinkle generously with cheese, then pour cream around the edge of the egg and add a dash of pepper.
6. Bake 10-14 minutes until egg is firm. Serve with salsa and fresh corn muffins.

Comments: For a low-fat version, omit cream and butter and use low-fat cheese.

❧ ❧ ❧

Country Cottage B&B
Country Cottage Scones

Yield: 8 large scones

2 cups unbleached flour	4 tsp. baking powder
1 tsp. salt	1-2 Tbs. sugar
1/2 cup Scotch oatmeal	1/4 cup shortening
1 cup milk	3/4 cup Sultana raisins

1. Preheat oven to 450°.
2. Mix all dry ingredients together, then cut in shortening.
3. Form a well in the dry mixture and add milk and raisins.
4. Mix together, knead, and roll into a ball.

5. Flatten the ball into a 8-12" circle on a greased cast iron skillet. Cut into quarters, then eighths.
6. Bake until golden on top and firm to the touch.

Comments: Serve with butter, blackberry jam or aged cheddar cheese, either warm out of the oven or cooled.

🐞 🐞 🐞

Country Willows B&B
Baked Stuffed Peaches

Yield: 8 servings

8 macaroon cookies (choose crunchy, not chewy cookies)

3/4 stick unsalted butter	1 Tbs. sugar
1 tsp. cherry extract	1 egg yolk
6 Tbs. sliced almonds, toasted	8 firm, ripe peaches
3 Tbs. melted butter	

1. Preheat oven to 375°F.
2. Crunch macaroon cookies into very small pieces and set aside.
3. In a medium-size bowl, beat softened butter and sugar until light and velvety.
4. Add egg yolk and cherry extract and beat again.
5. Beat in the cookie crumbs and the almond slices.
6. Cut each peach in half. Remove the pit. Using a melon baller, scoop out a small amount of flesh and discard.
7. Mound the stuffing into the peach cavities. Place peaches in a roasting pan.
8. Brush melted butter over the top of each peach, being sure to cover the exposed flesh.
9. Bake for about 15 minutes until the stuffing begins to brown.

Comments: This recipe may be prepared up until baking one day in advance; cover the baking pan with plastic wrap and refrigerate. The butter seals the peach to prevent discoloration. Country Willows Bed & Breakfast Inn serves these Baked Stuffed Peaches (or sometimes Nectarines) as a first course. Choose firm, ripe fruit. Serve with a dollop of vanilla yogurt and garnish with a sprig of mint or an edible flower, such as pansies or nasturtiums.

Flora's Lake House B&B
Aunt Bobbie's Sticky Bun Cake

Yield: 12 servings

1 package Rhodes frozen Texas or dinner rolls
1 package Jell-O Butterscotch Pudding mix (Cook n' Serve kind)
1/4 cup melted margarine or butter   1/2 cup brown sugar
chopped nuts–pecans or walnuts   cinnamon

1. Sprinkle chopped nuts on bottom of greased bundt cake pan.
2. Layer frozen rolls on top (1/2 package or about 12-14 rolls).
3. Dump package of dry pudding mix around on top of rolls.
4. Mix together brown sugar and melted butter, pour on top.
5. Sprinkle rolls with "loads of cinnamon" (you may need to go around twice).
6. Let raise overnight in cold oven (or covered on counter).
7. In morning bake in preheated 350°F oven for 18-20 minutes.
8. Let cool for about 2 minutes then dump upside down onto plate.

❦ ❦ ❦

Green Gables Inn
Anne's Crustless Quiche

Yield: 6-8 large servings

12 eggs, separated   1 cube butter 1/4 lb.
1/2 cup flour   1 tsp. baking powder
1 lb small curd cottage cheese   1 lb jack cheese, shredded
Optional: green chilies, vegetables, crab, ham, etc.

1. Separate eggs, beat whites stiff.
2. Melt butter and blend with yolks and cottage cheese in blender.
3. Add flour and baking powder.
4. Blend in egg whites.
5. Add shredded cheese.
6. Bake at 350°F for one hour in two Pam-sprayed 9" pie plates.
7. Cool for fifteen minutes before serving.
8. Top with choice of salsa, shredded cheese, green onions, etc.

Comments: Optional ingredients added after the shredded cheese (a small quantity of Swiss cheese adds zest).

❦ ❦ ❦

Greystone Manor
Orange Raisin Muffins

Yield: 12 muffins

1 orange with peel—cut up into chunks
1/2 cup orange juice   1/2 cup raisins
1/2 cup butter or margarine   1 egg
1 3/4 cups all-purpose flour   3/4 cup white sugar
1 tsp. baking powder   1 tsp. baking soda

1. Combine orange pieces and juice in blender. Puree.
2. Add raisins, egg and butter to blender. Blend. Pour into bowl.
3. In separate bowl, mix flour, sugar, baking soda and baking powder. Pour over orange mixture and stir to combine.
4. Fill 12 greased muffin tins.
5. Bake at 400° for 20 minutes.

❦ ❦ ❦

Groveland Cottage
Groveland Cottage Hot Cereal

Yield: 6 servings

Combine in a large container equal parts of rolled: thick oats, triticale, rye, barley and red wheat to make 2 cups. Mix very thoroughly.

4 cups water   2 cups mixed grains
1 Tbs. cinnamon   1/4 tsp. salt
1 apple grated   1/4 cup golden raisins
1/4 cup dark raisins   1/4 cup currants
1/2 cup chopped walnuts

1. Boil the water and add cinnamon, salt, grains, apple, raisins and currants. Mix well.
2. Add the walnuts but do not stir in—just place on top.
3. Turn heat to low and steam for 30 minutes.
4. Serve with brown sugar, milk or cream, plain yogurt or fresh berries.

🍎 🍎 🍎

Harbinger Inn
Sauce for Fresh Fruit

Yield: 8 servings

1 cup sour cream
1/4 cup powdered sugar

1/4 cup orange juice

1. Whip ingredients together gently.
2. Serve over fresh peaches, blueberries or raspberries

🍎 🍎 🍎

Hudson House B&B
Eggs Cristoff

Yield: 4 servings

4 baked croissants sliced lengthwise
1/4 lb. (about 8 medium) mushrooms sliced
1 diced shallot (or one small onion and a sprinkle of garlic)
2 Tbs. butter   1 tsp. dried chives
4 large eggs   salt and pepper to taste
4 Tbs. water   1/4 tsp. dry mustard
White Cheddar Sauce (see following recipe)

1. Beat eggs in small bowl with salt, pepper, water and dry mustard. Set aside.
2. Sauté mushrooms and shallot in butter for one minute over medium heat.
3. Add chives and egg mixture, scramble until just set (about two minutes—do not overcook).

4. Place a quarter of the mixture on each croissant bottom, allowing some to spill around the croissant, and cover with the croissant tops.
5. Generously blanket stuffed croissants with White Cheddar Sauce and garnish with a sprinkle of grated cheddar and a fresh dill sprig, if desired.

White Cheddar Sauce

3 Tbs. butter
1/8 lb. (2 oz.) Velveeta cheese
1/4 tsp. salt

3 Tbs. all-purpose flour
1 1/2 cups hot milk
1 dash cayenne pepper

1. Blend flour and butter in a saucepan over low heat; cook for one minute.
2. Add heated milk, salt, cayenne and Velveeta and stir constantly until sauce thickens and Velveeta is completely melted.

❦ ❦ ❦

Inn at Penn Cove
Nantucket Cranberry Pie

Yield: 1 pie

2 cups cranberries (if frozen let thaw first)
1/2 cup walnuts
2 eggs
1 cup flour

1 1/2 cup sugar
3/4 cup vegetable oil
1/4 tsp. almond extract

1. Preheat oven to 350°.
2. In the bottom of a greased springform pan, place cranberries, walnuts and 1/2 cup sugar.
3. Mix together until smooth the eggs, oil, flour, almond extract and remaining 1 cup sugar.
4. Pour mixture over cranberries,
5. Bake for 40 minutes until golden on top.

Inn at Swift's Bay
Inn at Swift's Bay Crab Cakes with a Lemon Tarragon Sauce

Yield: 8-10 servings (16-20 crab cakes)

6 cups fresh crab meat
2 tsp. ground celery seed
3 Tbs. finely chopped red bell pepper
6 Tbs. chopped fresh chives
2 tsp. lemon juice (more to taste)
1/2 cup mayonnaise (depending on moisture level of crab)
6 Tbs. country-style Grey Poupon mustard
6 eggs (or all egg white equivalents), beaten
5 dashes Worcestershire sauce
2 tsp. Old Bay Seasoning (available at most supermarkets)
2 tsp. tarragon leaves
1 1/2-2 cups bread crumbs to bind (Italian style with cheese and herbs work well)
8-10 eggs for poaching
Hollandaise Sauce
4 Tbs. sweetened rice flour (available at Asian markets)

1. Combine first 12 ingredients and let sit for at least 30 minutes—overnight is preferable—allowing all the liquids to be absorbed.
2. With your hands, work the mixture into patties about 3" round and 1/2 to 3/4" thick.
3. In a lightly buttered pan, with a touch of olive oil to avoid burning, brown the patties quickly on both sides. Place in oven to keep warm and start poaching eggs.
4. While poaching eggs, make Hollandaise Sauce, adding a little extra lemon juice, 1 tsp. tarragon leaves and the sweetened rice flour.
5. Place a poached egg on top of each crab cake and spoon a heaping Tbs. of sauce over each egg.
6. Serve 2 crab cakes per person, garnished with fresh flowers and a dash of nutmeg.

Comments: Broiled tomatoes with herbs, bread crumbs and freshly grated parmesan cheese are excellent with these.

Johnson House B&B
Johnson House Sweet Onion Tarts

Yield: 12 servings

Basic pastry crust (three 8" crusts)

3 cups sifted flour

2 sticks plus 2 Tbs. unsalted butter

6-7 Tbs. chilled water

pinch of salt

1. Mix flour and butter in food processor until mixture resembles a very coarse oatmeal—not uniform crumbs, but bits and pieces.
2. Shake mixture into large bowl and add chilled water, stirring with large spoon until well blended.
3. Shape dough into three balls. Put into rounds and refrigerate for an hour or so.
4. Preheat oven to 400°.
5. Roll out dough on floured board (not too thinly) and shape into 8" tart pans. Prick thoroughly. Line dough with aluminum foil and place pastry weights in center.
6. Bake for 10 minutes.
7. Remove foil and weight and bake until lightly golden (all moist spots gone).

Onion filling

2 large onions (Walla Walla, Vidalia or yellow) thinly sliced

2 Tbs. unsalted butter

2 cups heavy cream or Half and Half

2 or 3 grinds of fresh nutmeg

2 Tbs. Romano cheese, grated fine

1 cup Gruyere cheese, grated coarse

7 egg yolks

2 whole eggs

dash of cayenne pepper

1/2 cup chopped basil

1. Preheat oven to 375°.
2. Melt butter and sauté onions about 5 minutes (do not let onions brown). Drain onions in colander, reserving butter.
3. Whisk egg yolks, eggs, cream and seasonings until well-blended.
4. Sprinkle tart shells with gruyere cheese.
5. Divide basil evenly in shells atop cheese.
6. With slotted spoon, place the onions in the shells.
7. Ladle butter over onions.
8. Sprinkle lightly with Romano cheese.

9. Bake 35 minutes (until custard is solid and top lightly browned).
10. Cool 10-15 minutes before cutting. Serve warm.

Comments: This is also delicious served chilled the next day.

🐀 🐀 🐀

Lara House B&B
Lara House Puffy Pancakes

Yield: 3 large pancakes

1/2 cup flour	1/4 cup sugar
1/2 cup milk	1/2 tsp. orange rind
1/8 tsp. nutmeg	2 eggs
Glazed Banana (see following recipe)	

1. Combine all ingredients and mix well.
2. Coat three 6" Ramekins with cooking spray. Put pan in pre-heated oven at 475° for 1 min.
3. Pour mixture evenly into hot pans.
4. Bake at 475° for 5 minutes.
5. Reduce heat to 450° and bake an additional 7 minutes.
6. Remove from oven and serve with Glazed Banana and powdered sugar.

Glazed Banana

1 Tbs. brown sugar	1/2 cup orange juice
1 sliced banana	

1. Cook all ingredients in small sauce pan until banana is soft and sauce has thickened.
2. Serve over Puffy Pancake.

Manor Farm Inn
Manor Farm Inn Crumble

Yield: 16 servings

Filling
6 granny smith apples, peeled, cored and sliced
2 lbs. fresh blackberries or 2 bags frozen berries
1 cup sugar   2 tsp. cinnamon

Topping
3 cups flour   3 cups brown sugar
1 1/2 cups oatmeal   3 sticks butter, melted

1. Crumble the first three filling ingredients together in the bottom of a 12" by 14" deep pan.
2. Sprinkle cinnamon on top.
3. Combine all the topping ingredients together and spread over filling.
4. Bake at 350° for 1 hour or until golden brown on top.

Comments: Can also be served as a dessert with ice cream on top!

❦ ❦ ❦

Miller Tree Inn
Beef Jerky

3 lb. roast of beef cut in thin slices   1/2 cup soy sauce
1 Tbs. Worcestershire sauce   1/2 tsp. onion powder
2 tsp. seasoning salt   1/2 tsp. white pepper
1/2 tsp. garlic powder   1 Tbs. Liquid Smoke

1. Marinate beef in all other ingredients in the refrigerator for three days, stirring well daily.
2. Shake off excess moisture and spread over oven racks.
3. Cook at 175° for 5-6 hours OR overnight with a knife in the oven door to keep it open a crack.

North Cascades Basecamp
Whole Wheat Maple Waffles

Yield: Six 9" waffles

2 eggs
1/2 cup butter or margarine, melted
2 cups whole wheat pastry flour
1/2 tsp. salt

1 3/4 cups milk
4 tsp. baking powder
2 Tbs. maple syrup

1. Heat waffle iron after spraying with oil.
2. Beat eggs, then beat in remaining ingredients.
3. Cook according to waffle iron instructions.

❦ ❦ ❦

Olympic Lights
Olympic Lights Scones

Yield: 12 scones

2 cups flour
2 tsp. baking powder
1/2 tsp. salt
1/2 cup frozen blueberries
1/2 cup buttermilk

2 Tbs. sugar
1/2 tsp. baking soda
6 Tbs. cold butter
2 eggs

1. In large bowl sift together flour, sugar, baking powder, baking soda and salt.
2. Cut in butter and then stir in blueberries.
3. In a separate bowl, beat together eggs and buttermilk.
4. Combine the contents of both bowls, mixing as little as possible.
5. Turn dough onto floured surface and pat into 1/2 inch thick round.
6. Cut into 12 wedges.
7. Brush with buttermilk and sprinkle with sugar, place on ungreased cookie sheet.
8. Bake in the top third of the oven at 425° for 12 minutes.

Pine Lodge Farm
Orange-Date Muffins

Yield: 6 large muffins

1 whole unpeeled orange	1/2 cup orange juice
1/2 cup chopped dates	1 egg
1 1/2 cups all-purpose flour	1 tsp. baking soda
1/2 cup butter or margarine	1 tsp. baking powder
1/2 tsp. salt	3/4 cups white sugar

1. Cut the orange into pieces to remove seeds.
2. Drop pieces into blender with orange juice and whirl until peel is finely chopped.
3. Drop in the dates, egg and butter. Give blender a short whirl.
4. Stir together the flour, baking soda, baking powder, salt and sugar. Cut in butter or margarine.
5. Pour the orange mixture over the dry mixture and stir together only until moistened.
6. Pour into muffin tins and bake at 375° for 15-20 minutes.

Comments: Raisins may be substituted for dates for an equally delicious muffin.

ਦ ਦ ਦ

Rainbow Inn
Lemon Yogurt Bread

Yield: 2 loaves

3 cups flour	1 tsp. salt
1 tsp. baking soda	1/2 tsp. baking powder
1 Tbs. lemon zest	3 eggs
1 cup vegetable oil	1 3/4 cups sugar
1 pint lemon yogurt	1 Tbs. lemon extract
1 cup finely chopped blanched almonds	

1. Preheat oven to 325°.
2. Sift together flour, salt, baking soda and baking powder.
3. Stir in lemon zest and almonds. Set aside.

4. In large bowl beat eggs, then add oil and sugar and cream well.
5. Add lemon yogurt and lemon extract.
6. Combine wet and dry ingredients and blend thoroughly.
7. Spoon batter into two well-greased 9" by 5" loaf pans.
8. Bake 1 hour, or until toothpick inserted in center of bread comes out clean.
9. Cool in pan for 10 minutes, then turn onto wire rack and continue cooling.

❦ ❦ ❦

Run of the River
Country Pepper Potatoes

Yield: 6 servings

1/2 cup diced green pepper
1 fresh Chorizo or Italian sausages
1/4 cup chopped green onions
1/4 tsp. pequin pepper (more for a longer ride—these hummers are hot!)
Johnny's Seasoning Salt to taste

2 Tbs. olive oil
1 Tbs. fresh parsley
6 medium baking potatoes

1. Bake or microwave potatoes ahead of time. When cool, peel and dice into small chunks.
2. Cut sausage into small pieces.
3. In a large skillet, heat olive oil and sauté onions, green pepper and sausage. Cook until sausage is browned and sizzling.
4. Add potatoes and seasonings, continue cooking on high heat for approximately fifteen minutes or until potatoes are golden.
5. Reduce heat, cover and allow flavors to mingle.
6. Serve on a large platter with parsley garnish and a dash of paprika. Include a side dish of your favorite salsa for more zest!

Comments: For a high-nutrition, low-calorie alternative to nachos, save the peeled potato skins for your next nacho plate. Layer the skins on a plate with grated cheddar cheese on top. Adorn with fresh cilantro, bacon bits and seasoning salt. Enjoy!

Schnauzer Crossing
"Bluebarb" Crunch

Yield: 8 servings

Filling

4 cups rhubarb in 1" pieces	2 cups blueberries
1 cup sugar	1/2 cup flour
1 tsp. cinnamon	1 tsp. lemon juice
1/2 cup water	

Topping

1 cup flour	1 cup brown sugar
1/2 cup Snoqualmie Falls oats	1/2 cup walnuts
1/2 cup melted butter or margarine	

1. Preheat oven to 375°.
2. Mix together rhubarb, blueberries, sugar, flour, cinnamon, lemon juice and water for the filling.
3. Mix together flours, brown sugar, oats, butter and walnuts for the topping.
4. Pour rhubarb-blueberry mixture into a greased 9" by 12" baking dish and sprinkle with topping.
5. Bake 45 minutes or until rhubarb is tender.

❦ ❦ ❦

State Street Inn
Fruit Crepes

Yield: 20 crepes

20 cooked crepes (use any crepe recipe)
4-6 green apples (Granny Smith, etc.) cored and chopped

2 cups fresh or frozen blueberries	1 Tbs. honey
2-3 bananas peeled and diced	2 Tbs. butter
1 Tbs. brown sugar	1 tsp. cinnamon
1 tsp. nutmeg	1/2 tsp. cloves

1. Melt butter in large skillet.

2. Stir in brown sugar, honey and spices until dissolved.
3. Cook apples in butter mixture over medium-low heat covered until soft, stirring frequently.
4. Stir in bananas and blueberries and remove from heat.
5. Fill crepes with 2-3 Tbs. of filling in each crepe—do not overfill or crepes may tear when rolling.
6. Roll crepes and place on baking sheet.
7. Bake covered 10-15 minutes in 350° oven until warmed.
8. Serve topped with whipped cream and fresh nutmeg.

🐝 🐝 🐝

Sunnyside Inn
Santa Fe Rollups

Yield: 6 servings

12 flour tortillas
1/2 cup sour cream
1 firm medium tomato, chopped fine
1 ripe red pepper (sweet) chopped fine
1/2 cup chopped cilantro or parsley (or both)
1 bunch chopped fresh chives or green onion

8 oz. light cream cheese
garlic powder to taste

1. Lay tortillas out flat.
2. Mix sour cream and cream cheese together, spread on tortillas.
3. Sprinkle all other ingredients on top of tortillas and roll up each tortilla.
4. Slice each roll into 1" segments and place on end on serving platter.
5. Serve with salsa and jalepeños.

🐝 🐝 🐝

Sutil Lodge
Cornbread with Apples and Maple Syrup

Yield: 12 large wedges

1 1/2 cups yellow cornmeal
2/3 cup sugar

2 cups flour
6 tsp. baking powder

1 tsp. salt	2 cups milk
2 eggs	1/4 cup melted butter

2 small coarsely grated tart and firm apples
1/4 cup maple syrup

1. Preheat oven to 450°.
2. Mix cornmeal, flour, sugar, baking powder and salt.
3. Place two 9" cast iron skillets in oven.
4. Mix eggs, milk, maple syrup and butter.
5. Add the ingredients in step 4 to the dry mixture and blend well, then stir in apples.
6. Brush heated skillets with butter and spoon in batter.
7. Bake for 20 minutes or until bread springs up when touched and top is lightly browned.
8. Cool for 2-3 minutes, then cut in wedges and serve.

The Old Farmhouse
Omelette Soufflé a' l'Orange

Yield: 6 servings

5 egg yolks	5 egg whites
4 Tbs. sugar	1 Tbs. Cointreau
1 oz. butter	1 tsp. lemon juice

1 orange, with peel grated and set aside
powdered sugar

1. Beat the egg yolks with the sugar until frothy.
2. Mix in the Cointreau and orange peel.
3. In a separate bowl, beat the egg whites until stiff, then fold in the egg yolk mixture.
4. Grease an oven-proof dish generously with butter and sugar, then pour egg mixture into the dish.
5. Cut the peeled orange into thin slices and decorate the soufflé with them.
6. Sprinkle with powdered sugar.
7. Bake at 400° for 18 minutes.
8. Serve immediately.

Tudor Inn
Tunisian Eggs

Yield: 4 servings

2 medium onions, minced	2 Tbs. lemon juice
6 Tbs. melted butter	1 1/4 cups minced parsley
1/4 tsp. cinnamon	1/4 tsp. pepper
8 sheets phyllo dough	8 eggs
1 tsp. Tabasco	fresh chopped chives
ground pepper	

1. Cook onion in lemon juice and 3 Tbs. butter in a frying pan over medium heat until onion is limp (15 minutes). Stir often.
2. Mix in parsley, pepper, cinnamon and Tabasco. Stir until parsley is just wilted, about 2 minutes.
3. Lay 1 phyllo sheet on a flat surface, brush lightly with some of the remaining butter. Stack 3 more phyllo sheets on the first, buttering each layer.
4. Cut into 4 equal rectangles, then cut in half.
5. Fit and pleat each rectangle into a buttered muffin cup, letting edges extend above pan. Take care not to tear dough.
6. Repeat steps 3-5 to use remaining phyllo dough.
7. Spoon the parsley mixture into each phyllo cup equally.
8. Break an egg into each cup, and sprinkle fresh chives and ground pepper on top.
9. Place muffin tins on cookie sheet and bake at 400° on bottom rack of oven for 12-14 minutes, or until eggs are set to your liking.
10. With small spatula, carefully loosen phyllo cups from pans and transfer to serving plates. Allow 2 cups per serving.

❦ ❦ ❦

Turtleback Farm Inn
Smoked Salmon Torte

Yield: 6-8 servings

1/2 lb. smoked salmon	6 oz. cream cheese
1/2 cup sour cream	1 Tbs. capers

1 1/2 tsp. Dijon mustard   1 tsp. fresh dill
5 large cooked crepes (use any recipe)

1. In a food processor, blend cream cheese and sour cream until smooth.
2. Add salmon, capers, mustard and dill and process until just blended. The filling should have some recognizable pieces of salmon and the capers should be whole.
3. Place a crepe flat on a plate and spread some filling on top. Continue stacking crepes and spreading filling until you end with a crepe on top. Reserve some filling.
4. Cut into wedges and serve each slice with a dollop of filling, sour cream and dill on top.

❦ ❦ ❦

Youngberg Hill Farm
Austrian Pancake

Yield: 4 servings

1 cup flour   2 Tbs. sugar
4 egg whites   4 egg yolks
1 cup milk   2 Tbs. butter or margarine
1/2 cup raisins   powdered sugar

1. Preheat oven to 350°.
2. Whip egg whites and sugar until stiff.
3. In separate bowl, beat egg yolks, milk and flour together.
4. Melt butter in the oven in an oven-proof skillet.
5. Add melted butter to egg yolk mixture and pour into warm pan.
6. Gently fold in egg whites, then sprinkle raisins on top.
7. Bake for 20-30 minutes, until toothpick or fork can be inserted and comes out clean. Should look like a soufflé.
8. Dust with powdered sugar, cut in wedges and serve with raspberry or marionberry syrup.

WE NEED YOUR HELP!

The information contained in this book was as accurate as could be determined at the time of publication. But roads change: housing developments spring up, towns decide to make through roads dead end, or new roads are built. And even occasionally, an error by a researcher, writer, editor or publisher manages to make it to print.

That's why we at White Meadow Press rely on you, our readers, to help us keep our guidebooks up to date. If you see something on your bicycle that does not correspond to what's in this book, whether it be a cue sheet turn, description, line on a map, or text, please do not hesitate. When you get home from your ride, jot it down and send it off to us in a letter (be sure to pedal to the post office!). We will acknowledge your efforts with a return letter and a coupon good for one free book with your next purchase directly from the publisher.

Send your comments and notes to:

Publisher
White Meadow Press
P.O. Box 56
Boonton, NJ 07005

ALSO:

If you enjoy writing and researching bicycle routes, we want to hear from you at the above address. We are always looking for new authors to expand our line of guidebooks, both local RIDE GUIDEs and our Bed, Breakfast and Bike series. Thanks!

ORDER THESE OTHER BICYCLING GUIDES
FROM WHITE MEADOW PRESS!

Bed, Breakfast & Bike/New England	$12.95
Bed, Breakfast & Bike/Mid-Atlantic	$12.95
Bed, Breakfast & Bike/Northern California	$14.95
Bed, Breakfast & Bike/Pacific Northwest	$14.95
RIDE GUIDE/North Jersey/2nd Edition	$10.95
RIDE GUIDE/Central Jersey	$ 9.95
RIDE GUIDE/South Jersey	$ 9.95
RIDE GUIDE/Hudson Valley and South Shore	$ 7.95

Please send me the following books:

Qty.	Title	Amt.
_____	_____	_____
_____	_____	_____
_____	_____	_____
_____	_____	_____

Shipping:	$2.00
Subtotal:	_____
NJ residents add applicable sales tax:	_____
Total:	_____

Send books to*:

Name: _____

Address: _____

_____

*If this is a gift, please note your address as well.

Make checks payable to **White Meadow Press** (please pay with U.S. funds drawn on U.S. bank). Send this form and payment to **White Meadow Press, P.O. Box 56, Boonton, NJ 07005**. Sorry, no C.O.D., credit card or billed orders.